Marc-Antoine Caillot and the Company of the Indies in Louisiana

Marc-Antoine Caillot and the Company of the Indies in Louisiana

Trade in the French Atlantic World

ERIN M. GREENWALD

Louisiana State University Press
Baton Rouge

Published by Louisiana State University Press

Manufactured in the United States of America
First printing

Designer: Laura Roubique Gleason
Typeface: Whitman
Printer and binder: Maple Press

Library of Congress Cataloging-in-Publication Data

Names: Greenwald, Erin.
Title: Marc-Antoine Caillot and the Company of the Indies in Louisiana : trade in the French Atlantic world / Erin M. Greenwald.
Description: Baton Rouge : Louisiana State University Press, 2016. | Includes bibliographical references and index.
Identifiers: LCCN 2015035737 | ISBN 978-0-8071-6285-9 (cloth : alkaline paper) | ISBN 978-0-8071-6286-6 (pdf) | ISBN 978-0-8071-6287-3 (epub) | ISBN 978-0-8071-6288-0 (mobi)
Subjects: LCSH: Louisiana—Commerce—History—18th century. | Compagnie des Indes—History—18th century. | Caillot, Marc-Antoine, 1707–1758. | Compagnie des Indes—Officials and employees—Biography. | France—Commerce—History—18th century. | Atlantic Ocean Region—Commerce—History—18th century. | Louisiana—History—To 1803. | Louisiana—Social life and customs—18th century. | French—Louisiana—History—18th century. | France—Colonies—America—History—18th century.
Classification: LCC HF3161.L8 G74 2016 | DDC 382.06/5763—dc23
LC record available at http://lccn.loc.gov/2015035737

The paper in this book meets the guidelines for permanence and durability of the Committee on Production Guidelines for Book Longevity of the Council on Library Resources. ♾

In memory of Sarah R. Doerries

Contents

Acknowledgments xi

Introduction 1

1
The Company in France 11

2
Approaching the Atlantic World 43

3
Tropical Baptisms 69

4
Stopping Over: Provisioning and Acculturation 94

5
Louisiana: A Company Colony 112

6
A Colony Fit Only for a King? 141

Epilogue: Embracing India 153

Notes 161

Bibliography 195

Index 215

Figures and Tables

FIGURES

1. Title page of Marc-Antoine Caillot's memoir 4
2. Promotional broadside circulated by the French Company of the Indies 32
3. Detail view of company headquarters in Paris 37
4. Advertisement for sale of Indian Ocean goods at company warehouses in Nantes, 1730 58
5. Plan of Gorée Island 71
6. The *Durance* 74
7. Saint-Domingue, 1710 98
8. The Balize, 1731 108
9. Section of Caillot's map of New Orleans, dated February 14, 1731 115
10. Pondicherry, 1705 156

TABLES

1. Company-Owned Slave Population by Site, Sex, and Family Status 124
2. Company-Owned Slave Children by Site and Age Group 124
3. Occupations of Male Company-Owned Slaves 127

Acknowledgments

In the fall of 2007, Jessica Dorman, director of publications at The Historic New Orleans Collection, asked me to review first draft translations of an eighteenth-century manuscript under consideration for eventual publication. That manuscript, written by Marc-Antoine Caillot, a clerk working for the French Company of the Indies in Louisiana between 1729 and 1731, changed the course of my academic career. I spent the next six years researching the document and its author, situating Caillot's experiences in a broader context, and learning a great deal about the French Atlantic world in which he lived, loved, and worked.

Research tied to Caillot's memoir first bore fruit in 2013 with the publication of *A Company Man: The Remarkable French-Atlantic Voyage of a Clerk for the Company of the Indies*, edited by me, translated from the original French by Teri F. Chalmers, and published by The Historic New Orleans Collection. The present study extends the research undertaken for *A Company Man* and takes a critical look at the founding and development of the French Company of the Indies, particularly in the context of its trade and agricultural operations in the Atlantic world. This book would not exist without the many individuals who provided professional and personal support along the way.

At The Historic New Orleans Collection, many thanks go to Jessica Dorman, Alfred Lemmon, Mark Cave, Priscilla and John Lawrence, and some of the best colleagues one could ever hope to have, including Dorothy Ball, Daniel Hammer, Mary Mees Garsaud, Anne Robichaux, Teresa Devlin, Elizabeth Ogden, Melissa Carrier, Keely Smith, Lauren Noel, Rebecca Smith, Daphne Derven, John Magill, Joseph Shores, and the late Sarah Richards Doerries, whose friendship, snarky commentary, and excellent editorial advice are greatly missed.

Farther afield but no less critical to advancing this book project is the team of professional historians that shepherded me through my graduate studies at Ohio State University. Alan Gallay, a key ally and intellectual mentor, deserves heartfelt thanks. Alan's patience and his belief in my ability to switch course enabled me to embark upon the research and writing journey that produced this book. Thanks to Alan also for reminding me of the importance of maintaining balance in life and scholarship.

Kenneth Andrien, John Brooke, Dale Van Kley, and Kevin Boyle offered much-needed support and advice on everything from *ancien régime* historiography to prose style. The late John Conteh-Morgan introduced me to the francophone world and the people and histories of the African diaspora in the French Atlantic. Amy Overmyer, Nicole Jackson, Joe Orser, Alison Efford, Ray Ball, Robert Bennett, Carrie Greene, John and Molly Maass, and Christianna Thomas Hurford made the graduate student experience a rich and welcoming one.

Financial support from Ohio State University's history department, graduate school, and college of humanities, the United States Naval Academy, l'École nationale des chartes, and The Historic New Orleans Collection underwrote multiple trips to French archives. The reference staffs of the Archives nationales; Archives nationales d'outre-mer; Bibliothèque nationale de France; Archives de la ville de Lorient; Service historique de la Défense, Fonds de la Marine, Lorient; and Archives départementales des Hauts-de-Seine, Loire-Atlantique, Morbihan, and Seine-Maritime provided invaluable assistance and made sure I had access to relevant collections. Yevan Terrien, Nathalie Dessens, and Malick Ghachem generously used some of their own precious research time abroad to secure digital copies of documents from French archives I needed to complete this project.

In New Orleans, Sarah-Elizabeth Gundlach and Greg Lambousy of the Louisiana State Museum, Lee Leumas of the Archdiocese of New Orleans, Lee Miller of Tulane University's Louisiana Research Collection, and Mary Lou Eichhorn, Daniel Hammer, Jennifer Navarre, Eric Seiferth, Bobby Ticknor, and Matt Farah facilitated the use of court and sacramental records, rare books and pamphlets, microfilm, and other reference materials from their respective institutional holdings.

Danna Agmon, Kenneth Banks, Emily Clark, Shannon Dawdy, Catherine Desbarats, Alexandre Dubé, Malick Ghachem, Gwendolyn Midlo Hall, Jean Hébrard, Heidi Keller-Lapp, Herbert Klein, Phyllis Martin, George Milne, Larry Powell, Gordon Sayre, Rebecca Scott, Daniel Usner, and Sophie White sat through various readings of my work and/or helped me flesh out my narrative. The anonymous reader assigned by Louisiana State University Press offered thoughtful commentary and recommendations, many of which have been incorporated into this book. I also owe a great deal to Alisa Plant, senior acquisitions editor, and Catherine Kadair, senior editor, at Louisiana State University Press, for taking on this project and seeing it through to publication, and to Elizabeth Gratch, who provided a masterful copyedit of the manuscript.

Finally, the largest debt of gratitude goes to my family. My parents, Charles and Sandy Greenwald, introduced me to New Orleans and instilled in me a curiosity about the world and its inhabitants. My brother, Charles, makes forever sure I don't take myself too seriously—a useful contribution. Thanks also to my grandmother, Victoria Grodevant, who has always been a source of warmth and encouragement, and to Alexandria McCoy, whom I've watched grow into an extraordinarily kind, compassionate, and brilliant young woman in the course of writing this book.

The contributions of my husband, Vasy McCoy, and daughter, Acadia, to this project and my life are immeasurable. I quite literally could not have done it without them. Vasy has been particularly patient in reading, rereading, critiquing, and even listening to me read various chapter drafts. Acadia has helped just by being herself. They have both lived under the shadow of this book for longer than I care to admit. Thanks to both of them for always believing in me.

Marc-Antoine Caillot and the Company of the Indies in Louisiana

Introduction

In 1729 the French Company of the Indies (Compagnie des Indes) operated more than two dozen coastal and riverine *comptoirs*, or trade outposts, along waterways ranging from the Upper Mississippi Valley to the West African coast to the Bay of Bengal in South Asia. The company, administered by an assembly of Paris-centered directors, shareholders, and syndics, stood on the verge of initiating self-directed changes that would simultaneously diminish its functional and geographic scope and place it on firm financial footing for the first time since its mid-seventeenth-century inception.

As the company's focus shifted from the Atlantic to the Indian Ocean in the 1730s, so too did the life courses of individuals whose fortunes were bound up in the company's trade, colonization, and agricultural mission in the Americas. Unlike the Dutch and English monopoly companies, the French Company of the Indies prior to 1731 did not restrict its mission to trade alone, nor did the company limit its operational sphere to the East Indies. Instead, the company spread its ships, bureaucrats, soldiers, laborers, and cargoes across the Atlantic and Indian Oceans, leaving a staggering quantity of paper in the form of decrees, inventories, account books, and eyewitness accounts—both sanctioned and unsanctioned—in its wake.

Louisiana, claimed in the name of Louis XIV in 1682 but not settled until the first decade of the eighteenth century, was a late addition to France's colonial portfolio. By the time of the colony's settlement, France, through the commercial networks established by the predecessors of the French Company of the Indies, maintained a presence not only in Canada, the Caribbean, and West Africa but also in Bengal,

India, Mocha (present-day Yemen), and the Mascarenes. Much as the experiences of the Dutch East India Company had informed the development of the Dutch *West* India Company in the 1600s, Indian Ocean models provided by the French experience in Asia shaped French companies' expectations and behaviors in the Americas. This was particularly true for Louisiana during the second and third decades of the eighteenth century, when company hopes for the establishment of a hybrid colony based on trade and agricultural extraction ultimately failed.

This study examines Louisiana in a new way—as a colony of the French Company of the Indies—and places the development of the colony within the context of the company's global trade network.[1] From 1717 to 1731 the company maintained exclusive domain over trade (in goods and peoples), defense, settlement, and development in Louisiana. As a colony whose output was based not only on trade but also on hopes for agricultural expansion, Louisiana during this period can be seen as a hybridization of colonial models established the previous century in Canada and the French West Indies.

The company's presence in the colony was comparatively brief, and by 1731, when company directors unanimously agreed to withdraw from North America, the Louisiana endeavor had provided company officials and administrators with a clear, negative example of a productive trade environment. Whereas its operations in the Indian Ocean, and even in the Caribbean, relied on the presence of preexisting supply lines to fulfill trade objectives, its attempt to make Louisiana into a profitable entity was based on the creation and maintenance of a complete agricultural complex. Rather than rely on extant supply lines, such as furs and pelts available in the American Indian trade, the company in Louisiana sought unsuccessfully to create a French version of the Chesapeake. In its attempt to serve not as a trade facilitator but as a colony builder, the company expended more than twenty million livres yet never succeeded in turning a profit from Louisiana's limited output.

Between 1712 and 1729, first Antoine Crozat and then the Company of the Indies promoted the Louisiana colony to French investors as something it was not. For a time, commercial companies succeeded in convincing the French public (and themselves) that silver, gold, copper, and finally tobacco might be extracted from Louisiana's vast lands.

If only Louisiana had access to settlers, laborers, and investment funds, some argued, the colony could soon rival its silver- and tobacco-rich counterparts in New Spain and the Chesapeake. Yet for all the metropolitan efforts to convince investors of Louisiana's potential worth, those who lived in the colony, whether as colonists, soldiers, or administrators, soon realized that Louisiana's prospects had been grossly overblown. As for the involvement of the Company of the Indies and its efforts to turn Louisiana into France's largest tobacco producer, colonists could more easily support themselves through local trade than through large-scale tobacco production, a reality that thwarted company efforts to encourage agricultural expansion.

The example of Louisiana proved the proverbial last straw for a company already operating as the global trade underdog and prompted a definitive shift in the company's mission and geographic focus. Following the Natchez War of 1729–30, administrators relinquished their hopes for the colony. Its colony-building mission there was a poor fit for long-term stability, and continued investment in the colony threatened to undermine more profitable lines of trade in the Indian Ocean. Only after the company retroceded Louisiana to the Crown in 1731 did it become a stable, profitable trading company. By limiting its geographic scope and focusing on pure trade (as opposed to colonization) schemes, the Company of the Indies emerged from its failure in Louisiana as a competitive economic entity in the Indian Ocean.

In this study, the institutional history of the French Company of the Indies and the macro view of the French Atlantic world are brought to ground level through the lived experience of Marc-Antoine Caillot. In 2004 The Historic New Orleans Collection acquired an unpublished eighteenth-century manuscript titled "Relation du voyage de la Louisianne ou Nouvelle France" (fig. 1), which was subsequently translated into English, annotated, and released as *A Company Man: The Remarkable French-Atlantic Voyage of a Clerk for the Company of the Indies* in 2013.[2] Written by a company clerk as an account of his travels from Paris to and residency in New Orleans from 1729 to 1731, Caillot's account provides a rich window onto the commercial networks of the French Company of the Indies.[3]

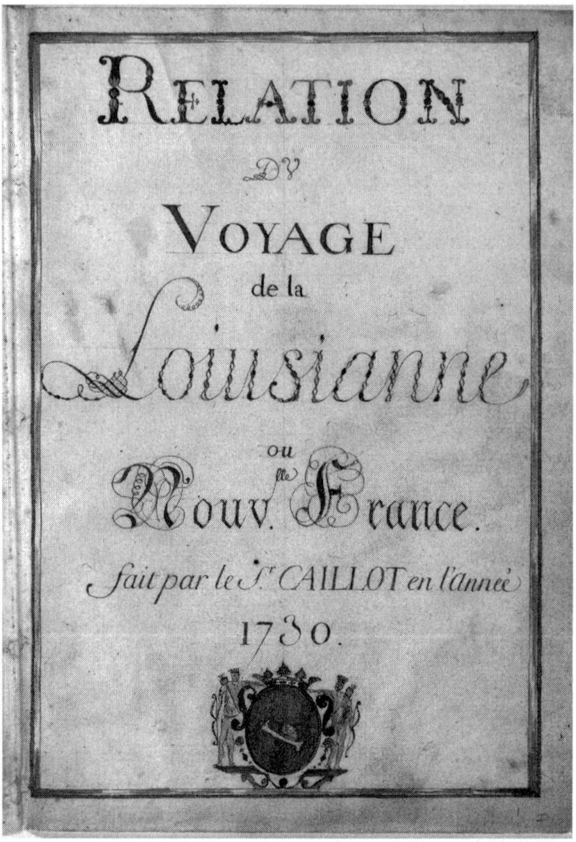

Relation
du
Voyage
de la
Louisianne
ou
Nouv.lle France.
fait par le Sr CAILLOT en l'Année
1730.

Fig. 1. Title page of Marc-Antoine Caillot's memoir. (Courtesy of The Historic New Orleans Collection, 2005.0011.)

Much as Laurel Thatcher Ulrich in *A Midwife's Tale* and Robert Harms in *The Diligent* respectively employed a midwife's account book/ journal and a ship officer's log as narrative backbones for much broader historical inquiries, I have used Caillot's experience in Louisiana as a structural through line in *Marc-Antoine Caillot and the Company of the*

Indies in Louisiana.[4] By examining Caillot's account in its entirety, from his departure from Paris in winter 1729 to his travels to the coast to his voyage at sea, rather than concentrating exclusively on his experience in Louisiana, I look beyond the artificial focus on his "destination" and instead bring the inherent connectivity of various points along the Atlantic Ocean circuit to the fore. At the same time, I have incorporated details pertaining to Caillot's life in France prior to 1729 and in India after 1731 to extend the narrative and track the history of the Company of the Indies through the lifetime of a single individual.

Caillot's account of his travels and time in Louisiana is an intimate one, but he was not alone in reporting his trials and tribulations to family, friends, or an even broader readership. The company period is eighteenth-century Louisiana's most fertile for the sheer number of voices documenting life in the colony. Although the company ultimately failed in its efforts to make Louisiana profitable, it succeeded in carrying more individuals—enslaved and free—to the colony during its fourteen-year tenure than any other public or private initiative in the entire history of the French Atlantic.[5] Nearly six thousand Europeans and more than sixty-seven hundred Africans boarded ships bound for Louisiana between 1717 and 1731. Not all of them survived the passage, but among those who did were literate engineers, administrators, soldiers, priests, nuns, craftsmen, bureaucrats, colonists, and scientists, some of whom left behind written accounts of their lived experience of the eighteenth-century Atlantic. Many of those accounts appear in this book, sometimes as counterpoints to official company narratives, others as voices that shed new light on well-known events in Louisiana's early history.

Shannon Dawdy refers to these Louisiana "*mémoires*, letters, and travel accounts" as "a 'useful' kit of knowledge called *histoire*." A combination of "both 'story' and 'history,'" *histoires* "were often a mixed-bag of natural and administrative history, astronomy, fashion and culinary critique, and good old-fashioned storytelling in which the tall tales spun by the writer were at times self-serving aggrandizements, or worse, gross distortions of reality."[6] Robert Darnton, too, acknowledges the frequent tendency toward exaggeration in eighteenth-century personal narratives. In analyzing the memoir left by the Parisian journeyman Jacques-Louis Ménétra, Darnton stresses that Ménétra "presents his life as a series of pranks," which all demonstrate that "no matter what he does, he comes out on top."[7] The same sentiment might easily be applied to Caillot's account, yet despite the inherent difficulties in taking these histoires at face value, their viewpoints provide a narrative skeleton upon which scholars can layer the musculature of additional sources to produce a fuller, more balanced account of the past.

Published in 1758, Antoine-Simon Le Page du Pratz's three-volume *Histoire de la Louisiane* is arguably the best-known histoire-hybrid from the eighteenth century (at least for Louisiana), yet dozens of other published and unpublished histoires have helped scholars breathe life into a narrative of French colonial history constructed from relatively drier sources.[8] From the letters of young Ursuline novice Marie-Madeleine Hachard to the picaresque mémoire of Jean-François Benjamin Dumont de Montigny, these sources offer a detailed view of an environment plagued by pernicious insects and scheming colonists. On a more functional level, they help students and scholars better understand the political and administrative contours of France's overseas colonies. But the same sources, when examined not exclusively as eyewitness accounts of life in colonial Louisiana, can serve as testimonies to the creation of—or at least of imperial attempts to create—a French Atlantic world. Although histoires flow from individuals, they can be one of the best vehicles for exploring an emergent French Atlantic.

Caillot's account, unlike those written by his contemporaries Dumont de Montigny and Le Page du Pratz, provides an uncensored view that was not written to impress his superiors or to secure a pension. His is not a propaganda piece, nor is it an effort to convince readers of his heroic bearing in the face of colonial hardships. "Relation du voyage de la Louisianne" is a unique encapsulation of the curiosity of the times, when the natural and day-to-day history of strange lands and their strange inhabitants, native or otherwise, piqued the interest of an educated metropolitan audience.[9] It is also a deeply personal reflection on how Caillot perceived himself and how he wished others—his male social peers chief among them—to perceive him. In satisfying the "autobiographical urge," Caillot positioned himself as a witty, quick-thinking, and sexually competent Frenchman whose experiences in the Atlantic world might serve as entertainment for readers in France but also as a lesson to those bound for the far-flung corners of France's overseas empire.[10] Unlike many of his better-known and published peers, Caillot wrote "Relation" for intimate circles. The nature of Caillot's writing and the baldness of his observations suggest he likely intended his account to be circulated among his peers, among fellow clerks, ships' officers, storekeepers, and family members.

Through Caillot's eyes, the inherent conflicts between official company aims crafted by administrators in Paris and the difficulties of their execution on the ground in the Americas is made strikingly clear. His account and extended life story allow for an exploration of how a common clerk of limited means experienced the Atlantic and how such a figure navigated the complicated web of patronage, service, and bureaucracy that stood between him and his own personal advancement.[11]

While the Caillot manuscript provides a way into the volatile world of the French Company of the Indies during its years in Louisiana, a host of other archival and printed primary sources bring a multilayered perspective to my understanding of the circuit that stretched from France to Senegambia to the French West Indies to Louisiana and back. For the John Law period, the holdings of The Historic New Orleans Collection are exceptional, given that many records from Law's *Système* were burned during the company's 1723 reorganization. For the post-1723 period archival materials relative to the company reside in three repositories. The Fonds de la Marine, Service historique de la Défense, in Lorient house all company outfitting and maritime personnel records. The Archives nationales in Paris maintain all correspondence and reports between company officials in Lorient or Paris and the minister of Marine, king, and other royal ministers based in the French capital and Versailles, and the Archives nationales d'outre-mer (ANOM) in Aix-en-Provence house internal company correspondence, mémoires, and decrees; correspondence between company officials in France and administrators in overseas company comptoirs; passenger lists for company ships; personnel records for company bureaucrats; and comptoir-by-comptoir budgets and expense reports.

Also useful for fleshing out Caillot's identity and the patronage circles in which he and his fellow bureaucrats operated were notarial and sacramental records. The departmental archives of Hauts-de-Seine in Nanterre provided a wealth of information on Caillot's life and family connections, as did notarial records and correspondence from his later life in Pondicherry and Bengal housed in the ANOM and Archives nationales. Additional background on colonists, passengers, and company personnel derives from admiralty court records, tax rolls, and sacramental records in the departmental archives of the Loire-Atlantique in Nantes, Morbihan in Vannes, and Seine-Maritime in Rouen, as well as the city archives of Lorient.

On travel and sightseeing in eighteenth-century France, the Bibliothèque nationale de France is a rich source for early travel guides, postal schedules, and visual depictions of seventeenth- and eighteenth-century towns and villages. The Cassini maps, also housed at the Bibliothèque nationale and available online through the combined efforts of the Bibliothèque nationale, École des hautes études en sciences sociales, Centre national de la recherche scientifique, and Institut national d'études démographiques, allowed me to quite literally reconstruct Caillot's early-1729 voyage from Paris to the Brittany coast.[12] On the slave trade and the role of both the company and private merchants in its perpetuation, the *Trans-Atlantic Slave Trade* database developed by David Eltis and others is an invaluable resource that helped me understand the volume of human cargo taken from Africa between 1717 and 1731.[13]

In Louisiana, Superior Council records housed at the Louisiana State Museum's Louisiana Historical Center helped clarify how conflicts were resolved (or not) and under what circumstances trouble within company ranks, among its employees and bureaucrats, spilled over into a more public arena. Sacramental records from births, deaths, and marriages on this side of the Atlantic reside with the Archives of the Archdioceses of New Orleans and Mobile. These records remain an invaluable source for mapping out social networks and, in the case of records pertaining to the enslaved, for illuminating the deviations between the legal doctrine of the *Code noir* and the actual practices of slaveholders.

This book is split into six chronologically ordered chapters and an epilogue that follow the Company of the Indies's operations on the France-Louisiana circuit from the establishment of its headquarters in Paris and Lorient to its near-complete withdrawal from the Atlantic world and finally to its expansion of operations in the Indian Ocean. The first chapter, "The Company in France," situates both the French Company of the Indies and the Louisiana colony in their historical contexts prior to 1717. Also key to this chapter is an exploration of the company during its management by Scottish finance guru John Law, under whose guidance the company became a global conglomerate. A third focus of chapter 1 is the structure of the company's headquarters in Paris and the composition of the company's metropolitan labor pool. Company clerk Marc-Antoine Caillot steps onto the page at the end of this chapter as part of the discussion of patronage within company ranks.

Chapter 2, "Approaching the Atlantic World," follows Caillot on his overland journey from the company's Paris headquarters to its outfitting port at Lorient. Caillot's trek to the coast spanned more than two weeks and included stops in Palaiseau, Chartres, La Flèche, Angers, Ancenis, and Nantes, among others. Using contemporary maps and travel narratives/guides, this chapter gives readers both a sense of travel in eighteenth-century France and popular opinion or imaginings of life (and death) in the Louisiana colony. A thorough discussion of Nantes illuminates the Breton capital's role in the transatlantic slave trade and as the site of the company's annual merchandise sales until 1734. This chapter also addresses the establishment and development of the company's home port, Lorient.

Chapter 3, "Tropical Baptisms," focuses on the company's operations in Lorient and uses the outfitting of three ships—one each bound for Senegambia, India, and Louisiana—to explore the diversity of the company's comptoirs and the interconnected nature of their trading activities. The Louisiana-bound ship *Durance*, its passengers and crew, and their experiences of life at sea in a transatlantic crossing receive close attention. Upon arrival in Louisiana, passengers-turned-colonists, soldiers, or bureaucrats filtered their initial understanding of the colony and its populace through a lens developed, at least in part, by interactions at sea. This chapter examines how sickness, shared experiences, and rituals such as the Baptism of the Tropics ceremony served as literal and figurative rites of initiation that marked passengers' journey into the French Atlantic world.

The fourth chapter, "Stopping Over: Provisioning and Acculturation," examines the role of Caribbean way stations in shaping newcomers' perceptions of the French Atlantic and the history of French companies on the island of Saint-Domingue. A look at the voyages of two slave ships, the *Galathée* and *Vénus*, highlights the sometimes lethal nature of company slaving operations and the dangers posed during the last leg of the transatlantic journey to Louisiana.

In chapter 5, "Louisiana: A Company Colony," I look at the company's presence in Louisiana between the company's post-Law reorganization in 1723 and its retrocession of the colony to the Crown in 1731. The company during this period, acting as colonizer, slaveholder, and commercial entity, attempted to develop the colony as a large-scale tobacco producer whose output would ultimately satisfy demand throughout the French Atlantic world. Also key to this chapter is a demographic and occupational analysis of the company-owned enslaved population residing in Louisiana.

Chapter 6, "A Colony Fit Only for a King?" analyzes the company's failure to reconcile its desire to transform Louisiana from a frontier-exchange to an agriculture-based economy, with its corresponding inability to maintain stable trade relationships with the colony's numerous Indian groups. Company administrators' decision to withdraw from North America in 1731 was not a given but, rather, resulted from the company's failure to adapt the structure of a global trading company to the demands of governing and developing a colony. Only in retroceding Louisiana and shrinking its global presence was the company able to concentrate on productive trade relationships in the Indian Ocean.

Marc-Antoine Caillot and the Company of the Indies in Louisiana closes with an epilogue, "Embracing India," that summarizes the tangible results of the company's decision to reconsider its mission and geographic focus in light of failures in Louisiana. The epilogue also traces Caillot's post-Louisiana career and considers the parallel tracks of success and failure experienced by both clerk and company.

1

The Company in France

From the fifteenth through the early seventeenth centuries, significant improvements in maritime technology—and a corresponding increase in hydrographic knowledge—led a core group of Europeans to embark on far-reaching programs of exploration. For the Spanish, these explorations resulted in the colonization and exploitation of much of Central and South America. While Spain's treasury grew heavy with silver and gold extracted from Peruvian and Mexican mines, Portugal—whose initial forays into Atlantic exploration predated all others—pursued an alternative to Spanish-style colonization: global trade. From the time Portugal established its first offshore settlement in the Madeira Islands in 1419, Portuguese navigators and traders continued to sail down Africa's coast, depositing *feitorias* (fortified trading posts or factories), some of which later served as the initiating sites of the Atlantic slave trade.[1] Typically located alongside extant communities, feitorias were sanctioned by commercial treaties between Portuguese representatives and local rulers. A feitoria's success depended on access to preexisting manufactories or supply lines, such as textiles from India or slaves from Kongo. By the mid-sixteenth century, a network of feitorias and occupied zones of influence stretched from Lisbon to São Tomé to Brazil to Nagasaki. These sites, along with the thousands of merchants, country traders, administrators, slaves, servants, and sailors who lived in or frequented them, formed the basis of a sprawling commercial empire fueled by trade in gold, spices, slaves, wine, dyes, textiles, and a host of other commodities.[2]

Over the course of the next two centuries, Spain colonized significant portions of modern-day Central and South America, while other European powers, including England, the United Provinces, and France, incorporated elements of the Spanish and Portuguese models of exploration and overseas expansion. Early French blue-water maritime expeditions centered on the New World and sought to replicate Spanish successes. But those led by Nicolas Durand de Villegaignon (1555) to southeastern Brazil and by Jean Ribaut (1562) and René de Laudonnière (1564) to Florida (modern-day Florida, Georgia, and the Carolinas) brought an increase in neither wealth nor territory to the French Crown. Historian Philip Boucher attributes French failures in Brazil and Florida in part to France's inability to conceive of models of "conquest and exploitation" that deviated from well-publicized Spanish examples.[3] In the sixteenth century, only the Canadian expeditions of Jacques Cartier (1534, 1535, and 1541) and Jean Roberval (1541) led ultimately to a New World settlement. And even then, more than seventy years passed from the time of Cartier's initial arrival before a permanent colony, established at Acadia in 1604, took root.[4]

Throughout the seventeenth century, settlement- and agriculture-based colonization projects in the Americas, in locales such as Brazil, the Chesapeake, and the Caribbean, coexisted with trade-focused endeavors in other places, including New Amsterdam and New France. While Europeans competed for territory in the Americas, the English and Dutch sought to bypass Portuguese trade networks in Africa and the East Indies by establishing competing East Indian trading companies. For the English in particular, this was perhaps partly a response to the needs of already settled colonies in the Americas. By increasing access to key commodities, such as slaves from Africa and textiles from India, the English were better positioned to serve their agriculture-based colonies. Textiles purchased in India, for example, paid for (and later clothed) African slaves, whose labor in the Americas produced cash crops sold in Europe. The liquid assets generated by the sale of these crops were then commonly reinvested in trade goods bound for Asia, completing the global trade circuit.

The Dutch East India Company (Verenigde Oostindische Compagnie, or VOC), a consolidated amalgam of multiple small, specialized companies, was chartered in 1602 in response to England's creation of its own umbrella company, the English East India Company (or EIC) in

1600.[5] By the mid-seventeenth century, the VOC and EIC had broken Portuguese domination of trade in the East, and the tide of globalization—one that swept up people, products, and ideas for the next three and a half centuries—had broken upon the shores of Africa, Europe, Asia, and the Americas. In the first decades of their presence in India (and later China), the English and Dutch companies relied on "existing mechanisms of supply and marketing which were controlled by indigenous brokers and merchants."[6] Local networks of weavers, dyers, traders, and merchants, which had been in place for centuries before the establishment of Portuguese feitorias along the Indian peninsula, for example, remained in place when the Dutch and English arrived.[7]

By 1650, the VOC had become the model of a successful East Indian trade conglomerate, with multiple trade factories scattered across the Indian Ocean; a central control structure for supply, organization, management, and distribution located in the Indian Ocean at Batavia (established in 1619 at present-day Jakarta, Indonesia); and a well-established network of investors, maritime workers, warehouses, and merchants operating out of Amsterdam. Based in London, the EIC was one of several English joint-stock companies engaged in overseas trade. As such, its assembly of twenty-four directors competed for investment funds with companies promoting a variety of New World ventures. Despite the competition, however, the EIC was a financial success, sending out an average of thirteen vessels each trading season from London to the East Indies between 1658 and 1688.[8]

The French were latecomers to the trade paradigm established by Portuguese and later replicated by Dutch and English merchant companies. When the French committed to chartering a company to compete with the VOC and EIC, their entrance into global trade was inauspicious, despite the increased opportunities for trade in Africa and Asia that resulted from the Portuguese empire's decline.

In the French Atlantic world, several companies backed by small, merchant-financier groups received charters to operate in places such as Saint-Christophe, Guiana, and Martinique in the Caribbean and in New France. But most of these companies held charters giving them control over very limited geographic areas. The entire island of Saint-Christophe, overseen by the Compagnie de Saint-Christophe from 1626 to 1635, for example, took up only sixty-eight square miles.[9] None of the companies in the French Atlantic remotely resembled in scale or administration the Dutch or English operations in the East Indies. Nor did they look much like the Puritan-led Massachusetts Bay Company, whose mission attracted individuals and families who willingly settled in the New World. Attracting settlers who sought permanent relocation to France's overseas colonies (as opposed to those who sought to make their fortune abroad and then promptly return to the metropole) remained a challenge throughout the colonial period. Yet the French monopoly companies that were granted charters in the Americas before the eighteenth century all faced some sort of settler-importation clause requiring them to help populate colonies under their control.

The French Crown insisted that chartered companies play a role in populating its New World colonies because it had shifted the burden of colonization away from a state treasury drained by Continental wars, especially those initiated by Louis XIV. Also key to population policies was France's claim that part of its objective in the Americas was to proselytize and convert the natives, a mission requiring the presence of both priests and Catholics who might serve as examples for potential converts. The settler clause was necessary, too, to the development of agriculture-based settlements, a category that included all of France's New World colonies outside of New France, where the focus was on the fur trade.

In settlements lacking preexisting commodities, such as furs in New France or silver in Peru, colonists and colonial administrators often turned to agriculture as a means of extracting wealth. But in addition to land and a stable political environment, agricultural production requires knowledge of given crops; manpower to oversee and carry out clearing, cultivation, and processing; and an established shipping network to bring the commodities to market. And slave labor—the most common form of labor in Louisiana after 1719—could not be "maintained on the cheap like mere imperial trading posts." "Slave economies," writes historian Paul Cheney, "required heavy internal policing, maritime protection, and a framework of imperial trade that could make these considerable outlays a profitable proposition for the nations [and I would add companies] that made them."[10] Perhaps most important, agricultural production requires sustained investment and patience; significant profit realization from new agricultural ventures might take years. Unlike the VOC and EIC, whose operations in the East Indies relied primarily on preexisting supply lines and trade in finished or partially finished goods, French companies in the Americas often faced the daunting task of creating exportable agricultural commodities from scratch.

In the Indian Ocean, the first serious French attempt to establish a large-scale, monopoly trading company occurred in June 1642, when Louis XIII granted exclusive rights to East Indian trade to the Compagnie française de l'Orient. The Compagnie française was not the first East Indian venture chartered by the Crown, but it was the first intended as a state-sponsored monopoly company to actually send out an expedition. Several smaller companies run by merchant collectives from Atlantic ports, including Dieppe, Rouen, and Saint-Malo, had been chartered prior to the Compagnie française de l'Orient. There were also a number of short-lived, narrowly focused charters granted to companies active in Canada and the Caribbean.[11]

Under Crown authority, the Compagnie française initiated a number of changes to better allow them to compete with the Dutch and English companies. To avoid being preyed upon by competitors on voyages around the Cape of Good Hope, cargo ships were often accompanied by one or more well-armed naval vessels. Adequate seaborne defenses were critical to the success of long-haul trading voyages. Yet in spite of a recent buildup in the French naval fleet, the Compagnie française failed to establish a single productive trading outpost, in large part because Cardinal Richelieu (Armand-Jean du Plessis), Louis XIII's chief minister and the company's greatest advocate, directed all of the company's meager resources into poorly executed colonization schemes in Madagascar.[12] Richelieu ignored evidence of the successive failures of three competing European trade entities active in the Indian Ocean. None had been able to make any inroads in Madagascar since 1500, when a Portuguese fleet found itself blown off course and onto the island's shores.[13] Instead of attempting to establish a multisite network of comptoirs in the Indian Ocean, Richelieu tried first to create an operational and provisioning base in Madagascar modeled after the VOC's base in Batavia.

Richelieu died within six months of the company's official birth, but company-funded attempts to colonize the island continued until the mid-1650s. By then, company coffers were empty, tropical diseases and hunger had ravaged the small colonial population, and relations between the French and native Malagasy peoples were openly hostile. The company charter was renewed in 1652 in the midst of the Fronde—a series of civil wars that took place between the Crown and regional judicial authorities (*parlements*) during the regency of Louis XIV—but shareholders distracted by civil unrest in Paris had little interest in stabilizing the company or its Madagascar base at Fort Dauphin.

Within a dozen years of the failure of Richelieu's company, another Paris-based strongman in the service of the new king devised a plan to create a series of monopoly companies intended to set the French on equal trade footing with England and the United Provinces. Jean-Baptiste Colbert came to power as minister of finances and advisor to Louis XIV in 1661, at a time when more textiles and spices from the East Indies were consumed by France than any other European power. Hoping to turn the trade table to France's advantage, Colbert attempted to gain merchant support for the creation of a new French East India company. But most French merchants seemed content to limit their economic engagement to the internal distribution of domestic goods or foreign imports, which arrived in port cities along France's Atlantic and Mediterranean coasts on foreign ships. Dutch merchants in particular capitalized on French demand for foreign goods—and a corresponding lack of French overseas traders—by setting up shop in French Atlantic ports. They even infiltrated the domestic scene, making significant inroads in cities such as Bordeaux, where they acted as the primary distributors of one of France's most lucrative commodities: wine.[14]

The reluctance of French merchants to engage in overseas commercial ventures can be attributed at least in part to the lack of a unified French economy. Unlike British and Dutch merchants, who operated within coherent spheres of nationwide financial systems, French merchants faced domestic barriers to trade. An archaic system of tolls, taxes, and tariffs meant that seventeenth-century France was more an amalgam of confederated fiefdoms than a nation-state. When it came to overseas trade, the decentralized nature of France's economy gave greater power to the port cities than to landlocked Paris, a disadvantage that made raising funds in the capital for large-scale maritime investments difficult.

For Colbert, self-sufficiency in trade was essential to stabilizing and eventually improving France's economy. Louis XIV employed traditional methods—namely warfare—in his quest to expand French territory and consolidate his power. But Colbert recognized that economic warfare could prove equally productive. In August 1664 he organized the leading merchants of Paris into a council of commerce, in part to help generate interest in his proposed company.[15] He then hired academician François Charpentier to pen a pamphlet touting the benefits of French trade with the East Indies and commissioned Pierre-Daniel Huet to write a guide to developing a trading company based on the Dutch model.[16] Charpentier stressed that the French consumed at least a third of "the goods brought out of the Indies" by the Dutch, English, and even the smaller Danish and Swedish companies and argued that the French would pay at least 12 percent less for the same Indian goods "if we fetched it ourselves."[17]

Despite the minister's promotional efforts, Colbert brought in only eight of the fifteen million livres needed to start the new company. Three of those eight were provided by the king, and much of the balance flowed in only as a result of political pressure applied on less-than-willing members of France's merchant class.[18] By comparison, Louis XIV drained forty-six million livres from the treasury for the design, construction, and appointment of Versailles, with over 1.6 million *livres tournois* (livres) spent on the main palace from 1664 to 1665 alone.[19]

The resulting French Company of the East Indies, then, officially chartered as the Compagnie des Indes orientales on September 1, 1664, was persistently underfinanced and entangled with the state.[20] It was dependent on the state treasury for many of the funds its directors managed to secure throughout the seventeenth century. Unlike Richelieu's company, however, the new company went beyond limited colonization schemes in Madagascar (although organizers continued attempts to create a provisioning base there) to form a basic model for trade in the East Indies that relied upon a network of strategically placed comptoirs scattered along the Indian coast from Surat to Bengal.

The company was but one aspect of Colbert's attempt to pry French trading interests from the hands of the Dutch and, to a lesser extent, the English. His approach was multifaceted and required a tremendous expenditure of resources. When Colbert came to power as finance minister, the entire French naval fleet consisted of three dozen vessels, including four cargo ships and six galleys. In 1664 the minister counted only "200 seaworthy ships" in the entire merchant marine, while English and Dutch merchant ships numbered in the thousands.[21] As part of his efforts to reform French trade, Colbert oversaw a massive buildup of naval forces. Ships were purchased from the Dutch, raw materials were amassed from northern Europe, shipyards were established along the Atlantic coast, and funds and manpower were dedicated to improving port facilities.[22]

Colbert also directed state finances into hydrographic explorations, which resulted in the 1693 publication of *Le Neptune françois*. Published simultaneously in Paris and Amsterdam, the atlas included more than seventy charts depicting Europe's Atlantic and Mediterranean coasts. Increases in cartographic knowledge and maritime resources were essential to Colbert's master plan to establish a seaborne commercial enterprise to help shore up France's weak financial system.

Colbert allotted some of the ships acquired during this period to the recovery of the carrying trade between France and its Caribbean colonies—a trade then largely controlled by the Dutch West India Company (Geoctroyeerde Westindische Compagnie, or WIC). Chartered in 1621 to undermine Spanish power in the Atlantic world through trade and charter-authorized seizure (privateering) of Spanish cargo ships, the WIC was meant to achieve in the Atlantic what the VOC had done in the Indian Ocean. The two companies' spheres of influence converged at the Cape of Good Hope, with the VOC charged with trade to the east and the WIC with trade to the west.[23] By the 1660s Colbert estimated that WIC ships carried three million livres' worth of sugar, tobacco, indigo, and cotton away from France's Caribbean colonies each year. In establishing a French West India Company (Compagnie des Indes occidentales) endowed with an exclusive monopoly on all Atlantic trade, including the slave trade, Colbert hoped to realize his mercantilist dream of a full-circle colonial trading empire: French raw materials grown in the colonies and carried to French ports by French ships would be exchanged for finished goods produced by industries within France.[24]

The mercantilist approach looked good on paper but in reality was far from perfect. French industries were insufficiently developed to furnish the colonies with the variety of goods required to sustain the population or their agricultural ventures, and France was not yet in a position to supplement local goods with those procured from the East Indies.[25] Despite efforts to improve roads and reform France's archaic system of interregional tolls and customs, moving trade goods within France as well as from the interior to the coast remained difficult. Worse, mercantilist policy mandated that only raw goods could be produced and exported by the colonies. For French sugar producers sending their crop to France from Saint-Domingue and Martinique, this arrangement was highly problematic.

French refineries, accustomed to processing only limited quantities of sugar because Dutch processors had previously handled the bulk of refinement, were flooded with unrefined sugar.[26] To offset plummeting sugar prices, Colbert issued orders demanding that West Indian producers dedicate less land to sugar cultivation. This directive left some planters with the difficult choice of either transitioning their fields and laborers from sugarcane to tobacco cultivation or continuing to grow the same quantities of cane as before the directive, in hopes of selling illicitly to foreign merchants.

Shifting land to tobacco cultivation posed its own set of problems. Demand within France was low. In the second half of the seventeenth century, domestic producers were already growing and processing enough tobacco to satisfy domestic demand. Outside of France, particularly in Holland and England, where merchants consolidated imported tobacco from the Chesapeake and West Indies for reexportation and sale to northern Europe and the Baltics, demand was higher. But even in high-demand regions—and eventually even in France—the style of tobacco produced by French growers was largely eschewed in favor of that grown in the Chesapeake style. French-style tobacco was often produced *en carotte*, a style of curing and packing the leaf into a rolled cylinder that resulted in a product better suited to snuffing than smoking. Fully dried leaf tobacco, such as that produced in the Chesapeake, weighed far less than the rolled variety and was therefore less expensive to import than French West Indian tobacco, even after factoring in the added costs of trade tariffs and shipping.[27] Conversely, French colonial planters were paid by the pound for their tobacco rolls, which discouraged them from adopting English processing methods that resulted in a far lighter product. Rather than stimulate trade, then, the French West India Company and Colbert's monopsonistic policies stifled sugar production and failed to convince colonial planters of the benefits of shifting from sugar to tobacco. By the close of the seventeenth century, the French West India Company had collapsed.

Colbert's desire to wage economic warfare through trade was further undercut by Louis XIV's thirst for Continental territory. Within just eight years of the founding of the Company of the East Indies, the Dutch War—instigated against the Dutch by Louis XIV—had spread across Europe, drawing many of France's already meager resources away from investment at sea, crippling the company in its infancy.[28] The 1678 Treaty of Nijmegen ended the Dutch War, but the damage had been done. Financial woes incurred during the war persisted. From 1675 to 1706 the company, whose funds were entangled with those of the state, experienced a series of bankruptcies and reorganizations. Unable to piece together enough funds to keep the company fleet afloat, shareholders leased the company's monopoly privileges to private merchants in 1706.[29]

By the beginning of the eighteenth century, there were five monopoly trading companies operating under French charters; none of them was especially effective. In the Far East, Colbert's floundering company was joined by the Royal China Company (Compagnie Royale de la Chine), and in Africa the French Atlantic slave trade fell to the Senegal, Guinea, and Saint-Domingue Companies, which had taken over the trade in the Caribbean from the defunct French West India Company. In Louisiana, the Crown granted a single financier, Antoine Crozat, monopoly rights to the entire colony in 1712, guaranteeing his domain over mining, the fur and pelt trade, and the cultivation and processing of silk, indigo, wool, and leather.[30] The terms of the monopoly also established Crozat as the exclusive supplier of French goods to the colonial population, which by contemporary estimates appears not to have exceeded 360 settled individuals, including no more than 200 French soldiers, civilians, and sailors; between 100 and 150 Indian slaves; and a handful of African slaves.[31]

In 1682 explorer–fur traders René-Robert Cavelier de La Salle and Henri de Tonty, along with an expeditionary team of twenty-three Frenchmen and eighteen Indians, sailed from New France through the Great Lakes drainage system into the Mississippi River, reaching the river's mouth in the Gulf of Mexico on April 9, 1682. Aware of the strategic benefits to be gained by controlling the river system connecting France's territories in Canada and the Illinois country to their tropical counterparts in the circum-Carribean basin and hopeful that the territory's proximity to Spanish Mexico might afford opportunities for mineral extraction (whether mined or plundered), La Salle claimed the river and the vast swath of territory that bounded it in the name of Louis XIV.[32]

Yet in the thirty years before Louis XIV awarded monopoly control of the colony to Crozat, the addition of Louisiana to France's overseas empire yielded few tangible benefits. After La Salle's initial descent of the Mississippi River, he sojourned briefly in Quebec before returning to France, where he secured permission and funds to plant a settlement upriver from the Mississippi's mouth. He took with him a group of some three hundred soldiers, laborers, and colonists. In 1684 the expeditionary force set sail for Louisiana with instructions from the king to erect a fortified base from which French ships could harass the Spanish. Unfortunately for the French, La Salle overshot the Mississippi and landed at Matagorda Bay, along the present-day Texas coast near Galveston. The mission did not end well: only a handful of the colonists survived the failed settlement experience. Six soldiers eventually made their way to Canada, while another half-dozen took refuge with a group of East Texas Indians. La Salle was murdered by his own men in 1687.[33]

Twelve years passed before another attempt was made to secure French claims on Louisiana. Aware of the territory's strategic importance in preventing unchecked English expansion westward from the Carolinas, French minister of the Marine Louis Phélypeaux, comte de Pontchartrain, renewed plans to occupy Louisiana following the 1697 Treaty of Ryswick. Between 1698 and 1702, Pontchartrain and his successor and son, Jérôme Phélypeaux, comte de Pontchartrain, authorized and funded the outfitting of three expeditions led by Canadian adventurer Pierre Le Moyne d'Iberville. The first departed from Brest, France, on October 24, 1698. After a stopover in Saint-Domingue and a brief anchorage off Mobile Bay, the expedition's three ships sailed into Biloxi Bay in early February 1699.[34] By the end of 1702, Iberville—along with his brothers, Jean-Baptiste Le Moyne de Bienville and Joseph Le Moyne de Sérigny, and contingents of soldier-laborers from Canada and France—had established three fortified outposts along the Gulf Coast: Fort Maurepas (established in 1699, reinforced in 1700) on Biloxi Bay; Fort de La Boulaye (1700, also known as the Fort of Mississippi) on the east bank of the Mississippi River, approximately eighteen leagues from the river's mouth; and Fort Louis (1702) on Mobile Bay.[35]

In the first decade of settlement, French colonists struggled against climate, disease, and hunger to maintain possession of the three forts and explore the territory's interior. Across the Atlantic, France found itself caught up in yet another Continental war: the War of Spanish Succession (1701–14). For the barely established Louisiana outposts, France's entrance into the war meant that ships intended to supply the fledgling colony with provisions, laborers, and soldiers were diverted to naval campaigns. For the Le Moyne brothers, prospects in Louisiana looked bleak. As early as the spring of 1700, Iberville recounted his disappointment to Rochefort's intendant Michel Bégon. He lamented the poor quality of the soil surrounding Fort Maurepas, the "miserable" nature of a native population, which was "incapable of making any valuable contribution to the development of the land," and the generally "uninteresting" local produce, which would be of no "great use" in trade.[36] Pontchartrain, aware of the French Marine's inability to support the colony while its ships, manpower, and finances were otherwise engaged, used the occasion of Iberville's death, in 1705, to begin casting about for investors. He planned to form a merchant company, modeled after those active in the previous century in the French Caribbean, to take over Louisiana's management.[37]

Pontchartrain spent more than a half-decade attempting to broker such a deal. One by one negotiations fell apart: with merchant Antoine Alexandre de Rémonville, naval supplies director Jean-Baptiste Duché, Rochefort port official Paul Bigot, and many others.[38] By the time Crozat was persuaded to accept monopoly control over the struggling colony in 1712, four years had passed since a French ship had appeared upon its shores. Bienville wrote repeatedly to French ministers of the need for provisions and trade goods from France; lacking provisions, colonists turned to the local Mobilian and Tahomé Indian villages surrounding

Fort Louis for sustenance. Some fifty men stationed at the fort, including ship carpenter André Pénicaut, left the post entirely, choosing to live and trade among the coastal Indians until supplies arrived from France.[39]

Crozat, who by the time he took on Louisiana had garnered more than twenty years' experience financing and promoting commercial schemes around the globe, began his career as a clerk in the offices of Languedoc's treasurer-general of estates, Pierre Louis de Reich de Pennautier. From that clerkship, Crozat rose through the ranks of public finance via his service in a series of purchased offices. By the 1690s, his investments in wide-ranging commercial ventures, including the Saint-Domingue and Guinea Companies, made him a well-established figure in French financial circles.[40] Much like the English Lords Proprietors, to whom Charles II awarded the Charter of Carolina in 1663, Crozat, at the time of his receipt of the Louisiana monopoly, had followed potential profits wherever they appeared. From 1697—when Crozat became one of nine partners granted the French tobacco monopoly—to 1712, the former clerk from Languedoc was, as one historian noted, "mixed up in virtually every risky commercial venture from South America to China."[41]

In Louisiana, Crozat intended to reap maximum profits through the company set up in his name with minimal personal investment. The charter gave Crozat control over "all settlements, ports, harbors, rivers, and especially the port and harbor at Dauphin (formerly Massacre) Island; the Saint Louis (formerly Mississippi) River from the coast to the Illinois country, including the Saint Philip (formerly Missouri) and Saint Jerome (formerly Ouabasha) Rivers, as well as all the territory, lands, lakes, and rivers that flow directly or indirectly into the Saint Louis River."[42] His primary focus, however, was mineral extraction. Rumors of copper and silver deposits in the Upper Mississippi Valley had been circulating in France since around 1695, when Pierre-Charles Le Sueur first recorded the presence of copper and lead traces along the Green River.[43] The rumors persisted through the first decades of the eighteenth century. In 1710 Pontchartrain received further word of Louisiana's mineral wealth from then-governor Bienville and commissioner Diron d'Artaguiette, who had in turn heard repeated reports of deposits from Indians in the Missouri and Upper Mississippi Valleys.[44] To persuade Crozat to invest hundreds of thousands of livres in Louisiana, Pontchartrain had enlisted the aid of Antoine de La Mothe de Cadillac. The time Cadillac had spent in the Great Lakes region and as governor of the Detroit settlement was intended to give weight to his observations. He dispatched an aide-mémoire to Crozat outlining "Louisiana's vast riches," which included "mines of gold and silver" and a wealth of "fine pearls."[45] Cadillac's mémoire alone was unlikely to have persuaded Crozat to accept the Louisiana monopoly—though his persistent boasting about his role to Pontchartrain suggests he thought otherwise—but it did contribute to Crozat's flawed perception of the colony's potential.

Crozat's charter guaranteed him the right to explore, extract, and sell any mineral deposits found "in the territory bounded by New Mexico and English Carolina," the Gulf of Mexico and the Illinois country. The colony's mining prospects were thought to include silver, copper, and possibly gold, and the Crown also held out hope that Crozat's company might find precious stones buried deep within the uncharted territory between the Missouri and Mississippi Rivers.[46]

For all the high hopes and persistent rumors of Louisiana's vast untapped mineral wealth, by the end of his five-year tenure Crozat had almost nothing to show for his efforts to ascertain the precise location of rumored deposits. Exploratory mining confirmed the existence of significant lead deposits in the Kaskaskia region, but no serious attempts at either extraction or smelting took place until 1719, two years after Crozat had relinquished the colony. The remaking of Louisiana into a "French Mexico" remained an elusive dream.[47]

The failure to find and extract mineral wealth in the early years of Louisiana's colonization represented a turning point for French designs there. Instead of pursuing extraction, officials in Louisiana looked increasingly to the plantation system established in South Carolina. The two regions shared similarities in climate and latitude, and both had experimented locally with high-value crops, including tobacco. Plantation agriculture required laborers, and in the colonial South the preferred laborers were African slaves. As dreams of finding gold and silver faded, French colonists and administrators flirted briefly with a capital-raising scheme popularized in early South Carolina and based on the sale of mainland North American Indians to the Caribbean. With profits realized in the Indian slave trade, the French could generate the capital needed to purchase African slaves. Thus commenced Bienville's now notorious two-for-one deal, whereby the governor procured Indian slaves (often through his network of Indian allies) to be sold to the French West Indies at a rate of two Indians in exchange for one African. The paucity of French settlers in Louisiana and French reliance on neutral, if not amicable, relationships with many of the territory's native inhabitants, however, made the practice of Indian slavery unsustainable in the long term. Indian nations that made war against other nations in order to generate slaves had the potential to destabilize already tenuous alliances throughout the Mississippi Valley. And most administrators recognized the folly in enslaving local Indians, whose knowledge of the terrain and proximity to kinsmen made them likely runaways.[48]

Attracting willing settlers and supplying the colony's inhabitants with much-needed provisions proved an insurmountable obstacle for Crozat. The financier was only obligated to send twenty "young men or women of his choosing" to the colony each year, and he failed to meet even that quota.[49] He saw the necessity of increasing Louisiana's population but was unwilling to pay the costs of transporting settlers from France. He turned instead to the Crown with the view that France might use forced emigration to rid itself of its poor and debauched—to Louisiana's advantage. Louis XIV refused to endorse Crozat's scheme.[50] Moreover, the king's comptroller rejected payment of passage even for prospective colonists who willingly desired to make the Atlantic crossing.[51] In granting the Louisiana monopoly to Crozat, the Crown believed it had discharged its financial responsibility for the colony; royal officials remained reluctant to expend any funds on its development.

The dearth of colonists, particularly skilled laborers, contributed to Louisiana's failure to thrive and undermined efforts to develop infrastructure that might support lead mining or even agricultural endeavors. The years of Crozat's monopoly were some of the most desperate for colonists in Louisiana. Crozat banned local and circum-Caribbean trade, extinguishing opportunities for self-sufficiency that had existed for Mobile residents selling homegrown produce and chickens to the neighboring Spanish in Pensacola and coastal residents selling lumber to passing ships.[52] Extreme poverty and hunger plagued the French population at the Mobile and Dauphin Island settlements, forcing colonists and soldiers time and again to depend on aid from neighboring Indians.

As in the years prior to Crozat's involvement, Frenchmen continued to seek refuge among the Indians, who fed and clothed them.[53] The terms of Crozat's charter mandated that he send to Louisiana two ships per year carrying twenty-five tons of provisions, munitions, and other necessities.[54] But the needs of a colony unable to produce even the most basic provisions, such as flour, were so great that even when Crozat sent the required supplies (as he did during the first two years of his charter), the quantity proved insufficient. Worse, Crozat stopped sending ships with any regularity after 1714, aggravating colonists' already fragile hold on life in Louisiana.

Crozat ultimately failed to make a fortune in Louisiana. In 1716 the newly formed French Chamber of Justice levied a retroactive tax on individuals who had profited personally from French colonial expansion projects during the reign of Louis XIV; Crozat was assessed 6.6 million livres.[55] Furious at being taxed for his role in expanding France's commercial empire and uninterested in investing the capital necessary to develop Louisiana, he ceded his monopoly to a company recently resurrected by France's rising star—the Scotsman John Law—as partial payment against his debt.[56]

John Law and the Consolidated Company

Since the late 1680s, efforts to resurrect Colbert's vision of an overseas trading empire had been limited primarily to false starts in Louisiana and expansion of the number of comptoirs operating in Bengal and southern India. The Lorient port facilities of the defunct Company of the East Indies had been requisitioned by the French navy at the start of the War of Spanish Succession in 1701, as had most of what remained of its fleet, but a contingent of company bureaucrats and administrators remained in South Asia.[57] In 1689 André Bourreau Deslandes, son-in-law of François Martin, high administrator of the company's Indian Ocean interests, oversaw the development of French comptoirs along the Ganges and its tributaries at Hugli (a former Portuguese enclave across the Hugli River from the EIC base at Calcutta), Cassimbazar, and Patna as well as a way station in Balassor, along the Bay of Bengal.[58] The following year Deslandes embarked on a successful campaign to court favor with Mughal officials and Ibrahim Khan, the local nawab (provincial governor) of Bengal's capital, Dacca. The company had acquired land and trading rights in Chandernagore, a village just north of Calcutta, from Khan's predecessor, Shaista Khan, in 1674, but it was not until Deslandes's intervention that the French began actively participating in Bengal's extensive textile trade.[59]

As with its entry into the Indian Ocean more generally, the French company arrived late to Bengal. The Portuguese were the first Europeans to establish a settlement in India's easternmost province in 1580, and though the Mughals expelled the Iberians in 1632, Portuguese merchants remained active in the province through the first half of the eighteenth century. The Dutch and English arrived in the 1630s and commenced trade at Pipli, Balassor, Hugli, and Dacca. Calcutta—future seat of the British Empire in India—had been established as a permanent English base in 1690, following a two-decade-long hiatus in the province that resulted from political and military tensions between the British and the reigning Mughal authorities. All of the European traders conducting business in Bengal found themselves enmeshed in an active and competitive textile market, whose experienced local merchants, agents, and weavers often had the upper hand with regards to credit and output. Over the next half-century, Bengal's high-quality silks, lightweight *indiennes*, and muslins made up the majority of the French company's cargoes sailing from the Bay of Bengal.[60]

In southeast India, François Martin reestablished the company's presence in Pondicherry, which had been regained from the Dutch following the signing of the 1697 Treaty of Ryswick. When the Dutch decamped, Pondicherry quickly became the capital of France's Indian Ocean trading network, a position it held until the late 1750s. As French comptoirs multiplied and became more established, opportunities increased for country trade, port-to-port trade that occurred within the confines of the northern Indian Ocean. Yet there was no corresponding expansion of maritime support—no new ships, no dedicated crews or outfitting ports—from France. Trade stayed within Asia, with little benefit to the metropole. With no company ships making the East Indian circuit, there was no profit to be made from the circulation of the region's high-demand trade goods in France. But that was soon to change.

John Law arrived in Paris in the summer of 1714. A Scotsman with a reputation for gambling and worse—he had escaped from London's

King's Bench prison, where he had been incarcerated and sentenced to death for killing a man in a duel some nine years earlier—Law set out to remake himself in France's capital. He took up residence with his common-law wife, Katherine Seigneur (née Knowles), in a lavishly furnished house on the exclusive Place Louis-le-Grand (now Place Vendôme).[61] He likely chose this newly constructed square because the residences lining it were home to some of the most influential financiers in Paris. Antoine Crozat lived just down the square from Law, as did Paul Poisson de Bourvalais, secretary of the Council of Finances, and Claude-François Paparel, treasurer-general for the war ministry. For a man intent on wheeling and dealing his way into Parisian society, a residence on Place Louis-le-Grand afforded Law a prime location from which to entertain.

Law had a reputation as a gambler, but as economic historian Antoin E. Murphy has shown, that appellation is misleading.[62] Law was more statistician than gambler. In his time at the tables in Amsterdam, Paris, Venice, and Genoa, Law played the role of banker, who was "in modern terms the equivalent of bookkeeper, able to exploit the gambling weaknesses of those who played against him."[63] He used his mathematical genius to his advantage, amassing a substantial fortune by the time he took up permanent residence in Paris. But Law had accumulated more than monetary wealth during his time spent in Europe's urban centers. He had also gained an understanding of financial systems and banking and of how they might be used to stabilize economies on a large scale.

By the time he settled in Paris, the Scotsman was on his way to establishing himself as one of the period's most influential economic theorists. In 1705 he published *Money and Trade Considered with a Proposal for Supplying the Nation with Money,* a treatise Law hoped would cure his native country's economic ills.[64] He was not alone in the effort to right Scotland's economy, which had fallen to pieces in the wake of the collapse of the Company of Scotland, or the Darien Company, whose primary mission had been to establish a colony on the isthmus of Panama that would act as a base for trade. That colonization attempt failed spectacularly, and the trading company's demise created a severe shortage of specie in Scotland. Law's proposal centered on the creation of a land bank that would by design alleviate the country's specie shortage through the issuance of paper money backed by the value of land. Although Law published the treatise anonymously, his authorship was well known by the time the proposal was considered—and rejected—by the Scottish Parliament in the summer of 1705. His reputation as a gambler and escaped convict had preceded him.

The following year Law sought an audience with Louis XIV in France, where a severe specie shortage, repeated military engagements, and mounting state debt combined to put Europe's most populous nation on increasingly precarious financial footing.[65] In "Mémoire touchant les monoies et le commerce" (Mémoire concerning Money and Trade), Law proposed the creation of a French national bank that would issue paper money, expand available credit, and promote trade (objectives known collectively as "Law's System"), but he failed to get the proposal past the king's controller general.[66] In 1707 Law's second and third submissions—both variations on the first—seem to have reached the king, but they were also rejected. Not until Law established himself in Paris were any of his proposals entertained in earnest by the French king and his ministers. Yet just as Law faced the prospect of seeing his financial plans adopted by a European ruler, Louis XIV died, on September 1, 1715.

The king's death left France in the hands of his five-year-old great-grandson, whose reign would be overseen by the regent Philippe, duc d'Orléans, until the dauphin reached the age of majority at thirteen. The regent inherited a financial crisis of epic proportions: France's treasury was bankrupt; state debt topped two billion livres, not including annual interest payments of ninety million livres to its creditors; and the treasury had borrowed against future tax revenues through 1718.[67] The entire financial system was on the verge of collapse, a situation that left the regent predisposed to consider Law's proffered solutions.

Law's ascent following the death of Louis XIV was meteoric. Within two months, his proposal to create a national bank was heard before the finance council. By the following summer, the Banque générale had become a reality.[68] The establishment and legitimization of the bank was the first phase of Law's ambitious financial reform program. The second required the creation of a powerful—and successful—trading company.

Crozat's relinquishment of his Louisiana charter, following his penalization by the Chamber of Justice in November 1716, proved propitious. It allowed Law an opportunity to form his own company, one whose financial backers, according to Law, would be quickly rewarded for their support with a healthy return on their investment. Crozat, like Pontchartrain and Cadillac before him, spun a fantasy for the prospective charter holder, expounding on the glories of Louisiana and the ripeness of the colony's soil for tobacco cultivation.

Tobacco was grown during Crozat's tenure but only in quantities fit for private consumption and local trade. Crozat blamed much of his own failure in Louisiana on the impossibility of securing colonists and slave laborers to clear and work the land. He faulted the slave trading companies for inadequate supplies and colonists in the more successful French Caribbean colonies for snatching up Louisiana-bound slaves before they could reach the mouth of the Mississippi. That Crozat had failed to establish a single tobacco plantation anywhere in the colony during his tenure seems to have been left out of his sales pitch.[69]

It is unclear just how much of Crozat's tale Law swallowed; he may simply have recognized the wider salability of Crozat's claims, choosing to embrace the picture of a Louisiana blanketed with tobacco fields as a promising promotional device. Or he may have seen tobacco as the perfect commodity through which he might justify the consolidation of other, preexisting trading companies (and trade monopolies) into his own.

However Law understood the colony's actual tobacco prospects, in August 1717 his newly formed Company of the West (Compagnie d'Occident, also known as the Mississippi Company) received a twenty-five-year monopoly over fur trading, mineral rights, and the distribution of goods in Louisiana.[70] A year later, in September 1718, the regent awarded the company a nine-year monopoly of the coveted and lucrative tobacco farm.[71] That December, Law's bank became a royal entity known as the "Banque royale," bringing Law and the Company of the West closer to the state. At the same time, the Company of the West took over the ailing Senegal Company—which itself had already absorbed the Saint-Domingue and Guinea Companies—with the professed objective of using the slaving company's eleven seaworthy ships and trading network to carry slave laborers from Africa to Louisiana's yet-to-be-established tobacco fields.[72]

To raise working capital and fund the acquisition and absorption of smaller companies, the Company of the West issued a series of shares, which allowed the ten newly appointed company directors—Jean-Baptiste d'Artaguiette, François Castanier, Jean-Baptiste Duché, Simon Gilly, Louis Boyvin d'Hardancourt, Law (who served as director in chief), René Moreau, François Mouchard, Jean Piou, and Antoine Raudot—to invest in improving long-neglected infrastructure in Paris, Lorient, and the surviving comptoirs. This money-raising scheme was authorized by the state, which benefited from the arrangement by the elimination of some of its floating debt. The initial 1717 offering of 200,000 shares (called *mères*, or mother shares) could be purchased only with *billets d'état*—the paper notes of credit issued by the Crown, whose valuation was prone to violent fluctuations. The government's intent was to decrease the number of unstable billets in circulation while promoting the sale of shares in what Law and the Crown viewed as a more stable alternative. In exchange, the company received 4 percent interest from the Crown on the billets d'état, a lower rate than what the Crown paid to most of its creditors.

To Law's disappointment, sales of the first shares issued were sluggish; more than a year passed before all the stock subscriptions were filled. Part of the difficulty stemmed from the stipulation that shares be purchased exclusively with billets d'état. Sales were also slowed by rumors that the regent was helping artificially prop up the scheme by purchasing a significant number of shares on behalf of the king (he had in fact bought 40 percent of the first issuance). For Law to realize his dream of creating a powerful trading company while providing financial stability to the French state, it was imperative that he find a way to create enthusiasm and trust among prospective subscribers.

By the summer of 1719, Law's company had absorbed the remnants of Colbert's Company of the East Indies, the Royal China Company, and the Africa Company (Compagnie d'Afrique). Acquisition of the Royal China Company gave Law's company exclusive domain over French trade "from the Cape of Good Hope to all the seas of the East Indies, the islands of Madagascar, Bourbon, and France, Africa's coast of Sofala [Mozambique], the Red Sea, Persia, Mongolia, Siam, China, and Japan." Further acquisition of the Africa Company expanded company presence across North Africa.[73] The resulting conglomerate, the Company of the Indies (Compagnie des Indes), had the most far-reaching geographic scope in the history of European trading companies but also the least financial and administrative ability to sustain such an expansion.

To finance the aforementioned acquisitions, Law released two more share issuances in June (called *filles* and *petites filles*, or daughter and granddaughter shares) and eliminated the stipulation that they be purchased with billets d'état. At the same time, the Banque royale issued 50 million livres' worth of banknotes to ensure that there was enough cash in circulation to cover new share purchases, and Law pledged to personally underwrite the new shares. A month later, on July 25, 1719, the bank released an additional 240 million livres in banknotes. Loosened subscription requirements, an increased money supply, and Law's personal investment of 25 million livres bolstered public confidence.

In order to convince the public that Louisiana was worthy of investment, Law's company engaged in a propaganda campaign whose mission was not only to promote the sale of shares but also to encourage immigration to Louisiana.[74] Two promotional posters published around 1719 lauded Louisiana's natural resources and fertile farmland. The first, printed in Paris and titled *Le Commerce que les Indiens du Mexique font avec les François au port de Missisipi* (Trade Conducted by Indians from

Fig. 2. Promotional broadside circulated by the French Company of the Indies in hopes of encouraging immigration to Louisiana. (Courtesy of The Historic New Orleans Collection, 1952.3.)

Mexico with the French at the Mississippi Port [fig. 2]), describes the colony as an idyllic land of plenty, with "mountains full of gold, silver, copper, lead, and quicksilver." The future capital at New Orleans was, according to promoters, already home "to more than six hundred well-built houses" and a "magnificent" port.[75] In reality, New Orleans in 1719 was little more than a partly cleared mud pit, home to a few dozen hastily built shacks and only primitive port facilities.

A German-language broadside and accompanying map published in Liepzig and titled *Geographische Beschreibung der Provinz Louisiana in Canada von dem Fluß St. Lorenz bis an den Ausfluß des Flusses Missisipi* (Geographical description of the Louisiana province in Canada from the St. Lawrence River to the mouth of the Mississippi) also focused on Louisiana's bounty and unparalleled fertility, encouraging prospective settlers to book the next possible transatlantic passage. According to its anonymous author, "the open fields of this wild land are filled with buffalo, deer, bears, partridge, quail, parrots, woodcock, turtle doves, beaver, otter, marten, and many other birds and game," "wood to build ships is available in abundance," "hemp grows without being planted," and there is "so much copper and lead that one could provide for a whole kingdom." To help investors take the plunge, the author highlighted the benefit of stock value based on actual transferrable plots of land in the colony—a value not carried by Dutch or English company stock—and "the potential for great trade there."[76]

Law's promotional efforts worked. By mid-June 1719, the value of first-issue shares had risen 30 percent, and shareholders began to reap dividends on their investments, prompting a rapid rise in the sale of new subscriptions. With the supply of filles and petites filles exhausted and their corresponding valuations on the rise, demand for more shares and speculation on those already in circulation soared. On September 4, 1719, first-issue shares were valued at five thousand livres, an increase of 900 percent over the original purchase price, and by then Law had managed to gain even more control over the direction of France's finances.

In July the company acquired rights to the mint's profits for the following nine years. Weeks later, the regent canceled the existing lease of France's tax-collecting entity (known as the Ferme générale, or United Farms), then held by prominent financier-brothers Antoine, Claude, Jean, and Joseph Pâris, and transferred it to the company. With help from an enabling regent, Law hoped to streamline France's tax collection system and eliminate the myriad middlemen who reaped personal profit at the Crown's expense from the United Farms.[77]

The public's appetite for company shares in the fall of 1719 seemed insatiable. In the two-week span from September 26 to October 4, Law released four additional issuances (the first of petites filles, the next three of an issuance called *cinq cents*, or five hundreds) totaling 324,000 shares. Trade along the rue Quincampoix spilled over from the company's share sales office into the street, where the frenzied throng of investors and speculators was so thick that the city had to issue a ban on horses and carriages to prevent citizens from being trampled. The speculative fever popularly known as the "Mississippi Bubble" took hold of men and women from all walks of life. Through early 1720, share values continued to rise, peaking at over ten thousand livres per share just days after Law's January 5 appointment as controller general of France.[78]

Rather than ensuring the success of his system, Law's appointment to France's highest administrative office represented the beginning of its demise. Big investors, sensing an impending fall in stock prices, began to cash in their shares shortly before his appointment. In refusing to accept banknotes in return for their shares, they nearly emptied the Banque royale of specie. At the same time, rumors of the discouraging state of affairs in Louisiana—which had produced neither minerals nor tobacco—swirled, halting the slow stream of immigration to the colony. Distrust of Law grew; public confidence in his system wavered. As company stock plummeted, shareholders rushed to cash in, and the mint printed more banknotes to meet demand, causing widespread inflation. On November 27 the bank closed its doors. By December, Law's System had collapsed, despite efforts by the controller general to stabilize the credit market and restore public confidence.[79]

Law's Legacy

Law's fall from favor was as strikingly swift as his rise had been. By late December 1720 he had fled France, the nation's economic apparatus was in shambles, and thousands were left holding worthless paper notes. For the Company of the Indies, however, Law's tenure had brought about an unprecedented level of financial and operational stability. The collapse of his system, though spectacular in its speed and magnitude, did not spell an end to company operations. Instead, after a chaotic reorganization period following Law's expulsion, the company emerged in 1723 as a largely profitable entity.

Under the system, company directors oversaw the acquisition and outfitting of dozens of vessels for use in overseas trade. From 1717 to 1720 the company purchased existing ships from Brest, Hamburg, and Nantes and initiated construction of at least nineteen new ones at shipyards in Bayonne, Hamburg, La Rochelle, London, Marseille, and Nantes. Directors also invested heavily in new masts, rigging, hardware, and naval stores.[80] During that same period, ninety company vessels departed French Atlantic ports: nine for Peru, ten for the East Indies, three for China, twenty for the West African coast, five for the West Indies, and forty-three for Louisiana. At least three of those headed to Louisiana were brigantines with carrying capacities of less than 150 tons, commissioned specifically for use along the territory's interior and coastal waterways. The number of company ships that dropped anchor along the Gulf of Mexico's northern coast in the seventeen-month period from May 1719 to March 1721 far exceeded ships arriving in all previous years combined.[81]

By June 1720 the company had amassed a fleet of approximately seventy-five deep-draft sailing ships.[82] Outfitting continued during the reorganization as ships sent out in preceding years returned to Lorient laden with valuable cargoes. Forty-eight company ships departed French ports between January 1, 1721, and March 23, 1723, including twenty bound for Louisiana, sixteen for the West African coast, seven for the East Indies, two for the West Indies, and one each for Canada, China, and Peru.[83] Increased cash on hand from the sale of cargoes—including those of the *Amphitrite*, *Solide*, and *Vierge de Grâce*, which collectively generated over six million livres—facilitated the purchase of additional trade goods and prompted directors to expand the network of company bureaucrats in France and abroad.[84] By 1723 new comptoirs had been established on the islands of Bourbon (now Réunion), France (Mauritius), Madagascar, and Poulo Condore and in Mahé and Mocha, bringing the total number of comptoirs operating in the Indian Ocean to nine.

Investments in the nuts and bolts of trade—ships, trade goods, port facilities, and people (laborers, sailors, officers, slaves, clerks, and administrators)—left the company in a better position to weather its tumultuous reorganization; other entities drawn into the system, such as the bank and mint, did not fare as well. When the company reemerged in 1723, it did so under the direction of the newly formed Council of the Indies. The council reported to the new controller general, Charles-Gaspard Dodun, and comprised six councillors of state, four high-ranking naval officers, twelve syndics (to represent shareholders' interests), and ten professionals drawn primarily from the merchant class.[85] Day-to-day departmental operations were managed by twelve *négociants-directeurs* who reported to the council. Both groups were overseen by a team of four inspectors general from the king's council.[86] Such a diffusion of administrative power was meant to ensure that no single interest group or individual could initiate unilateral policy changes.

In Paris, the Council of the Indies met in a U-shaped structure acquired by Law in 1719 that had served as the company's headquarters since 1720 (fig. 3). Situated at the corner of rues Vivienne and Neuve des Petits Champs, the offices were flanked by the king's library and the Paris stock exchange.[87] Two storehouses—one housing merchandise collected from points across France and destined for outbound company ships, another storing (and selling) beaver pelts from North America—ran along the rue Vivienne. Cashiers' offices, open to the public, were also at street level, as was the company's central countinghouse.[88] The next level up, the mezzanine, or *entresol,* was home to a crowded tangle of offices.

Filling the space above the ground-floor warehouses were confiscated Indian textiles and Chinese silks smuggled into France in direct violation of the company's monopoly.[89] French protectionist policies allowed the company to distribute and sell imported white linen and muslin within the realm but expressly prohibited the sale of printed cottons and silks. An *arrêt* (judicial ruling) dated December 14, 1723, reiterated the general prohibition (first issued in 1686) on the importation of silk and printed cotton textiles and piece goods by any individual or noncompany entity. The presence of a dedicated confiscation office and the regular reissuance of the ban, which occurred more than thirty-five times between 1686 and 1759, attest to the frequent violation of this prohibition.[90]

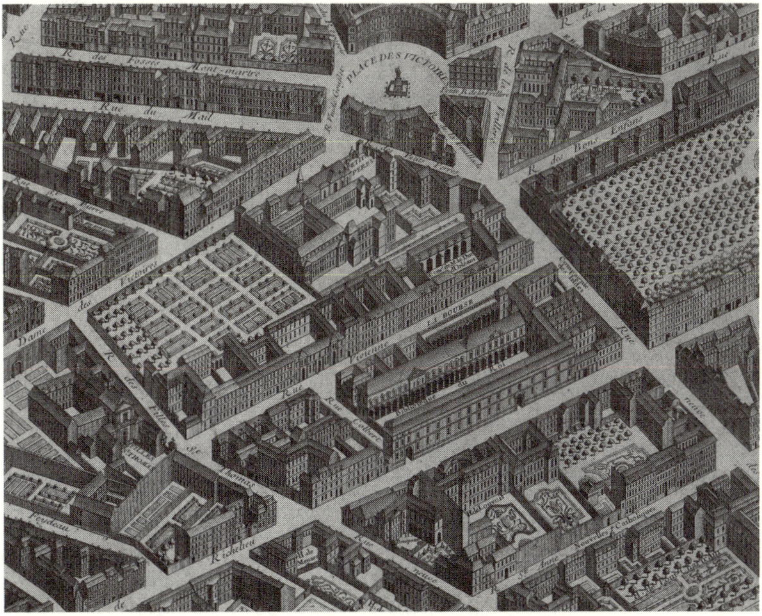

Fig. 3. Detail view of company headquarters in Paris. (Courtesy of The Historic New Orleans Collection, 2012.0206.)

Purchasing offices, whose agents were charged with procuring goods and specie in France that would be traded by company representatives abroad for high-demand goods, overlooked the central courtyard.[91] Agents had to keep up not only with trends within France but also with the nuances of supply and demand in the company's web of interconnected comptoirs. Both consumers and trading partners were fickle. Their shifting tastes had to be anticipated and monitored lest the company find itself stuck with a five-year supply of striped calicoes when checked prints were all the rage. Striking a balance between supply and demand was particularly difficult—and critical—in Africa, where textiles procured in Europe and India served as one of the primary commodities in the slave trade.[92] Purchasing agents kept tabs on which goods or combinations of goods gave the company a trade advantage and which might be written off as a waste of valuable cargo space.

Also overlooking the courtyard from the mezzanine were the company bookkeeping and copying offices. Bookkeepers and their clerks balanced the company's trade, administrative, and outfitting accounts and directed bookkeeping and auditing of company comptoirs around the globe. Next door, dozens of young clerks, or *commis*, whose only technical qualification was that they could write neatly, passed their time copying the hundreds of letters and memorandums in constant circulation among company directors, administrators, and shareholders in Paris; outfitters and ship personnel in Lorient; and comptoir bureaucrats. The same letter might be copied three times or more, depending on its intended recipients and destinations, while a single memo on company procedures might be reproduced by hand more than thirty times if, for example, it needed to reach representatives in all company outposts along the Indian Ocean.

To serve as copy clerk in the company's Paris offices was to hold the lowest available clerical position, requiring the least amount of knowledge. Yet the Paris copying offices were also a gateway to opportunity for the dozens of literate and often well-connected (but cash-poor) young men who cycled through, quill in hand, each year. From this labor pool copy clerks moved on to more specialized departments within the Paris headquarters. Some went next door to the bookkeeping wing, others upstairs to one of the half-dozen offices charged with site-specific correspondence. These work spaces, divided by region, served the Americas, China, India, Lorient, and Senegal, and were likely the last stop for clerks before they were sent to a comptoir.[93] French historian Philippe Haudrère has determined that for its Parisian offices the company typically drew personnel from among one of three general sources: "the Parisian financial sector," "the families of influential individuals involved in company policy making," and "the children or nephews of preexisting personnel."[94] In the 1720s, however, the company had not yet achieved the multigenerational stability in its comptoirs that made clerks from the latter group numerically significant. Haudrère's assessment holds true for personnel in overseas comptoirs as well, given that most cycled through the Paris offices before receiving new commissions. Paris was the training ground for clerks and administrators, but comptoir service was often the ultimate goal for those in the company's employ. Service abroad, especially in the more lucrative trade zones in India and China, brought opportunities for career advancement and increased wealth.

A company clerk, regardless of kinship or patronage ties, was unlikely to advance beyond his clerkship without the benefit of gaining firsthand experience in at least one, and better several, comptoirs. The path was relatively well defined: a stint as a commis in Paris often led to a commission, perhaps in an outpost the clerk had corresponded with during his time in the central offices. Professional advancement within the company hierarchy was not the only motivation for clerks to seek overseas commissions. Indeed, it may not even have been the primary one. A clerk in Paris might have access to a vibrant social and cultural scene after leaving the office, but a clerk in Pondicherry might use his professional connections and access to trade goods to his personal advantage in the country trade. Not all comptoirs, however, were created equal.

Sometime in the autumn of 1728, Marc-Antoine Caillot, a clerk in the company's Paris offices, received his first overseas commission. The following February, he was Louisiana bound. It was the sort of commission more likely to fill a twenty-one-year-old clerk with disappointment than with satisfaction. Compared to comptoirs in the East Indies, most of which were by the late 1720s stable, lucrative sites, those in Louisiana offered few rewards for company bureaucrats hoping to achieve personal gains through trade. Despite the sizable injection of capital and colonists that had taken place during Law's tenure, Louisiana remained largely unprofitable. The colony's capital, which had been moved from Biloxi to New Orleans in 1722, was unfortified and sparsely settled.[95] Mortality rates were horrific for newly arrived colonists, company employees, and slaves alike. And neither company nor colonists had yet realized a profit from the crop touted first by Antoine Crozat and then by John Law as the solution to Louisiana's long-term viability.

But Caillot was young and relatively well connected. Barring any number of sicknesses or accidents that might reasonably result in his death at sea or on land, he faced a career in the service of the company that was likely to offer more attractive prospects later on. His memoir, "Relation du voyage de la Louisianne ou Nouvelle France fait par le Sr. Caillot en l'année 1730" (Account of the Voyage to Louisiana, or New France, Made by Sieur Caillot in the Year 1730), written between 1731 and 1758, provides a rare glimpse of the life of a low-level clerk employed by one of the eighteenth century's most powerful global trading companies.[96]

The eldest surviving son of the footman of the eldest son of Louis XIV, this particular Louisiana-bound clerk was born Marc-Antoine Caillot in Meudon, France, on June 4, 1707, to Pierre Caillot and Marie-Catherine Blanche.[97] Named for his godfather, Marc-Antoine Balligant, an *officier de la bouche,* or table attendant, in the château de Meudon, Marc-Antoine spent his early years in a royal household in turmoil. Meudon's master, Monseigneur le Dauphin, died of smallpox, at age fifty-three, on April 14, 1711. His eldest son, Louis, duc de Bourgogne, then stood to inherit the Crown, but he died just over a year later, at age thirty. The series of deaths visited upon the royal house continued in 1714, with the death of Monseigneur le Dauphin's youngest son, Charles, duc du Berry, and in 1715, with the death of the Sun King himself, at the age of seventy-seven. At the time of Louis XIV's death, Marc-Antoine was eight years old, three years older than the heir to the French Crown.

Located a short carriage ride from Versailles, the château de Meudon was one of eighteen in the network of royal households whose entourage of religious, military, and domestic personnel was known collectively as the "Maison du Roi." Included among the sites in this network were Bellevue, Choisy, Compiègne, Fontainebleu, Madrid, Marly, Meudon, Montreuil, La Muette, Paris (including the Louvre, Luxembourg, and Tuileries), Rambouillet, Saint-Cloud, Saint-Denis, Saint-Germain, Saint-Hubert, Trianon, and Versailles.[98] Sharon Kettering, in her work on the development and maintenance of patron-client networks in seventeenth- and early-eighteenth-century France, has shown that service in noble households provided an exceptional opportunity for kin patronage. This was especially true for those in the service of the Maison du Roi, where multiple generations and branches of the same family often held a variety of appointed positions.[99] Those engaged in household service received a host of benefits, including exemption from direct, royal, and local taxation; legal protection from creditors; exemption from wartime military service; and room, board, and an annual salary.[100] Less tangible, but no less important, members of the Maison du Roi also held the status of trusted companion-attendants. Familiarity bred by attendants' physical proximity to royals often gave way to patron-client relationships beneficial to both attendants and their families.

The extended kinship network that Marc-Antoine Caillot's father and uncle joined ("joined" because the brothers married into families whose heads of household were already members of the Maison du Roi) during the first decade of the eighteenth century offered precisely these types of patronage opportunities. With the exception of the highest-ranking posts, which were filled directly by the king, positions in the Maison du Roi were purchased offices held for life by members of the nobility or by individuals who were ennobled via the purchase. Within Louis XIV's household, individuals filled as many as fifteen hundred venal offices, and this figure does not include the extended domain (households of the queen, royal offspring, and such) of the Maison du Roi.[101] Officeholders reported to the *grand maître de France* (superintendent of the Maison du Roi) and were known collectively as "domestiques commensaux," or the live-in nobility. Among those in support positions were the valets, table attendants, dance masters, stablemen, tutors, footmen, and many others who attended to every detail of the household's inner workings, from supervision of the king's or dauphin's toilette each morning to care of the household's horses, carriages, and hunting dogs. During the Regency, the purchase price of a footman's post in the household of the duchesse de Barry, the regent's daughter who resided at the château de Meudon from 1718 to 1719, was three thousand livres. In return, the footman received a stipend covering food and wardrobe costs and the *droit de manteau*, wages provided to individuals clothed by the king.[102] Through the first quarter of the eighteenth century, offices within the Maison du Roi were frequently passed down within families, creating familial dynasties that ran parallel to those of the royal family.

The generation in which Marc-Antoine and his siblings came of age, however, was a time in which multigenerational service in the Maison du Roi (and in large noble households in general) was coming to a close.[103] When Louis XIV's five-year-old great-grandson and his Paris-based regent succeeded to the throne, Meudon's role in the hierarchy of royal households was considerably diminished. It remained one of many châteaux owned by the king and later became a popular hunting lodge for members of the royal family, but it was no longer the primary residence of anyone in the line of succession.[104] Thus, its staff was no longer in the service of the Maison du Roi. For Marc-Antoine, his brothers, and their cousins, this shift meant that they were less likely to move into apprenticeship positions within the household as pages or members of the chapel choir. Instead, brothers Pierre and François Caillot used their standing to secure positions (and livelihoods) for their offspring outside the Maison du Roi. Among the immediate offspring of these two brothers, Marc-Antoine, the eldest surviving male, received a clerical appointment in the Company of the Indies's Paris offices; two sought their fortunes in Saint-Domingue; and four were awarded lifelong pensions in the name of their fathers' service.[105] For Marc-Antoine, his father's service in the Maison du Roi opened the door to a thirty-plus-year career with the Company of the Indies that began in Paris and ultimately spanned three continents.

2

Approaching the Atlantic World

In the winter of 1729, Marc-Antoine Caillot left the relative comforts of the Company of the Indies's Paris offices and set out on the first leg of a lengthy journey. His destination was a decidedly less hospitable outpost along the banks of the Mississippi River. By leaving France, he became one of the thousands of young men who left the Continent from France, Spain, the Netherlands, and most notably England for the Americas in hopes of bettering their economic standing.

It is important to note, however, that in comparison to other European powers of the late seventeenth and early eighteenth centuries, France's colonizing impulse was decidedly weak. At the height of the race to colonize and settle the New World, France was the most populous nation in Europe. But its teeming population did not translate into significant numbers of willing colonists eager to brave the climatic and cultural extremes of Canada and the circum-Caribbean colonies.[1] In Louisiana, for example, a series of ill-fated colonization schemes during John Law's tenure drew emigrants from among the metropole's least-desirable citizens, including the long-term unemployed, tobacco and salt smugglers, petty thieves, and prostitutes. Despite the actual number of colonists of questionable background being much smaller than the present-day historical imagination would suggest, contemporary knowledge of these schemes helped contribute to the struggling colony's reputation for debauchery. This reputation was further tainted by rumors of individuals (typically young men) being sent to the colony under *lettres de cachet*, royal decrees that offered well-connected wayward souls caught up in any number of scandals, from theft and gambling to sexual peccadilloes, a way out of incarceration in France.[2] The use of lettres de cachet was intended to benefit both the subject of the decree, who was expected to seize upon his exile as an opportunity for self-reform, and the subject's family, which might minimize potential scandal by sending the troublemaker across the ocean. Despite the rumors and persistent references to such individuals in contemporary accounts, however, there are only two individuals listed as arriving under lettres de cachet in contemporary passenger registers.[3] One, a Sieur Conians, arrived in 1717. The second, Sieur Ballay, arrived two years later aboard the *Saint-Louis*. Both sailed from La Rochelle.[4]

For Caillot, employment as a bookkeeping and copying clerk in the Company of the Indies's Louisiana offices did not result from any odious prior act but rather from simple economic necessity and a desire to secure a post where his service would likely result in future advancement. As a clerk, Caillot was among the hundreds of administrative representatives scattered across the globe whose collective charge was to advance the mercantilist and bureaucratic policies of the French state. Caillot left Paris for Lorient, the home port of the Company of the Indies, on February 19, 1729. From Lorient he would board a company ship that would carry him across the Atlantic to Louisiana. During the overland leg of his journey, he traveled with two companions, one of whom, a Sieur de Troyes, was also headed to Louisiana as a company clerk. Caillot did not identify the third traveler, but it may have been a man named Sieur de Bussy, another company employee who had received a commission as bookkeeper some two weeks earlier. All three received travel allowances.[5] The trio traveled primarily on horseback, following the network of *grands chemins*, or royal roads, that radiated outward across France from Paris to the Atlantic and Mediterranean coasts and to the southern, northern, and eastern frontiers. These grands chemins served as complementary appendages to the web of waterways that had long conducted goods, people, and information among the communities lining their banks.

Begun in the fifteenth century during the reign of Louis XI, the royal road system was expanded and improved upon in the seventeenth century as part of Louis XIV's efforts to centralize governmental power and authority.[6] The importance of the road system in maintaining ties between Paris and the commercial port cities along the Atlantic coast grew under Colbert.[7] In the late seventeenth through early eighteenth centuries, the expansion of ports serving as operational bases for chartered monopoly companies further prompted the expansion and regulation of the royal road system, as thousands of letters, reports, and decrees—not to mention trade goods—traveled back and forth between the king and his ministers, provincial governors, port administrators, merchants, company officers, stockholders, and the like.[8]

The first two days of the journey to the coast proved difficult for Caillot; he was filled with regret at leaving behind friends and family who had "only shown [him] manifestations of kindness."[9] Despondent and depressed, Caillot provided little detail on the passing countryside or meals taken during stops in Palaiseau, Bonelle, and Lauray Ford, choosing instead to wallow in the fear that he might never see his family again. But his melancholy was short lived. At the urging of his travel companions, he soon turned to the task of "erasing for a while thoughts of [his] parents and friends" by availing himself of what he described as "Bacchic liqueur."[10] The alcohol brought a welcome change to Caillot's spirits, but its effects on his judgment and physical coordination were less desirable. Driven to leave behind his sorrows in body as well as mind, Caillot pushed his "horse forward with such violence that one of its front feet slipped," sending Caillot flying "over his head" in a tangle of harness straps and stirrups, damaging his hunting horn and breaking his gun in half.[11]

Fortunately for the young clerk, there was little chance that his behavior would lead him too far from his charted path. For one, he had the company of Troyes and the other, unnamed traveler to help him stay the course. But more important, Caillot traveled on a network of royal roads that had by 1729 become synonymous with the royal courier, or mail, system. Royal mail couriers and travelers alike followed these grands chemins, traveling by coach or horseback from one postal exchange (*relais de poste,* or simply *poste*) to the next at set intervals. Coaches carried not only royal mail but also correspondence generated by individuals and institutional entities, such as France's religious and university communities, whose once separate mail services had by 1715 been absorbed by the royal courier system.[12] *Messageries* also operated on the grands chemins, transporting travelers and merchandise between postal exchanges. Because traveling with the mail coaches and messageries offered some protection against roadside attack and helped to ensure the timely arrival of the directionally challenged to their destinations, independent travelers often accompanied coaches, following timetables and stopover patterns dictated by postal schedules and established exchanges. Caillot and his traveling companions were no exception. The trio took full advantage of the itinerary published by the royal postal bureau. Each stop along their route corresponded with postes listed in the guide to royal mail service published annually by royal authority as *Liste générale des postes de France.*

Postes served as a sort of eighteenth-century precursor to travel plazas or rest stops, where travelers refreshed themselves and their horses, changed horses altogether, and gathered news of the road ahead. At postes there were travel amenities, including inns, taverns, stables, and churches. If travelers were unable or unwilling to keep pace with the mail coaches, they could use passing coaches to relay messages to postes down the line. In this way travelers announced their imminent arrival and often sent ahead word of their travel or lodging needs, so that innkeepers and stablemen might prepare rooms, meals, and stalls in advance. Coaches also relayed more specific needs: when Caillot and his companions reached the small village of Durtal on the first Sunday of their trek, they found the village priest, who had heard of their proximity from the morning courier, waiting for their arrival to say Mass.[13]

Overland distances were measured in *lieues,* or leagues. In the first half of the eighteenth century, the length of a French *lieue,* also called a *lieue de poste,* was set by the Crown under the direction of the general office of *couriers, postes et relais* at two thousand *toises,* or two *milles* (2.4221 miles). With the distance between postes averaging some 4.1 leagues (roughly ten miles), travelers who covered between eight and twelve leagues per day could depend on the presence of two postes en route each day.[14] Passing postes was one way that travelers—and early travel writers such as Claude-Marin Saugrain—marked distance traveled.[15]

After two days on the road, Caillot and his companions had passed three postes, and by late afternoon of the second day the trio had reached the fourth, at Chartres, passing into town through one of its nine gates. Split in two by the river Eure, Chartres was the capital of the duchy of Beauce, a region stretching from Paris southwest toward the Forêt d'Orléans, and the largest town the travelers had encountered since leaving the capital. Although Beauce's natural landscape was dominated by flat plains strewn with fields of wheat, the western (left bank) portion of Chartres was situated atop an embankment. Its approaches were notoriously steep, its roads narrow and winding. Caillot complained bitterly of the "appalling paths" made worse by winter conditions.[16] He made no mention of the town's massive cathedral, whose hulking presence dominated the skyline, but perhaps traveling twelve leagues (29.1 miles) by horseback in a single day had dampened Caillot's interest in the city's sights. The travelers left Chartres at daybreak and rode hard the third day, covering the thirteen leagues to Nogent-le-Rotrou, a prosperous hamlet on the Huisne River, known for its manufacture of leather goods and muslin cloth.[17]

The fourth day brought a slower pace. With stops in La Ferté-Bernard at midday and Saint-Marc in the afternoon, the travelers covered only seven leagues, a pace that offered riders and horses much-needed rest.[18] At Saint-Marc the three sought respite at an inn, where they were greeted by a servant whom Caillot described as a "plump, jolly girl" who "made sure we were lacking in nothing and took very good care of me." The inn sat at the "edge of a beautiful wood," and after days of jarring, body-numbing riding, the forest's sound-dampening canopy and "clusters of tall trees" proved irresistible.[19] Hunting horn in hand, Caillot left his companions and entered the woods to take a stroll and test the forest's acoustics. He soon encountered three locals of his age. All greeted him kindly—especially the two young women—and all welcomed the occasion Caillot's presence afforded them to hear news from Paris.[20] Two of them were a brother and sister who shared their surname, Saint-Marc, with the village. Caillot's status as a Parisian gentleman with clear connections to the court and a commission to the Company of the Indies's Louisiana comptoir apparently overrode any concerns the siblings may have had about Caillot's bedraggled appearance. For despite Caillot's own embarrassment at being "only as clean as a horseman who had just set foot upon the ground," who was boot-clad and "not at all as clean as [he] would have wished," he accepted the brother's invitation to join the Saint-Marc family for dinner.[21]

Caillot's dinner engagement at the Saint-Marc château was the first of several occasions during his journey to the Atlantic coast when his social status and familiarity with Paris garnered him invitations into people's homes or to semiprivate cultural events. In each instance, Caillot's observations reflect a Paris-centric outlook on life lived outside the Île-de-France. His attendance at dinners, theater performances, and musical spectacles en route afforded him an opportunity to compare his past experiences in Paris against preconceived expectations of life in France's villages, towns, and rural locales. During dinner with the Saint-Marc family, he found his notions about dining outside Paris challenged when he sat down at the table and was "attended to not like in the countryside but in the Parisian fashion—that is, very properly."[22]

Caillot's commentary on fashion, food, social customs, romance, and etiquette reveal his identification with the urban nobility in general and with Parisian nobility in particular. His writings also reveal a persistent undercurrent of anxiety over leaving the known world of Paris for the unknown world of Louisiana. For despite the fact that the colony was an oft-discussed topic at court and table—especially in the wake of the Mississippi Bubble's collapse—knowledge of the colony was often superficial and nearly always secondhand. Whatever else the French populace had heard about Louisiana, one detail seems to have struck a chord in their collective imaginings of the colony: Louisiana was an inhospitable and even deadly place.

Dinner with the Saint-Marc family had ended with a further extension of hospitality: Monsieur and Madame insisted that their Parisian guest make himself comfortable in their home for the night. At daybreak, following a breakfast of "soup and a selection of cold meats" in Monsieur de Saint-Marc's bedchamber, Caillot left to rejoin his companions. Madame lamented his departure, finding herself at a loss for reassuring words. She regretted that Caillot might "perhaps lose France forever, since [he] was going to a very dangerous environment."[23] With this bleak insinuation ringing in his ears, Caillot headed for the nearest poste, where he met his fellow travelers. They continued on to La Flèche, riding thirteen leagues before passing through its northern gate.

By the time the trio arrived in La Flèche, Caillot seems to have hit his stride, putting aside his melancholy at leaving France in favor of enjoying the pleasures of his homeland while he still could. Nestled in a deep valley on the banks of the Loir (a smallish river, not to be confused with the Loire), La Flèche was an established town of approximately six thousand souls, "filled with young people," "straight, expansive" roads, and "well-built houses."[24] According to Saugrain in his 1720 *Nouveau voyage de France*, the townsmen were "spirited" and the women "beautiful"; members of both sexes were "very sociable and well disposed to strangers."[25] Piganiol de la Force, a travel-writing contemporary of Saugrain known for his erudite, if less practical, style, painted a more restrained portrait of the town. In his 1724 travel guide, he restricted his descriptions of notable landmarks to the town's seigneurial château and its government and religious buildings. But even Piganiol de la Force, who may have been the target of Saugrain's critique of writers prone to "lengthy dissertations on each town's antiquities" at the expense of practical information, admitted that La Flèche was a "very agreeable town."[26] Indeed, by the end of their one-night stay, the travelers from Paris might have endorsed both accounts.

They arrived after dark, muddy, wet, and half-frozen. Five leagues from the town walls, Caillot's horse had stumbled on the rutted road, sending horse and rider into a "hole that had at least five to six feet of water in it." Shortly afterward, Troyes's horse threw him "quite hard" into one of the deep, muck-filled ditches that lined the road. Troyes managed to pull himself out but was "obliged to get out bare-legged," having been unable to pull his boots from the mud. They continued on with Caillot "frozen in [his] boots" and Troyes barefoot. Both were such a mess when they arrived in town that Caillot was grateful for cover of darkness, without which they "would have been greeted with catcalls by the children because we were so dreadfully covered in mud."[27]

Once they reached the inn, the travelers made a quick recovery, washing up, changing clothes "from head to foot," resting briefly, and then heading out for a night on the town. They went first to the theater, where Molière's comedy *The Imaginary Invalid* "was performed as well as could be expected."[28] They returned to the inn accompanied by a well-heeled young man they had met outside the theater, who insisted on ordering "a huge quantity of extraordinary fare," including a full range of desserts, wines, and liqueurs. Suspicious of their newfound friend's generosity, Caillot consulted the innkeeper, who warned him that the man was "related to him, but that he was a brawler and gambler" who "would try his best to lay traps for us in order to get at our money."[29]

In the wake of Louis XIV's death in 1715, the notion of gambling as a form of aristocratic sociability had gained increasing traction. The culture of gambling and chance that emerged during the Regency stood in stark contrast to the somber religious climate that dominated the last years of Louis XIV's reign.[30] Seen as a way of developing mental acuity, gambling, especially at cards, also offered its proponents an opportunity to exhibit cunning in a socially acceptable fashion (i.e., without fear of appearing inappropriately boastful or clever). Despite laws outlawing games of chance, gambling remained one of the "favorite distractions among the high society."[31] Lavish desserts, cheeses, and fine wines or liqueurs were at stake as often as money, with games ranging from billiards and roulette to card games with hundreds of variations. Outside Paris, taverns and inns served as the primary sites for gambling. Proprietors hoping to keep local authorities at bay insisted that without the ability to offer patrons on-site gaming tables and cards, their businesses stood no chance of survival.[32]

Having grown up in the midst of the courtly life at Meudon, whose boundaries touched those of Versailles and Saint-Cloud, Caillot was no stranger to card games. Time spent among members of Parisian high society reinforced his familiarity with popular games of chance. He fancied himself a capable gambler but took even greater pleasure in bluffing of a different sort: Caillot derived extreme satisfaction from outsmarting others—friends, associates, and strangers (and later in his voyage, ship captains and gullible, desperate young women).

Like other memoir writers of this period, Caillot depicted himself as a sort of knight-errant, sallying forth on episodic adventures much in the same manner as characters in contemporary picaresque novels. While Dumont de Montigny, writing of his experiences in Louisiana during the 1720s and 1730s, described himself as a sort of Robinson Crusoe, Caillot drew repeated comparisons between himself and Don Quixote and sometimes Quixote's sidekick, Sancho Panza.[33]

Women—from the "plump, jolly" serving girl who "took very good care" of Caillot at the inn in Saint-Marc to the party-throwing seneschal's wife in the town of Pontchâteau—receive special attention (of both the personal and literary varieties) from this self-styled Don Quixote.[34] As for those individuals not belonging to the fairer sex, Caillot took note of men who were gamblers or men of means, men who might be in some way outwitted. One of the most striking qualities of Caillot's observations is that he does not appear to have had any self-aggrandizing political or economic motives in writing his account (which may help explain why it remained unpublished). Rather, he was often more concerned with bragging about his exploits, such as duping someone into paying his supper or bar tab, than in painting flattering portraits of powerful men to whom he might have appealed for patronage. In his day-to-day interactions, his preference for cleverness over wealth or standing prevailed.

The "brawler and gambler" he encountered at the inn may have been a native of La Flèche, but it is also possible that he was an exiled gambler from Paris. Hundreds of notorious gamblers were banished from the capital to the provinces during the first half of the eighteenth century.[35] Whatever his origins, Caillot pegged him an easy mark. After confirming his suspicions about the young man's character with the innkeeper, Caillot "took it upon [himself] to make him play, not at cards, but the role of the dupe."[36] At the gambler's urgings, Caillot ordered "anything that [he] wanted to drink and eat," while cordially refusing to engage in any number of card games the gambler suggested. Finally, after the detritus of their feast had been cleared away and the bill settled by the gambler with the innkeeper's wife, Caillot "told him that as far as games went, [he] did not know any at all, except for 'brisquambille' [*sic*]," a card game played with between two and five players.[37] The two played until three thirty in the morning, when Caillot excused himself with a full belly and pockets heavier by "about twenty *écus*."[38]

At daybreak the trio mounted their horses and departed from La Flèche with the courier, stopping midmorning for Mass in Durtal, then continuing on to the poste at Suette, where they slept. From Suette they headed southwest toward Angers, where the utility of traveling on the unpaved grands chemins was supplanted by the mobility afforded by the Loire River and its tributaries. The road into Angers was lined on either side with dozens of wood-and-stone windmills. Quarries on the outskirts of town supplied slate in abundance. The prevalence of slate-roofed houses, churches, and other buildings earned the capital of the Anjou region the nickname "la ville noire." Caillot felt right at home there, describing the bustling city of more than twenty thousand inhabitants as "a second little Paris, where there is a thriving high society and where people are attended to very well."[39] He had little time, however, to enjoy the pleasures of Angers. He and his traveling companions left the morning after their arrival via a *cabanne*, a small, covered passenger barge. Like Chartres, Nantes, and many other mercantile cities in the eighteenth century, Angers was strategically located on one of the country's principal waterways. Split in two by the Mayenne (Maine) River, which flows directly into the Loire just southwest of the city, Angers's growth and prosperity were connected to its merchants' ability to float cargoes—especially heavy ones such as slate tiles, whose weight made overland transport impractical—downriver to other commercial centers.

Their eighth day of travel was spent on the Loire. As they made the 9.5-league passage from Angers to Ingrande, they passed small villages, fields of wheat, and expansive châteaux. Just before the town of Savennières, the river broke to make way for the dozens of small islands that dominate the lower Loire. Caillot and his companions continued into the marshland flanking the river's northern bank, then came upon the port and village of Ingrande, along a bend approximately ten leagues upriver from Nantes. Their arrival marked the travelers' entry into Brittany, then one of the most commercial regions in all of France.

Jutting out into the Atlantic, Brittany was the nexus of France's maritime operations. Shipyards, warehouse complexes, and fortified harbors in the region's coastal and riverine towns helped sustain France's Continental and global trade empire, as did the thousands of Breton men who manned the ships that made both trade and defense possible on the open seas. To the Paris-centric Caillot, rural Brittany and its people were objects of curiosity and sometimes scorn. The sights and sounds of the region seemed truly foreign. Breton, a Brythonic Celtic language related to Welsh and Cornish, was spoken throughout Lower Brittany. Breton is so unlike the French dominant in the Île-de-France that it must have seemed impenetrable to Caillot's ears. Women were dressed "handsomely enough"; on their heads most wore "sorts of mantillas . . . full of folds." In a pattern similar to his later descriptions of American Indian tribes in Louisiana, Caillot equated many of the cultural practices he witnessed in Brittany with backwardness. In Ingrande, after settling into his lodgings at the Trois Morts (three dead men) Inn, the sound of violins outside drew Caillot to the window, where he was "surprised to see that there were gentlemen and ladies there," dancing Breton dances. Caillot cringed to find his social peers engaged in "dances with the most bizarre steps that one could ever see."[40]

At dawn the travelers reboarded the passenger barge. The vessel took them as far as Ancenis, where Caillot noted that a gentleman whose acquaintance they had made in Angers "very kindly hosted us."[41] From Ancenis they again traveled by road, passing through the old-growth forests (long a source of shipbuilding timber) that lined the town's perimeter as they made their way to Nantes. The closer they got to the Atlantic, the more explicitly and visibly tied the cities and their industries were to the global trade system. By the time Caillot reached Nantes, he had traveled 78 of the approximately 110 leagues between Paris and Lorient.

The travelers passed into Nantes via the city's northeastern gate. Surrounded by ditch-lined ramparts from the southwestern to northeastern boundaries, with its remaining flanks bounded by the Loire River, Nantes had the deserved reputation as one of France's most commercial and fastest-growing cities. Its four *faubourgs* (suburbs)—Saint-Clément, le Marché, la Fosse, and Pirmil—were, according to Piganiol de la Force, "much more substantial than the city itself."[42] The fashionable and recently settled la Fosse district, home to the city's leading merchants, whose mansions afforded them a view overlooking the port, lay nestled against the city's western ramparts just outside the Porte au vin. The Quai (wharves) de la Fosse ran the length of this district; ships lined up along the docks connected Nantes and its merchant community to points across the Atlantic. To the quai "the Spanish bring wine, fine wool, iron, silk, oils, oranges and lemons; they leave with woven linen cloth, lightweight fabrics, hardware, and wheat," Saugrain wrote. "The Dutch bring salted fish, along with all sorts of spices; the Swedish their copper ware; the English their lead shot, pewter ware, coal, etc."[43] Saugrain's brief description offers a glimpse of the global trade networks that fueled the success of many Nantais merchants and propelled the Company of the Indies's ships—and with them clerks such as Caillot—across the seas.

When Caillot arrived there in 1729, Nantes was in the midst of an unprecedented construction boom. Work on the new Pont de Pirmil, which ran from Nantes proper across the Loire and the Île Beaulieu to the faubourg Pirmil, was completed in 1727. The new stock exchange was nearly complete. And some twenty-four nearly identical townhouses (*hôtels particuliers*) were in various stages of completion on the Île Feydeau.[44] Caillot found the city filled with a "great quantity of merchants" and "fashionable young people" who followed "the same styles as in Paris." He was impressed by the Quai de la Fosse, "where the people of Nantes go walking along the Loire."[45] The money he had won from the gambler in La Flèche helped him take full advantage of the city's cultural and social scene. During his five- to six-day sojourn, he attended two plays: Molière's *Don Juan, or, The Feast with the Statue,* which Caillot described as "not badly acted," and Philippe Néricault Destouches's *The Married Philosopher,* a play that had debuted in Paris two years earlier, which he said was "in general well received by everyone." He also attended the weekly concerts "given two times a week at the home of Monsieur Montaudoin, an important merchant of that city."[46]

René Montaudoin could well afford to host twice-weekly concerts for visiting members of the social elite and members of Nantais society at his expansive property near the Quai de la Fosse. In the early eighteenth century, Montaudoin helped establish Nantes as France's largest and most lucrative slaving port. Son of a prominent merchant by the same name who had financed his first trade expedition to the French Caribbean in 1676, Montaudoin was the largest outfitter of slave ships in France, sending out an estimated forty-five ships between 1706 and his death in 1731.[47] A 1726 tax audit of 230 Nantais merchants estimated their collective wealth at 18.8 million livres. A closer look at the audit results shows that an oligarchy of just 63 merchants from 56 Nantais families controlled the bulk of that wealth (58 percent), at more than 11 million livres. The wealth of the Montaudoins as a family unit topped 1.1 million livres, but René Montaudoin led the pack, with a personal fortune worth more than 600,000 livres (3 percent of the total wealth reflected in the 1726 survey).[48]

The precedent for leasing out trading privileges to private merchants was first established in 1681 during Jean-Baptiste Colbert's administration of the first Company of the East Indies. When the company proved unable to meet the demands of the East Indian carrying trade, Colbert authorized private merchants—first on company ships, then on privately owned ships—to engage in trade. In the Atlantic Ocean before

1716, the slave trade was controlled primarily by the Guinea Company, which was charged with the trade from Sierra Leone south to the Cape of Good Hope, and the Senegal Company, which operated in West Africa north of the Sierra Leone River.

In 1700 merchants in Nantes began openly agitating for the admittance of privately funded outfitters to the trade. That year, trade representative Joachim Descasaux du Halley appeared before the newly reorganized Council of Commerce in Paris and accused the Guinea Company of limiting the success of French ventures in the Caribbean by failing to supply adequate numbers of slaves.[49] Descasaux's lobbying met initially with limited success, but in 1701 the Guinea Company received the coveted Spanish *assiento*, the permit that granted its holder the lucrative privilege of supplying slaves to Spain's New World colonies. A 1480 treaty between Spain and Portugal barred the country from trading along the African coast, thereby necessitating third-party delivery of slaves to Spanish America. A provision of the Guinea Company's assiento-related reorganization allowed two privately funded slavers per year to supply France's Caribbean colonies.[50] Under that provision, in 1703 Nantais traders outfitted the first of the more than fourteen hundred slave ships that sailed from the city's port in the eighteenth century.[51]

Just as the Guinea Company had failed to meet the demand for slaves in France's own colonies in the last decades of the seventeenth century, it also failed to maintain supply to those operating under the Spanish Crown. The Guinea Company's inability to meet demand resulted in France's loss of the assiento in 1713 and the company's own liquidation. For Nantais merchants, however, the company's loss further fueled their argument that chartered monopoly companies lacked the ships, crews, and efficiency needed to satisfy the growing demand for slave labor in the Americas. Only by allowing private traders unfettered access to the slave trade would demand be met. The monopoly company's weaknesses, the merchants stressed, undermined the profitability of France's colonies and, in turn, France's own treasury.[52] Their rationale rested on the assumption that colonies such as Saint Domingue, Martinique, and Louisiana would prove wildly profitable to Crown and colonists only if planters had access to a steady supply of enslaved laborers to work actual and theoretical fields of indigo, tobacco, and especially sugar.

Their arguments did not fall on deaf ears. In 1713 Minister of Marine Jérôme Phélypeaux, comte de Pontchartrain, authorized the outfitting of twelve privately funded slave ships per year. Just over two years later, faced with mounting pressure from Caribbean colonists and coastal merchants, the French government issued *lettres patentes* that allowed merchants in Bordeaux, La Rochelle, Nantes, and Rouen to engage in the unlimited provisioning of slave ships bound for the Guinea Company's former trading posts in Africa.[53] From 1716 to 1720, Nantais merchants outfitted sixty-eight slavers. Most sailed for the French fort at Ouidah (or Whydah).[54]

The Montaudoin family financed all or part of thirty-one of the sixty-eight voyages, with René Montaudoin acting as the primary outfitter of twenty-one of the slave ships. In those four years, slavers financed by the Montaudoin family carried off more than seventy-eight hundred men, women, and children from the west coast of Africa.[55] Those who survived the crossing were deposited on French-controlled Caribbean islands or in Guiana. In exchange Montaudoin ships returned to Nantes laden with cargoes of indigo, cocoa, tanned leather and hides, exotic woods, and sugar.

By September 1720, however, John Law's successful consolidation of several ailing chartered monopoly companies into a reorganized, reinvigorated Company of the Indies prompted the Royal Council of State to revoke the 1716 lettres patentes. Council orders issued September 27, 1720, required that all slaving activities along the African coast be turned over to the company, provided that the company guaranteed delivery of a minimum of three thousand slaves per year to France's circum-Caribbean colonies.

Once again, the company monopoly on the slave trade was short lived. Only in the years immediately following the company's post-Law reorganization in 1723 and 1724 was it able to meet demand without the help of private traders. By August 1725 company directors caved under pressure from shareholders and from Minister of Marine Jean Frédéric Phélypeaux, comte de Maurepas (son of Jérôme Phélypeaux). Shareholders suspected that the investment needed to bulk up the company's slaving fleet in order to meet new Ministry of Marine demands—ninety-three hundred slaves delivered (eleven thousand embarked) to the islands per year—might bankrupt it. Maurepas, whose seat on the

Council of Commerce subjected him to the incessant lobbying of Nantais merchants eager to break the company monopoly, shared their suspicion and sought to open the trade. His proposed scheme, which would generate for the company a profit of twenty livres for each slave carried by private traders, made the dissolution of the company's monopoly over the slave trade more attractive to shareholders.[56]

The years 1723 to 1725 were the zenith of the French Company of the Indies's participation in the African slave trade. The next six years saw the company drastically curtail slaving expenditures. It was not alone. Over the course of the first half of the eighteenth century, as government-chartered monopoly companies failed to keep pace with the seemingly insatiable demand for slave labor in the Americas, the trade shifted increasingly to a host of privately funded slave outfitters and traders. By midcentury, private traders had eclipsed not only the French monopoly companies but their English and Dutch counterparts as well. An act of Parliament passed in 1698 forced the British Royal African Company to compete with private slave traders, and the Dutch West India Company (WIC) saw its monopoly punctured in 1730.[57] Merchants in Nantes were well positioned to accomplish what the company could not. Of the ninety-nine slave ships that departed from France in the second half of the 1720s, fifty-one of them departed from Nantes. The remaining forty-eight sailed from Lorient (fifteen), Saint-Malo (fifteen), La Rochelle (ten), Le Havre (four), Marseille (two), Bordeaux (one), and Dunkerque (one).[58]

Although the outfitting of slave ships continued to be a primary source of Nantes's wealth throughout the eighteenth century, it was not the city's sole source of commercial prosperity. Nor was the slave trade the only significant commercial connection between Nantes and the Company of the Indies. In 1729, when Marc-Antoine Caillot traveled through Nantes, the city was still home to the company's warehouses (and would remain so until 1734). At least some of the building and construction Caillot noted in his memoir was connected to Nantes's position as the exclusive site for company sales. Ships returning from comptoirs along the Indian and Atlantic oceans, Caribbean Sea, and Gulf of Mexico docked in Lorient, where their cargoes were unloaded, inspected, inventoried, and packed off to warehouses in Nantes. Each year merchants and factors flocked to the city from across the Continent to attend the annual sales of company goods. Printed notices announced the sale of an astonishing array of textiles—especially printed and specialty piece goods (*petites étoffes*), spices, agricultural products, and durable goods recently arrived from overseas comptoirs (fig. 4).

The principal sale was held each fall in stages, with the *grande vente*, featuring the most salable items, preceding the *petite vente*, which show-

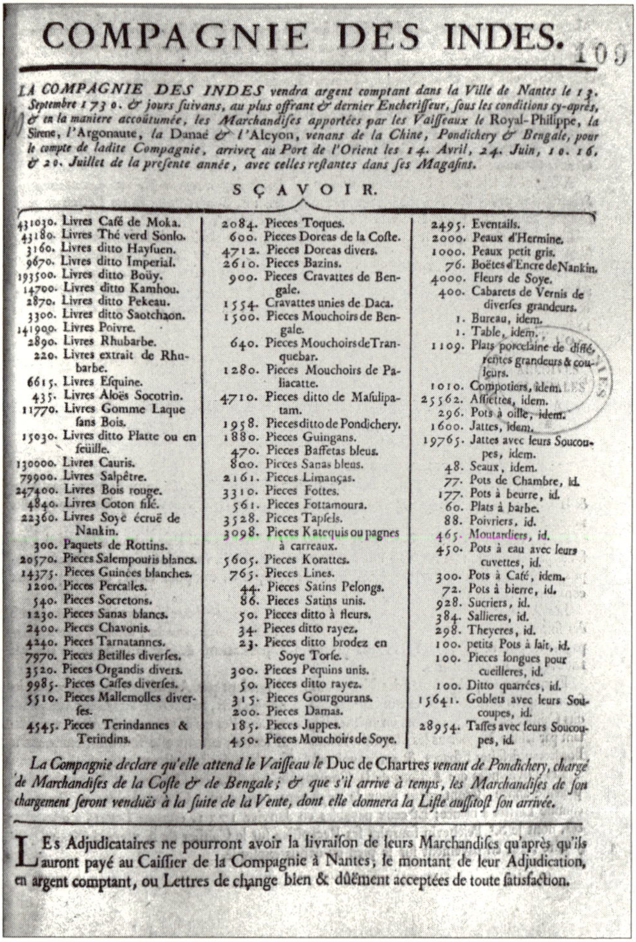

COMPAGNIE DES INDES. 109

LA COMPAGNIE DES INDES vendra argent comptant dans la Ville de Nantes le 13. Septembre 1730. & jours ſuivans, au plus offrant & dernier Encheriſſeur, ſous les conditions cy-après, & en la maniere accoûtumée, les Marchandiſes apportées par les Vaiſſeaux le Royal-Philippe, *la* Sirene, *l'*Argonaute, *la* Danaé *& l'*Alcyon, *venans de la Chine, Pondichery & Bengale, pour le compte de ladite Compagnie, arrivez au Port de l'Orient les 14. Avril, 24. Juin, 10. 16. & 20. Juillet de la preſente année, avec celles reſtantes dans ſes Magaſins.*

SÇAVOIR.

431030. Livres Café de Moka.
43180. Livres Thé verd Sonlo.
3160. Livres ditto Hayſuen.
9670. Livres ditto Imperial.
193500. Livres ditto Boüy.
14700. Livres ditto Kamhou.
2870. Livres ditto Pekeau.
3300. Livres ditto Saotchaon.
141900. Livres Poivre.
2890. Livres Rhubarbe.
220. Livres extrait de Rhubarbe.
6615. Livres Eſquine.
435. Livres Aloës Socotrin.
11770. Livres Gomme Laque ſans Bois.
15030. Livres ditto Platte ou en feüille.
130000. Livres Cauris.
79900. Livres Salpêtre.
247400. Livres Bois rouge.
4840. Livres Coton filé.
22360. Livres Soye écruë de Nankin.
300. Paquets de Rottins.
20570. Pieces Salempouris blancs.
14375. Pieces Guinées blanches.
1200. Pieces Percalles.
540. Pieces Socretons.
1230. Pieces Sanas blancs.
2400. Pieces Chavonis.
4240. Pieces Tarnatannes.
7970. Pieces Betilles diverſes.
3520. Pieces Organdis divers.
9985. Pieces Caſſes diverſes.
5510. Pieces Mallemolles diverſes.
4545. Pieces Terindannes & Terindins.

2084. Pieces Toques.
600. Pieces Doreas de la Coſte.
4712. Pieces Doreas divers.
2610. Pieces Bazins.
900. Pieces Cravattes de Bengale.
1554. Cravattes unies de Daca.
1500. Pieces Mouchoirs de Bengale.
640. Pieces Mouchoirs de Tranquebar.
1280. Pieces Mouchoirs de Paliacatte.
4710. Pieces ditto de Maſulipatam.
1958. Pieces ditto de Pondichery.
1880. Pieces Guingans.
470. Pieces Baffetas bleus.
800. Pieces Sanas bleus.
2161. Pieces Limanças.
3310. Pieces Fottes.
561. Pieces Fottamoura.
3528. Pieces Tapſels.
3098. Pieces Katequis ou pagnes à carreaux.
5605. Pieces Korattes.
765. Pieces Lines.
44. Pieces Satins Pelongs.
86. Pieces Satins unis.
50. Pieces ditto à fleurs.
34. Pieces ditto rayez.
23. Pieces ditto brodez en Soye Torſe.
300. Pieces Pequins unis.
50. Pieces ditto rayez.
315. Pieces Gourgourans.
200. Pieces Damas.
185. Pieces Juppes.
450. Pieces Mouchoirs de Soye.

2495. Eventails.
2000. Peaux d'Hermine.
1000. Peaux petit gris.
76. Boëtes d'Encre de Nankin.
4000. Fleurs de Soye.
400. Cabarets de Vernis de diverſes grandeurs.
1. Bureau, idem.
1. Table, idem.
1109. Plats porcelaine de differentes grandeurs & couleurs.
1010. Compotiers, idem.
25562. Aſſiettes, idem.
296. Pots à oille, idem.
1600. Jattes, idem.
19765. Jattes avec leurs Soucoupes, idem.
48. Seaux, idem.
77. Pots de Chambre, id.
177. Pots à beurre, id.
60. Plats à barbe.
88. Poivriers, id.
465. Moutardiers, id.
450. Pots à eau avec leurs cuvettes, id.
300. Pots à Café, idem.
72. Pots à bierre, id.
928. Sucriers, id.
384. Sallieres, id.
298. Theyeres, id.
100. petits Pots à lait, id.
100. Pieces longues pour cueilleres, id.
100. Ditto quarrées, id.
15641. Goblets avec leurs Soucoupes, id.
28954. Taſſes avec leurs Soucoupes, id.

La Compagnie declare qu'elle attend le Vaiſſeau le Duc de Chartres *venant de Pondichery, chargé de Marchandiſes de la Coſte & de Bengale; & que s'il arrive à temps, les Marchandiſes de ſon chargement ſeront venduës à la ſuite de la Vente, dont elle donnera la Liſte auſſitoſt ſon arrivée.*

LEs Adjudicataires ne pourront avoir la livraiſon de leurs Marchandiſes qu'après qu'ils auront payé au Caiſſier de la Compagnie à Nantes, le montant de leur Adjudication, en argent comptant, ou Lettres de change bien & dûëment acceptées de toute ſatisfaction.

Fig. 4. Advertisement for sale of Indian Ocean goods at company warehouses in Nantes, 1730. (Courtesy of the Archives nationales d'outre-mer, C2 23 fo. 109.)

cased numerous goods damaged either at sea or during transport from Lorient to Nantes. The road between Nantes and Lorient was critical to commerce, but the stretch running from Hennebont to Lorient via Port-Louis was in disrepair. Improvements were made between 1724 and 1730 in an attempt to cut company losses resulting from damage incurred between the time trade goods left Lorient on carts or boats and their arrival in Nantes. Even after they arrived in Nantes, the pitiful condition of the warehouse complex's roofs sometimes exposed goods—especially textiles—to less than ideal conditions. Moldy, water-stained textiles were among the most frequently sold items at the petites ventes.[59]

The city also hosted company sales of specific agricultural products, such as monopoly-controlled coffee and tobacco, at specified dates throughout the year. These sales generally coincided with the seasonal arrival of company ships from Mocha (in present-day Yemen) or the circum-Caribbean.[60] The same sales featured trade goods brought back to France by ships' officers and crew through the use of the *port-permis* as well as any goods taken from vessels seized by the French navy. For Nantes-based merchants, company sales held locally were a boon. Unlike merchants from Le Havre, Saint-Malo, and beyond, who had to pay the freight costs associated with shipping their goods from Nantes to their home ports before outfitting could begin, merchants from in and around Nantes could outfit their ships on the spot. The elimination of freight charges and the ease of procuring trade items, such as cowrie shells and high-demand textiles, directly from the company also help explain the early dominance of Nantais merchants in the African slave trade.

The quantity and variety of goods available in Nantes made it one of Europe's leading trade cities. Annual sales, according to Nantes mayor Gérard Mellier, attracted between "five and six hundred merchants" to the city each year, and they were often accompanied by their servants and families.[61] Their numbers swelled the city's population of roughly forty-five thousand; their need for lodging, food, entertainment, and business services during their stay—which often spanned several weeks—accelerated the development of Nantes's hospitality sector.

Unlike Lorient, which was described during a 1719 company debate over where to house and sell company goods as a town "at the end of the world" with "no lodgings for even a dozen merchants," Nantes was home to a bevy of hotels, inns, and apartments or rooms for rent as well as an array of financial services and agents that facilitated international trade.[62] A growing number of entertainment venues—featuring theater, opera, and musical performances—complemented the city's expansive hospitality and financial services industries. Merchants whose business kept them in the city for weeks or even months at a stretch could join their local counterparts in the enjoyment of various evening spectacles. But for Caillot, who, after exhausting his *brusquembille* winnings, "had only just what was necessary to complete [his] voyage and no more," the presence of so many entertainment options served as a reminder of his meager finances.[63]

After five or six days in Nantes, Caillot and his fellow travelers returned to the road, traveling with the mail courier through Pontchâteau, La Roche-Bernard, Vannes, and Auray as they pushed on toward the coast. At Hennebont they returned their leased post horses and chartered a dinghy to take them two leagues down the Blavet River to Lorient. Their 264-mile journey from Paris had required nine days of active travel, nearly three weeks total. They had traveled over mud-lined roads, through Brittany's wheat-filled countryside, and down rivers to reach Lorient, a town whose unexpected and untidy expansion was taking France's coastal and Breton communities by surprise.

Established in 1666 as the home base of the second French Company of the Indies (Colbert's Compagnie française des Indes Orientales), Lorient had grown in fits and starts from the late 1660s until the creation of the third Company of the Indies in 1720. The site at the confluence of the Scorff and Blavet Rivers had not been Colbert's first choice for company headquarters. Company ships operated briefly out of Le Havre in 1664, but difficulty securing a parcel of waterfront property large enough to accommodate the necessary shipbuilding and outfitting facilities, offices, and warehouses forced the minister to consider alternative Atlantic ports. Le Havre's location also posed a security risk: English ships preyed on company vessels laden with valuable cargo in the narrow confines of the Channel. Colbert then looked to Bayonne, but it too was ill suited as an operational base.

As the possibility of setting up base at an established port faded, Colbert sent Guillaume de La Motte, a king's lieutenant based in Hennebont, to survey a site along the Brittany coast near the Gulf of Morbihan. Four navigational pilots from Hennebont and three from Port-Louis accompanied La Motte to an unnamed expanse of scruffy, uninhabited land on the right bank of the Scorff. From there they surveyed the convergence of waterways and land, which created a natural harbor long used as a place of refuge for ships engaged in the coastal trade. Within six months of La Motte's initial survey, Colbert sent three additional teams of bureaucrats, engineers, and naval officers to the site. By the summer of 1666, company director Denis Langlois had arranged the purchase of seven hectares (17.3 acres) of land from Breton noble Louis XII de Rohan, prince de Guéméné.[64]

The company settlement quickly became known as "L'Orient"—a name synonymous with the geographic location of the company's primary trading hubs in the Far East. Company goods arriving in Paris, Nantes, or elsewhere in France were said to be "from l'Orient," an ambiguous statement providing no clear distinction between the use of *l'Orient* as a geographic designation for the Far East and the town along the Brittany coast. For consumers of these goods, perhaps there was no distinction. It remains unclear whether the town name was popularized by the company or by the consumers of its trade goods, though some historians posit that the name derives from an abbreviation of *Le Soleil d'Orient*, the name of the first ship built on-site (completed in 1671). Whatever its origins, the town name L'Orient was adopted readily by residents and company administrators alike. Within four years of the company's 1666 land purchase, L'Orient was used as the location of birth in the settlement's baptismal registers.[65]

Although the land upon which the company built its operations had been previously uninhabited, it was not isolated from Brittany's well-developed port complex. Just across the bay from the enclosure sat Port-Louis, a small fortified settlement that was itself home to shipbuilding and food-processing facilities and, in the late seventeenth through early eighteenth centuries, to a series of monopoly companies, including the slave-trading Senegal and Saint-Domingue Companies. Hennebont, located two leagues up the Blavet River, housed a busy commercial port and served as a hub for overland transportation. Goods flowing through Hennebont were often disbursed via one of the six major roads that intersected there—a positional benefit that allowed the company to tap into an already established supply-and-distribution network. And the presence of Pont-Scorff, a village located less than two leagues up the Scorff River devoted primarily to wheat processing and bread production, helped ensure Lorient's sustenance in its early years.

Despite Lorient's prime location, a number of bankruptcies and reorganizations between 1675 and 1706, and again following the collapse of Law's system in 1720, impeded company claims to the port. Beginning in 1685, the site was partially shared by the navy, and by 1701 it was fully requisitioned as a naval base during the War of Spanish Succession. Naval authorities recognized Lorient's value as a secure port and used the site for outfitting and shipbuilding throughout the war. With the company reorganized and consolidated in 1721, directors took the site and its improvements back from the navy.[66]

The seventeen acres purchased in 1666 formed the original footprint of the company enclosure. By the time of the company's 1721 reorganization, improvements to the enclosure included warehouses (1669); forges (1671); a chapel (1675); a ropewalk, bakery, and windmill (1677); a four-hundred-bed barracks (1691–92); a hospital and rationing facilities (1720); and numerous offices charged with outfitting, bookkeeping, and personnel management. Outside the enclosure, a hodgepodge of more than three hundred mud-and-straw huts housing workers and their families stood alongside a handful of more solidly constructed stone structures.[67]

From 1720 to 1740, the town's growth far outpaced any similar expansion of infrastructure. The company went from outfitting no ships in Lorient in 1719 to provisioning an average of twenty-two ships in each of the next five years.[68] Laborers, craftsmen, seamen, and their families poured into the town, filling in the land surrounding the enclosure with makeshift tents and poorly constructed huts as they scrambled to secure their footing in an environment filled with opportunities. The number of company and royal officials, administrators, and low-level bureaucrats rose apace. In 1706 Lorient was home to no more than six thousand individuals. Some thirty years later, its population had more than doubled, having increased to fourteen thousand.[69]

But urban development was slow to arrive in Lorient, despite attempts by royal engineers to bring order to the chaos. There was little company willpower to address the needs of a town that had sprung up seemingly overnight alongside the enclosure. Complicating the systematic management of the company town was a lack of clear jurisdiction: the company controlled what took place within the enclosure's walls, but it was less clear who had authority over the town. The Rohan-Guéméné family maintained seigneurial rights over the land it had sold to the company. The family held baking and bread-making monopolies in the town, oversaw its courts and policing, and collected duties on a variety of supplies passing through Lorient.[70] It took a series of fires that consumed dozens of residences near the enclosure in the early 1720s to prompt the company to issue building regulations. In 1724 it issued the first of several ordinances intended to regulate construction materials and reduce the risk of fire, requiring that all new structures be of stone or slate. Seven years later, the company strengthened its fire prevention attempts, issuing a general prohibition against thatched roofs.[71]

Outside the enclosure, Lorient's streets remained unpaved and overcrowded. The population had expanded so quickly in the first decades of the eighteenth century that the town lacked an established grid. Royal engineers failed in their early efforts to bring order to the streets; the influx of people was simply too great. Even the road leading into neighboring Port-Louis from Hennebont was in disrepair, which may help explain why Caillot traveled by dinghy from Hennebont to Lorient rather than by horse.

By the winter of 1729, company ships sailing from Lorient called at dozens of ports spread across five continents. Some ports of call, such as the Spanish-controlled Canary Islands off Africa's northwest coast, served exclusively as provisioning stopovers. Others served as trading ports run principally by local interests, as was the case with the Canton post in China, where company ships dropped anchor to conduct trade directly with local populations. But many of the ports called on by company ships were home to permanent company comptoirs. The scale of these comptoirs and the number of resident company laborers and bureaucrats in each depended largely on the volume and type of trade or agricultural goods that passed through a given port.

In a handful of locales, a type of capital-comptoir served as on-the-ground headquarters for multiple trading establishments or outposts in a region. This was true of both Pondicherry, a company settlement on the southeastern coast of India, and New Orleans, the chief port and capital city of the company's vast Louisiana colony. Each served as operational capital for company affairs and was charged with the administrative and financial oversight of lesser comptoirs located throughout the region at key trade and agricultural sites. For comptoirs in India and Louisiana, official company-controlled correspondence traveled by courier from Paris to Lorient and was then loaded onto ships bound for the capital-comptoirs, where councillors and clerks oversaw the conveyance of relevant news, correspondence, and directives to outlying comptoirs. Overseas comptoirs generally followed the same communication chain but in reverse. In order to fulfill their operational mandates, capital-comptoirs required the presence of a good number of competent bureaucrats and clerks to carry out bookkeeping, copying, and cashier's duties.

Caillot's own appointment to a clerking position in New Orleans took place against a backdrop of failed efforts to maintain a reliable cadre of low-level administrative workers in the Louisiana colony. From 1723 to 1730, company directors in Paris received incessant complaints from Jacques de La Chaise, the company's director and chief financial officer in Louisiana, on both the degenerate quality and insufficient quantity of clerks working in the Louisiana offices. La Chaise arrived in 1723, in the wake of John Law's collapsed financial scheme, with the mandate to clean up the colony's administrative affairs and set the company's finances in order. The previous year the capital of Louisiana had moved from New Biloxi to New Orleans, after work on the settlement had progressed far enough to provide shelter to the goods and people necessary to the company's commercial activities. When La Chaise arrived in New Orleans, he faced the near impossible task of rectifying warehouse inventories against long-neglected account books and reining in endemic corruption among company administrators, warehouse keepers, and council members. The challenge was made more difficult by a perpetual shortage of hard currency, which encouraged colonists and company personnel alike to take what they could, when they could, from company stores or to bypass financial interaction with the company altogether in favor of trade with local Indians.[72]

One of La Chaise's first efforts to bring order to the bureaucratic chaos of the company's Louisiana offices centered on the creation of a workable administrative structure that connected the colony's central offices in New Orleans to its coastal and riverine outposts at Mobile, Natchez, Natchitoches, and elsewhere. To La Chaise, staffing the bookkeeping, storehouse, and inspection offices in the capital with capable personnel was critical to the company's success. His goal was to standardize bookkeeping and inventory practices and establish clear administrative and financial boundaries between offices. In La Chaise's view, this objective could be met only through the appointment of bureaucrats and clerks with training specific to a given office's function. La Chaise's approach to Louisiana's administrative reorganization might be traced to his own past work experiences in Lorient. In the years prior to his arrival in Louisiana, he had served as chief clerk to Gilles Le Brun de La Franqueri in the company's outfitting storehouse there, and he had participated in a similar administrative cleanup that targeted questionable port management, storekeeping, and inventory practices. His successes in Lorient recommended him to company directors eager to see the mismanaged Louisiana colony turn a profit. (Ironically, La Franqueri was himself recalled in 1726 after he was found to have repeatedly smuggled goods onto company ships to be sold for personal profit.)[73]

Within weeks of arriving in New Orleans, La Chaise wrote company directors in Paris: "Gentlemen, be so good as to send at once, if you please, a bookkeeper, an assistant bookkeeper, and five or six clerks who know how to work. There is not one here who can be used." He further urged them to provide incoming clerical workers with "reasonable salaries for if they are mediocre they will not have enough to live on and will perish here as the others have done."[74] La Chaise repeatedly echoed his request that the company send qualified, adequately compensated personnel to Louisiana. He also encouraged the directors to take care to supply the colony's treasury with copper or silver money with which to pay the bureaucrats already serving there.

The colony's chronic specie shortage left La Chaise, and the company, in a difficult position. In April 1727 La Chaise and Governor Étienne Périer (a former ship captain in the company's fleet) reported to the directors on the "sad condition" of the colony's treasury, which had "been without one sou for some time."[75] Company warehouses stocked with goods and provisions from France saw little trade with colonists because the specie shortage meant that the company was unable to pay colonists for crops, livestock, and provisions raised and produced locally. Only debtors were able to turn over their rice crops to company storehouses; those who expected payment for their crops looked elsewhere for trade opportunities.[76] French mercantile policies required that colonists purchase (in cash or trade) all nonlocal supplies, including tools, agricultural implements, and slave laborers, directly from the company at predetermined prices. Colonists' inability to sell their produce to the company, however, made French mercantile policies rather difficult to enforce.[77]

The empty treasury sometimes led company employees to choose between starvation and graft. The company owed back wages "to clerks, workmen, and sailors" and was repeatedly forced to borrow money from passengers arriving from France to avert an uprising of the colony's soldiers stationed in New Orleans.[78] With no cash to pay wages, there was little incentive for employees to remain loyal to company objectives but great temptation to skim off what they could from incoming receipts. In 1728 three clerks working in the company's cashier office in New Orleans were involved in a scheme to circulate forged paper banknotes among the colonists. The ringleader, a clerk named Maisonneuve, confessed under torture to forging La Chaise's signature and was sentenced to imprisonment for life. Rather than dismissing the affair as the work of dishonest clerks, La Chaise laid the blame for Maisonneuve's actions on the company for not sending specie as promised. "If you had sent us the 50,000 livres in silver money that you have been promising us for two years," wrote La Chaise, the forgery "would not have happened."[79]

La Chaise achieved some success in expanding the colony's clerical labor pool. From 1722 to 1728, staffing levels in the company's New Orleans offices grew by 21 percent, with the overall number of clerical positions, including bookkeepers, warehouse or storekeepers, inspectors, and clerks, increasing from nineteen to twenty-three and that of clerks assigned to bookkeeping, council, storehouse, and inspection offices from nine to thirteen. During the same period, the annual budget allotted to payroll expenses for clerks rose from 7,200 to 12,800 livres.[80] By 1729 staffing levels in the New Orleans and Balize offices were roughly equal to levels found in Lorient and Pondicherry.[81]

The number of employees may have increased, but staffing the offices with well-trained, diligent workers remained an unrealized dream.

In the seven years of his tenure in Louisiana, La Chaise described various members of the colony's clerical staff as fraudulent, thieving, disorderly, lazy, incorrigible, and dissipated, stressing to company directors in Paris that "the indulgence we show to the clerks comes from the necessity of our keeping the least bad for want of persons to replace them." After firing three wayward clerks in the summer of 1728, he wrote: "It is not here as in France. It is rare that one finds one of them by chance who is good."[82] When company directors in Paris received word of the clerks' dismissal, in October 1728, it is likely that they looked first to the pool of individuals employed in the company's Paris offices for replacements. The timing of Caillot's and Troyes's February 1729 departure from Paris suggests that they were two of the young men selected to fill the void.

Within months of their appointments, Caillot and Troyes found themselves at the end of their journey from Paris to the coast, arriving in Lorient around the first week of March. Lorient had grown considerably in the ten years since one observer had labeled it "a town at the end of the earth," but lodgings and food were still at a premium.[83]

After making an appearance at the company outfitting offices, where they collected a two-month salary advance, Caillot and Troyes ventured outside the enclosure to secure rooms at "one of L'Orient's best inns."[84] They lodged at an establishment run by gentleman-proprietor André Bachelier, whose inn was popular among visiting officials from both the Company of the Indies and the Marine. But within two weeks the impracticality of lodging with high-level officials on a clerk's salary became apparent. Caillot had exhausted the three-hundred-livre company allowance meant to cover his travel expenses between Paris and Lorient. At six livres per night, paying for lodging at Bachelier's proved unsustainable.[85] The stay had cost Caillot nearly seventy livres. His clerk's salary stood at six hundred. In the span of less than two weeks, he had spent more than 11 percent of his annual earnings, 70 percent of the salary advance he had received upon his arrival in Lorient. Homesick and nearing financial embarrassment, he packed his bags, bid his fellow lodgers adieu, and stepped out into the mud-lined streets of Lorient.[86]

Individuals awaiting passage on outbound trade vessels—including those directly in the employ of the Company of the Indies—often had to wait weeks or even months to depart. Three years earlier, in November 1726, Jesuit father Nicole-Ignace de Beaubois had pleaded with a company secretary, Monsieur de La Loë, for an advance after weeks of waiting in Lorient for the departure of his Louisiana-bound ship. Beaubois complained that each day he remained in port wrought havoc on his "modest purse" and made "the blood boil in [his] veins at every quarter of an hour."[87] For Caillot, a young man seemingly unaccustomed to solitude, the waiting period proved a disconsolate time. He wrote, "The anxiety of knowing the day of our departure, the sorrow of being away from my parents," coupled with "the sorrow of seeing my wallet get thinner right before my eyes without being able to do anything about it . . . made me feel an unparalleled commotion in my soul."[88] With his wallet thinning, Caillot sought out a dinghy that could carry him and his baggage to Penmanec, a small company-run harbor just south of Lorient at the confluence of the Scorff and Blavet Rivers. There preparations on board the *Durance* were well under way. Boarding on the ship, rather than in town, would afford Caillot the chance to save what little money he had left. His passage and meals on the *Durance* were underwritten by the company; his early arrival ensured a preview of the orchestrated chaos required to outfit a ship.

3

Tropical Baptisms

Outfitting a transatlantic vessel was an arduous and often dangerous process for the dozens of sailors, skilled laborers, and suppliers involved.[1] Depending on the ship's size, purpose, and destination, it took on average between three and six weeks to complete. In March 1729, three ships—the *Duc de Chartres*, *Espérance*, and *Durance*—lay in wait at Lorient's Penmanec roadstead as each underwent preparations for lengthy sailings. Although all were company ships, their pending expeditions differed greatly.

The 180-member crew of the *Duc de Chartres* faced the most complex outfitting. Crew members under the direction of Captain Jacques de Marquaysne scrambled to prepare the eight-hundred-ton ship for embarkation to the East Indies.[2] At an average time to completion of twenty-one months, the East Indian circuit was the lengthiest but also the most lucrative of the company's routes.[3]

Laden with casks of wine and brandy; ingots or pieces of silver, copper, lead, and gold; and crates of flat irons, glassware, and woven woolen cloth, company ships bound for the East Indies drew their cargoes from across France and, as was the case with commodities such as Canadian ginseng, its colonies.[4] In exchange, trade goods purchased from comptoirs in Chandernagore, Pondicherry, Surat, and other sites throughout the Indian Ocean circulated within the company's trade network. Silks, printed cottons, muslins, spices, indigo, rice, porcelain, all manner of petites étoffes (including collars, cuffs, shawls, and kerchiefs), coffee, tea, red wood, rattan, saltpeter for gunpowder, and cowrie shell ballast flowed from East Indian ports to company warehouses in France. From these warehouses the company redistributed the goods to the holds of ships bound for European, African, Caribbean, and North American ports. The East Indian trade allowed the company a symbiotic relationship with comptoirs around the globe. Trade goods from the East Indies, especially textiles and cowrie shells, underwrote nearly all of the company's slaving activities along Africa's Senegambian coast and fueled some of the trade with Native Americans in the Louisiana colony.[5]

The *Espérance*, a half-galley bound for Senegal, stood in stark contrast to the hulking shadows cast by the *Duc de Chartres*. At only 120 tons, the double-masted *Espérance* measured just over 120 feet long and 18 feet wide. Intended primarily as a coastal vessel (half-galleys were employed most frequently in the Mediterranean), the half-galley was ill equipped for carrying substantial cargoes across open ocean.[6] But though some features made galleys unlikely trade vessels—namely their small size and relative lack of cargo space—others made them ideal for maneuvering becalmed seas or shallow, narrow bodies of water. On the *Espérance*, banks of oars worked by an eighteen-man crew of *galériens*, or galley slaves, lined each side. When conditions allowed, two large lateen sails could be struck to supplement manpower with wind. Since 1723 the vessel had been in near constant service, sometimes making two journeys to Africa in the same year. The 1729 voyage was the *Espérance*'s eighth on the Senegambian circuit.

The company's Senegambian concession included three major slave-trading outposts: Saint-Louis (the concession headquarters), an island fortification in the mouth of the Senegal River; Gorée Island, just off the Atlantic coast to the south of Cape Verde (fig. 5); and Fort Saint-Joseph, an inland post in Galam accessible by way of the Senegal River. It was likely to this last post—which could be reached via a forty-day voyage upriver—that the *Espérance* set sail. Fort Saint-Joseph was of strategic importance to the company because it lay at the confluence of the Senegal and Feleme Rivers. This interior location allowed French traders to intercept slave caravans coming from eastern Senegambia and funnel them into the Senegal River, which flowed into a French-controlled *captiverie* at Fort Saint-Louis, thereby reducing the number of slave caravans bound for the English-operated Fort St. James at the mouth of the Gambia River. But reaching Fort Saint-Joseph from the Atlantic coast was tricky. Low water levels in the Senegal River limited access to a short window that ran from late spring to early fall. Each year, when the waters of the Senegal crested, the French sent small boats, such as the *Espérance*, inland. These support vessels shuttled captives, company employees, laborers, provisions, trade goods—including the gum Arabic so critical to textile production—and supplies to or between Forts Saint-Joseph and Saint-Louis.[7]

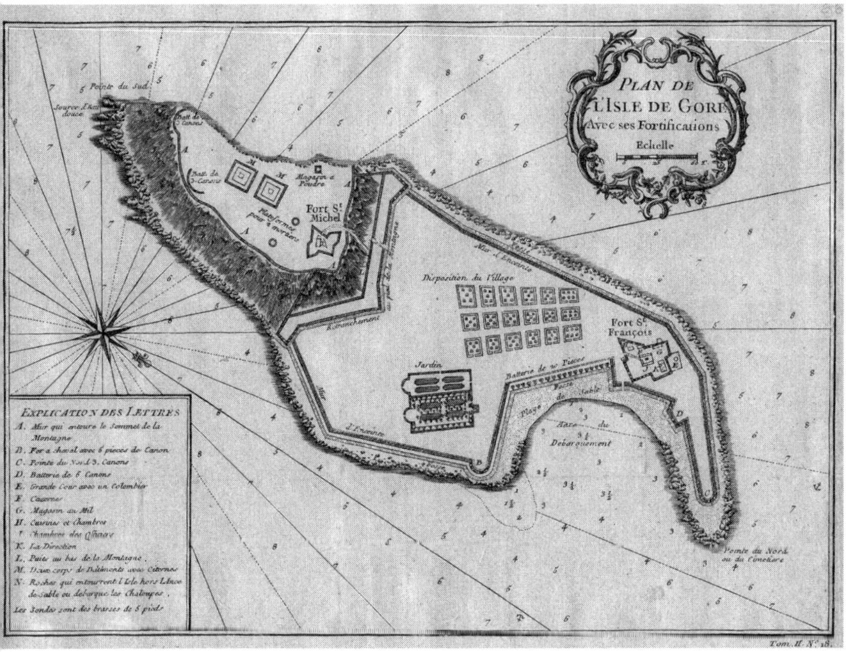

Fig. 5. Plan of Gorée Island. (Collection of the author.)

The *Espérance* was not a slaver in the usual sense. Unlike many of the ships bound for Senegal from Lorient, it was not directly engaged in the transatlantic transport of human cargo. But its service, like that of countless other longboats, canoes, and dinghies employed by the company on both sides of the Atlantic, facilitated the continued success and expansion of the triangular trade.

In 1729 the company increased its slaving activities along the Senegambian coast, sending more slavers to company-controlled trading posts that year than it had since the peak of the company's African trade, from 1723 to 1725, when the company had sent out a total of sixty-three ships—twenty-six to Senegambia, seventeen to Guinea, fourteen to Ouidah, and six to Angola—to Africa's west coast at an average of twenty-one per year. The number of Africa-bound company ships to sail during that three-year period was 44 percent of the total number sent by the company between 1720, the year following the company's absorption of the Senegal Company, and 1731, the year directors returned Louisiana to the Crown. By ramping up its slave-trading activities from 1723 to 1725, the company had hoped to prove to the Crown and Minister of Marine Maurepas that it could meet the colonies' need for slaves without opening up the African trade to private competitors.

The company failed in both its effort to meet Maurepas's projection of a needed eleven thousand slaves embarked per year on company ships and its fight to retain the *exclusif* over the African trade.[8] Shipwrecked slave ships, elevated mortality among slaves at sea and on arrival in the circum-Caribbean, and reluctance on the part of colonists to pay for slave purchases at the point of sale resulted in severe financial losses for the company. Colonists in Saint-Domingue, for example, owed so much money—over two million livres—for unpaid debts related to previous purchases of slaves and supplies that the company briefly ceased commerce with the colony in 1728.[9] Having failed to meet the demand for slaves with their own ships, the company agreed to reopen the trade south of the Sierra Leone River to private merchants in August 1725. The decision was financially sound. Private merchants paid a commission of 10 to 20 livres per slave for the privilege of helping the company meet its quota. By 1727 those commissions funneled some 350,000 livres per year into company coffers.[10]

Although the company was unable to maintain its monopoly over the slave trade, the readmission of private slave traders south of the Sierra Leone River did not result in the elimination of company-led expeditions. The company maintained exclusive control over trade in the Senegambian region and their fort at Ouidah, though at Ouidah, French ships competed side by side with vessels owned by other European powers. Out of the twenty-one company vessels that sailed from France the year of Caillot's departure, twelve were bound for the west coast of Africa—eleven for the company's Senegal concession, the twelfth for Ouidah. Two more sailed for India and the last for China. But only five of the Africa-bound vessels were directly engaged in the transatlantic trade; the *Annibal, Vénus, Duc de Bourbon, Saint-Louis,* and *Néréide* were destined to carry their slave cargoes across the Atlantic to the Louisiana colony. All but the *Néréide* visited multiple ports of call in the Americas, selling slaves in Saint-Domingue, Martinique, and Louisiana before returning to Lorient.

The four company ships bound directly from France for the Americas in 1729—the *Durance, Saint-Michel, Alexandre,* and *Baleine*—were engaged in the carrying trade. Direct trade ships ferried all manner of goods, company employees, soldiers, colonists, and correspondence between France and its American colonies. For company ships (slavers or not) on the Atlantic circuit in 1729, Louisiana was the primary and final port of call.[11]

The ship destined to bear Caillot across the Atlantic to a post of questionable importance in a colony known—at least in Parisian circles—primarily for its large and diverse Indian population, rudimentary settlements, inhospitable environment, and of course its association with John Law's failed financial scheme, was the *Durance* (fig. 6). The eighty-seventh such carrier of goods and peoples sent directly from France since the Company of the West gained control of Louisiana in 1717 and the twenty-fourth since the company's reorganization, the *Durance* was a flute, or *fluitschip.*[12] A Dutch-created vessel, the flute was an ideal freighter in times of peace. Its design maximized cargo-carrying capacity and minimized the number of necessary crew members. Flutes were also relatively lightly armed, a design aspect that made them attractive prey for pirates.[13]

A five-hundred-ton, triple-masted ship, the flute *Durance* was the largest—at least in terms of tonnage—of the four company vessels bound directly for the Americas in 1729.[14] The Company of the Indies measured tonnage by a ship's stowage capacity, rather than by the total weight a ship could bear without exceeding its maximum draft. A 1681 ordinance set the cubic tonnage measurement at 1.44 square meters (42ft^2) and assigned a corresponding weight of 2,000 pounds per ton. Tonnage measured by volume was an imperfect indicator of a ship's actual carrying capacity, as ships often bore lesser or greater burdens than the tonnage advertised by their builders.[15] Ships such as the *Duc de Chartres,* with higher carrying capacities of up to a maximum of 850

Fig. 6. The *Durance*. (Courtesy of The Historic New Orleans Collection, 2005.0011.)

tons, were engaged almost exclusively in trade with the company's most distant comptoirs—those in the East Indies—while those with minimal capacities of between 50 and 300 tons operated as slavers, shuttling human cargo from Africa to the Americas or as slave trade support. Mid-range ships, including the *Durance*, were the most likely to be found in the Atlantic carrying trade.

Constructed in Holland in 1718, the *Durance* had completed two full direct-trade navigations prior to the 1729 sailing. Its maiden voyage in 1721 took place under the guidance of Captain Gaultier, a maritime officer who in 1725 had the very rare distinction of being removed from his duties by the company due to his inability to properly control his crew. The next sailing, overseen by Captain Pierre de Brossy, carried trade goods, as well as 108 German-speaking immigrants, including 22 men, 33 women, and 53 children, to Louisiana. Brossy successfully completed the Lorient–Saint-Domingue–Louisiana circuit in 1727 but succumbed to a deadly tropical fever on his next navigation. All of the *Durance's* sailings in the 1720s were direct-trade voyages.[16]

On board the *Durance*, six cannon lined each side. During the outfitting, each cannon and its seating were inspected by Jacques Gouriou, a master gunner and one of the ship's nine noncommissioned officers. A native of Port-Louis, the twenty-one-year-old Gouriou also oversaw the stocking of la Sainte-Barbe, or powder magazine, where kegs of gunpowder and crates of cannon and other munitions were stacked from floor to ceiling. Above deck, barefooted sailors shimmied up and down the masts and out onto the booms, checking to be sure the maze of rope and cording was properly threaded through the countless blocks, hooks, and rings. Others readied the ship's sails to be unfurled the moment the captain gave the order to raise anchor.[17]

Dinghies or longboats ferried trade goods and supplies from shore to ship, where they were then loaded through the ship's hatch via a system of ropes and pulleys. In the hold, casks of water, brandy, olive oil, cured meats, and wine joined crates of cheese, rice, and dried vegetables that would sustain passengers and crew alike in the weeks and months ahead. Hardtack biscuit, baked at the company-run bakery in Lorient, was loaded into a tin-lined storeroom intended to prevent infestation and deter rodents.[18] With a view toward making Louisiana less dependent on imported provisions, the company entrusted a number of New Orleans–bound citrus plants to the *Durance's* captain.[19] More mundane supplies for everyday use were also brought on board. Bales of Genoa paper went in the hold to satisfy the great demand among company officials and private citizens for writing paper, as did 2,657 ells of fabric intended to help clothe Louisiana's slaves.[20]

High-demand trade goods destined for the Indian trade along the Gulf Coast and throughout the Mississippi Valley were also loaded into the hold. Gunpowder, cannons, bullets, hatchets, guns, "trading shirts for men and women," kettles, and sewing implements were among the most salable items employed in the Indian trade. But traders also peddled vanity and decorative items such as handheld mirrors "lacquered in the Chinese style," dyed red and blue socks, feathers in every possible color, and hats trimmed with fake gold or silver braid. In exchange, company traders would likely receive one of French Louisiana's only consistently available commodities: furs and pelts.[21]

In addition to space for the company's trade goods, each of the *Durance*'s officers received an allotment in the hold to be used on the return leg for his own personal stash of goods. Commissioned officer pay, though considerably higher than that of noncommissioned officers and sailors, did not represent the bulk of an officer's potential earnings.[22] Rather, maritime officers, and especially ship captains, tended to enrich themselves primarily through the use of a benefit that entitled them to company-sanctioned space on board ship. Known as the *port-permis*, this benefit allowed officers to bring on board a set amount of specie to be used in the colonies to purchase goods that could later be sold for personal gain in France. The financial allotment, along with a corresponding amount of cargo space on the return voyage, varied according to rank. Captains could board 3,000 piastres (silver coins of Spanish origin more commonly known as "pieces of eight"), invest them across the Atlantic in goods available through colonial comptoirs, and—barring shipwreck or takeover by pirates, in which case the port-permis was invalidated—carry the goods back to France free of charge on company ships. First lieutenants could do the same with 1,100 piastres, second lieutenants with 660 piastres, and so on.[23]

Items carried on board through the use of the port-permis were later sold in Nantes, alongside official company trade goods, at the annual company warehouse sales.[24] Officers could realize significant profit from the port-permis, although the greatest potential for increased extra-salary income was to be found on slave ships, where captains received a 13-livre per head bonus for slaves delivered alive to the Americas. Such bonuses averaged between 250 and 300 livres per sailing, a sum that surpassed captains' monthly salaries.[25]

While use of the port-permis to carry goods from the colonies to France on the return voyage was permissible, use of company ships to carry personal stashes of trade goods from France to the colonies was explicitly prohibited. In the 1720s, trade in French Louisiana was officially restricted to transactions and goods that flowed through the company. Mercantile policies embodied by the company's right to complete control over imports and exports rendered any alternative trading systems illegal, but as a number of historians have shown, actual enforcement of those policies in Louisiana proved difficult.[26] Not all of the goods loaded onto the *Durance* (or any other trade ship for that matter) could be considered legitimate.

Before stepping foot in the colony, Louisiana-bound passengers (not to mention ships' officers) ranging from high-level administrators to soldiers destined for the lowest ranks of a comptoir's workforce took every opportunity to fill their trunks with contraband trade items that might help them sustain or further themselves once they traversed the Atlantic. In a letter to a Lorient port official named Soret in 1720, recently arrived concessionnaire Gérard Pellerin insisted that any colonist who hoped for success in Louisiana "must bring with him if he has the means" a laundry list of trade items that violated the company's monopoly, including guns, bolts of limbourg cloth ("red is best"), lead shot, "white Venetian glass, absolutely no blue," large and small bells, mirrors on cards, and "brand new" trade shirts, among other items.[27] Even Caillot, whose meager allowance ran out before the *Durance* left France, managed to smuggle a small quantity of ribbons and lace onto the ship for future employ in the petty trade.[28]

Once crew members had finished loading all provisions and cargo (legitimate or otherwise), they then had to organize and reorganize the goods on board so that the cargo's weight was evenly balanced throughout the hold. Uncooperative weather conditions during the loading could delay a ship's departure for days or even weeks at a time, while the combination of choppy seas and precariously balanced cargo being hoisted on board sometimes produced fatal results and further delays for captains, who then had to scramble to replace injured crew members. Sacramental records for the Parishes of Saint-Louis (Lorient) and Riantec (Port-Louis) offer evidence of numerous armament-related deaths throughout the first half of the eighteenth century.[29]

Even Caillot found himself floundering about in the Atlantic after being thrown from a dinghy a few days before the *Durance*'s departure. Once he had boarded the *Durance*, boredom struck, motivating the young clerk to seek diversion. While the crews prepared the ships, Caillot and three officers from the *Duc de Chartres* set out on what might best be described as a pleasure excursion—a day trip—on a dinghy. The four young men left the harbor, sailing past the fortifications at Port-Louis and into the open Atlantic. They intended to sail south-southwest along the coast toward the island of Belle-Île, but a violent storm overtook them. A series of waves broadsided the dinghy, knocking the four men into the water. All four made it back to the boat and rode out the storm. It was Caillot's last dinghy excursion, though not his last unintended fall into the sea. Two days later, while helping the crew load livestock from longboats onto the *Durance*, Caillot was again plunged into the sea when the loading plank swung around and threw him overboard. The waters below were calm; the crew quickly hauled him back onto the loading deck.[30]

At the *Durance*'s helm stood the relatively inexperienced twenty-nine-year-old Louis-Laurent Aubin, Sieur du Plessis, of Le Havre.[31] Younger than the majority of his peers by some ten years, Aubin Duplessis (as he was referred to in company records) had first served as a ship's officer in 1727, when he sailed as junior lieutenant, or ensign, aboard the *Dromadaire*. The *Dromadaire* was also a cargo- and passenger-carrying flute on the Lorient-to-Louisiana circuit, a route and vessel that helped give Aubin Duplessis the experience necessary for his next voyage.[32] In 1729 Aubin Duplessis was commissioned as captain, due in part to his extensive familial connections. His father, Jean-Baptiste Aubin, Sieur Duchesne, was the artillery commander for both the city of Le Havre and its citadel.[33] His uncle Gilles Cambry *père* served as master shipbuilder in the French Royal Navy from 1720 to 1725 and as commander of the company's shipbuilding facilities at Lorient from 1730 until his death in 1739.[34]

Aubin Duplessis was joined by four additional commissioned officers. André-Jacques Bienvenu, a Lorient native who had served as captain of the *Espérance* on a 1724 sailing to Senegambia and as pilot in earlier sailings, was the *Durance*'s first lieutenant.[35] François Pardimene, also of Lorient, was ship's surgeon, while Jean-François Haumont of Saint-Malo, the youngest officer at twenty-two, filled the dual role of ensign and ship's scribe. Rounding out the commissioned crew was thirty-four-year-old Reverend Father Dennis O'Kelly ("Denys Oquely" in company documents), a prematurely gray chaplain who appeared on the crew register as an "Irish Jacobin" and whom Caillot described as a "waggish Irish rogue."[36]

The nine noncommissioned officers all hailed from the neighboring towns of Lorient and Port-Louis. They included a master attendant charged with overseeing docking, mooring, and equipping the ship as well as securing the rigging; a boatswain and his mate; a coxswain; a pilot and his assistant; a master gunner; a master carpenter; and a ship's steward. Apart from the noncommissioned officers, there were thirty-four additional crew members, including twenty-six sailors; three domestics charged primarily with food preparation; and five shipboys, or apprentice sailors, one of whom, Pierre Guyonard of Lorient, was the *Durance*'s youngest crew member, at age thirteen. The entire crew, save the Irish chaplain and sixteen-year-old shipboy Jean-Mary Blanche from Pontivy (an inland village), was composed of men from Brittany's coastal communities. Among the seamen and shipboys, four were from Saint-Malo and its immediate environs; seven from Lorient and neighboring Port-Louis; and nineteen from the naval hub surrounding Brest.[37] Many spoke Breton, a Celtic language prominent in southeastern Brittany, especially along the Atlantic coast. The seamen's linguistic disparity further reinforced the difference in dress, manner, and gait that separated them not only from the ship's uniformed officers but from even the lowest-ranking passenger.

Thirty-one passengers appear on the *Durance*'s passenger list, which can itself be seen as a microcosm of colonization efforts under the Company of the Indies. Caillot's shipmates represent a striking cross-section of travelers bound for Louisiana. Directly attached to the company were four *employés de la plume* (administrative or bureaucratic employees, literally "employees of the quill"), two physicians, and twenty skilled laborers who doubled as soldiers. Among the employés de la plume were three bookkeeping clerks: Caillot and his traveling companion Sieur de Troyes from the company's Paris offices and Charles Gontier from Lorient. A more senior employé de la plume from Paris, the commissioned bookkeeper Bussy, joined the three clerks.[38]

The *Durance* carried a higher number of administrative and clerical employees to Louisiana than any company ship since the *Comte de Toulouse* in 1718.[39] From 1717 to 1731, the company sent a total of five bookkeepers and nineteen clerks (including bookkeeping, tobacco inspection, and warehouse clerks) to the Louisiana colony. Only one, a warehouse clerk named Sieur Masclary, brought his wife.[40] None brought children. This near-total absence of accompanying family suggests that clerks' anticipated tenure may have been too brief to warrant company subsidy of spouses and children. Furthermore, the high turnover among young men working in clerical capacities may have further deterred company sponsorship of family members. The pool of clerks engaged in the company's overseas offices represented a notoriously unstable group. Typically young men under the age of twenty-five, clerks trained in the company's Paris offices, and their propensity toward laziness and unreliability made them the object of derision on both sides of the Atlantic. A 1731 report to Jacques Deshayes, one of the company's directors in Paris, mentions "an extraordinary number of useless clerks" scattered throughout the company's comptoirs as a contributor to bloated spending.[41]

In contrast to clerical employees, company administrators, engineers, physicians, and military personnel were more likely to cross the Atlantic accompanied by family members. Of the 5,625 Louisiana-bound passengers traveling on board company ships sailing from Lorient in the years 1717–31, 1,085 are listed on passenger registers as individuals engaged by the company in nonclerical capacities. They include a merchant, 6 administrators, 3 engineers, 2 surveyors, 7 surgeons (two of whom, Jean de Reytet and Jean Robert Chierdel, were on the *Durance*), 22 tobacco workers, 13 miners, 33 skilled laborers not affiliated with the military, and 989 military personnel. At least 74 (7 percent) of these men were accompanied by their wives. Fifty-two of their children also made the crossing. And like members of the civilian population, nonclerical company personnel already in Louisiana sometimes had family members join them after they had established themselves in the colony. Twenty such passengers sailed from Lorient to join husbands, fathers, uncles, or sons attached to the company in Louisiana.[42]

Military men made up the largest percentage of individuals within the company labor pool. They constituted 92 percent of *all* employees sent to Louisiana from 1717 to 1731. Among those sailing to Louisiana during this fourteen-year period were 174 officers and 815 soldiers, some of whom (17 percent) were also skilled laborers sent to Louisiana with Plantin's Company.

Named for its commanding officer, Plantin's Company was a military unit initially charged with protecting company holdings at Lorient. But what began in 1721 as a sort of local militia overseeing the defense of Lorient had by the mid-1720s expanded geographically to points across the French Atlantic.[43] Plantin's Company also emerged as the primary source of skilled labor for newly established or struggling comptoirs. French historian Philippe Haudrère estimates that 42 percent of Plantin's soldiers were artisans, while an additional 30 percent possessed some form of agricultural experience. The remaining 28 percent were unskilled laborers.[44] On board the *Durance*, the ratio of skilled to unskilled soldiers was even higher. Twenty soldiers from Plantin's Company sailed on the *Durance*. Seventeen were skilled laborers, including silk and metalworkers, weavers, ribbon and nail makers, carpenters, tanners, and candlemakers.[45] Those without skill were either too young to have learned a trade or had been impressed into service with Plantin's Company.

Also at the charge of the company was Mademoiselle Margueritte-Françoise Le Coq, a young woman of twenty-five who, according to Caillot, "was a very small specimen, with a very badly formed figure, golden blond hair, a long and sun-burnt face, a pushed-in nose," and "four teeth in her mouth, which ran one after the other."[46] The alluring Margueritte Le Coq, daughter of Suzanne Demorils and François Le Coq, hailed from the port city of Le Havre. Her father, a successful rope maker, had died in the early 1720s, likely putting his wife, Suzanne, who continued his rope manufactory on a much smaller scale, in a difficult financial position. Tax rolls from Le Havre provide a clear picture of the family's changed circumstances after François's death. In 1705 he had paid nine livres to the tax collector, while the average rope maker paid just over three. To put that sum in perspective, those with the highest income in 1705—ship captains and merchants—paid an average of fourteen livres annually, while innkeepers paid an average of eight and bakers six. After François's death the household's tax burden fell to two livres per annum.[47] His widow kept one daughter home to help with the rope manufactory and sent her other daughters off in hopes they might find means to support themselves. For Margueritte, one of the Le Coq family's middle children, this meant sailing for Louisiana as a prospective bride. When she boarded the *Durance*, she joined the ranks of dozens of women whose passage to Louisiana was underwritten in full or part by the company in an effort to balance the sex ratio between white male and white female colonists in Louisiana.

Regardless of where inhabitants settled, they faced a striking disparity in the sex ratio. Historian Daniel H. Usner estimates that for every 100 white women in French colonial Louisiana, there were 280 white men.[48] The ratio was even more lopsided among enslaved Africans, making women of all backgrounds desirable as domestic and sexual partners.

The French Crown was aware of what happened when an overwhelmingly male European population lacked an equal number of white female counterparts. In New France, French settlers and *coureurs de bois* had cohabited and intermarried with the native population beginning in the early seventeenth century. And in France's Caribbean colonies, where Africans far outnumbered Europeans, interracial unions—legitimated by marriage or not—were common. Because these unions sometimes led to freedom for the woman and/or the couple's offspring, a population of free people of color, who were often of mixed Afro-European descent, emerged.[49] In an attempt to eradicate such mixing across racial lines in Louisiana, in 1724 the Crown issued a revised and updated edition of the *Code noir* (the legal code regulating the treatment of slaves first issued by Louis XIV in 1685).[50]

The new code not only sought to ban interracial relationships by prohibiting "priests, missionaries, and even ships' chaplains" (art. 6) from marrying whites and blacks but also took preemptive measures to undermine the growth of any future free black or mixed-race population by denying its members the right to inherit land, chattel, or money from whites (art. 52).[51] Yet selective application of the code on the ground in Louisiana, where the sex ratio remained skewed throughout the eighteenth century, meant that relationships across the color line continued, as did manumissions of mixed offspring, which increased the total free colored population. Two years after the code was released, New Orleans parish priest and Capuchin superior Father Raphaël protested colonists' repeated violations, lamenting that "although the number of those who maintain young Indian women or negresses to satisfy their intemperance is considerably diminished, there still remain enough to scandalize the church and to require an effective remedy."[52]

The effort to balance the sex ratio and provide stability to the colony via the introduction of marriageable French women was not new in the late 1720s, nor was the practice limited to Louisiana.[53] As early as 1701, just two years after the colony's founding, Iberville pleaded with the minister of the Marine for "some families and a few girls" who could be "married off shortly after their arrival."[54] His requests for "sturdy" girls to temper the wandering tendencies of Louisiana's predominantly male residents and strengthen the colony's overall chance at survival continued, resulting in the arrival of the first of many ships carrying prospective brides in 1704.[55] Twenty-three single women and two families arrived on the *Pélican* from La Rochelle that year. The arrival of single French women in the Louisiana colony, however, was sporadic and the number generally insufficient even after the Company of the West (later the Company of the Indies) changed its approach and began the notorious practice of rounding up known prostitutes, criminals, and destitute, sickly women and carting them off to Atlantic port cities. Historian Marcel Giraud estimated that only about 160 of women in these categories, exiled by king's orders, ever made the crossing, and many died shortly after arrival. And during the company period only forty-four exiled women are identified as such on passenger registers. They include twenty banished for fraud, six for *libértinage*, and another eighteen for unspecified offenses. Although their numbers were small, their reputed presence in Louisiana loomed large in the collective memory of contemporary visitors and novelists alike.[56]

References to female colonists' dissolute nature appear frequently in contemporary accounts. Ship captain Valette de Laudun, after visiting Louisiana in 1720, surmised that "most of the women sent here are so unhealthy and so used up by past relations that they are sterile before they even leave [France]," while Ursuline novitiate Marie-Madeleine Hachard assured her father that in New Orleans "girls of bad conduct . . . are closely observed . . . and severely punished by putting them on a wooden horse and whipped by all the soldiers of the regiment that guards our city."[57] Despite such measures, however, Hachard admitted that the punishment did "not prevent there from being more [such girls] than would fill a reformatory."[58] La Chaise, too, complained about "a number of women . . . who are useless and who do nothing but cause disorder." The same women, he claimed, "are ruined with pox and ruin the sailors." As an alternative to keeping them in the capital, where they received rations from the company, he suggested the company order the Superior Council to have them sent "into the interior among the Indians."[59] For La Chaise, such a solution offered the best of both worlds: it rid the city of potential spreaders of venereal disease and relieved the company's burden of keeping them on the dole. But La Chaise was always on the lookout for ways to trim company allotments, and as Emily Clark has argued, critiques of middling and poor colonists made by members of the colonial elite should be treated with skepticism.[60]

By the time Caillot's ship sailed for Louisiana, the company had largely discontinued its efforts to round up women by volume over quality in favor of a more organic approach. The demand for marriageable white women remained high throughout the 1720s, but as the decade progressed and the overall population expanded, male inhabitants were far more likely to secure brides through the social and economic networks that tied individuals already in the colony to women in the metropole than through unions with banished prostitutes.[61]

The passenger survey reveals just thirty-two single women not classified as forced exiles whose passage was in some part subsidized by the company.[62] Subsidies ranged from full dining privileges at the captain's table to basic rations while on board. To further encourage male colonists to marry white Frenchwomen, the company sometimes provided modest dowries to single women bound for Louisiana. Thus, Margueritte Le Coq is listed on the register of the *Durance* with 270 livres of company-paid expenses "for her trousseau as well as her rations."[63]

Despite Caillot's unfavorable description of Le Coq, he believed she was in some way related to Louisiana's governor, Étienne Périer. He suspected, given this supposed tie, that she might carry a substantial dowry. In fact, Le Coq did have ties to Périer, but they were not direct (and the dowry was company sponsored). Rather, her sister, Marie-Louise "Catin" Le Coq, had traveled to Louisiana three years earlier on the *Baleine* as one of three European servants attached to the Périer household, who made the trip from France to Louisiana with the company ship captain turned governor.[64] Domestic servants such as Catin made up just 2 percent of passengers traveling from Lorient to Louisiana. Of the 107 individuals identified as domestics, 10 (9 percent) served religious orders, while 26 (24 percent) served households headed by company administrators. Military officers and engineers brought a total of 18 domestics (8 percent each) to Louisiana. Six servants had no documented affiliation, and the remaining 60 (56 percent) arrived with prospective colonists. Approximately 40 percent of domestics whose sex was noted on passenger registers were women.

Catin had arrived as Madame Périer's *femme de chambre*, or lady's maid, but left the Périer household shortly after her arrival to wed Joseph Chaperon, a Montreal native, in 1727.[65] For Margueritte Le Coq, too, the company's investment was sound. She married Joseph Larchevesque, a resident of upper Louisiana and native of Quebec, within four months of her arrival in New Orleans.[66]

Rounding out the passengers on board the *Durance* were two *fraudeurs de tabac*, or "tobacco cheaters," exiled by order of the king for violating the strict trade monopoly that allowed tobacco importation and sales in France to be carried out exclusively by the company. Unlike Louis XIV, his successors did not share an unwillingness to engage in forced emigration schemes. A 1719 royal decree issued during the Regency spelled out a detailed plan to round up undesirables, including *galériens* (galley slaves) and *les gens sans aveu* (individuals without professions or other means of support), and ship them to the colonies.[67]

John Law's company was not the first to make the export of social and economic outcasts to France's colonies a central tenet of a monopoly company's labor policy. Vagabonds and miscreants had been rounded up and sent to the French Caribbean colonies in the previous century. And during the course of the late seventeenth and early eighteenth centuries, the view that forced emigration was beneficial to the mother country (because it could be rid of the dregs of society) as well as to the social outcasts uprooted by the policy (because they would be given a chance to be productive in a new environment) had gained increasing traction.[68] From 1717 to 1731, 413 exiles arrived in the colony; nearly 25 percent of them were clearly identified as tobacco cheaters. They constituted the second-largest exiled group, outnumbered only by salt smugglers.[69]

Of the various occupational and demographic groups typically present on board company ships, colonists (be they concessionaires, independent tradesmen, or something in between), privately contracted laborers (domestics, contracted tradesmen), and clergy were not among the *Durance*'s passengers. Also absent from the *Durance*, as they were from most company ships by the late 1720s, were *engagés*, or indentured servants. In the early 1720s, hundreds of engagés had traveled to Louisiana to work large-scale concessions granted during John Law's tenure. Many migrated with their masters to the rich agricultural lands of the newly established Natchez outpost, where concessionaires hoped to establish tobacco plantations. Those who survived the three-year term of indenture often stayed in the colony, with some settling in New Orleans, where there were opportunities beyond farming, and some remaining in the Natchez area and establishing their own farms and plantations. By the mid-1720s, regular company shipments of enslaved laborers from Africa made the use of indentured labor, and its temporary nature, less attractive to prospective planters.

By March 14 the *Durance* was in the final stages of preparation for the Atlantic crossing. With all passengers and crew in place, Pierre Antoine de Fayet, commander of the port at Lorient, boarded the *Durance* to issue final instructions from the company's Paris offices and a revised passenger list to Captain Aubin Duplessis.[70] On March 16, 1729, the *Durance* set sail on what would be a seventeen-week voyage from Lorient, across the Atlantic to Saint-Domingue's La Caye Saint-Louis, through the Gulf of Mexico to the Balize at the mouth of the Mississippi River, and finally to New Orleans.

Historians have long acknowledged that for Europeans and Africans arriving in the Americas, the initial period of exposure to New World environments—especially in those colonies south of the mid-Atlantic region—was one frequently marked by sickness. Newcomers' ability to survive during the so-called seasoning period depended on a host of factors, ranging from the month of their arrival to their exposure to infectious diseases. But seasoning was not limited to the bodily transformations that resulted in death for some and increased stamina or immunity for others. Rather, *seasoning* is a term that can be applied in a more general sense to describe the complete range of physiological, psychological, and emotional responses of newly arrived men, women, and children as they struggled not only to stay alive but also to make sense of their surroundings.

The term *seasoning* is one associated primarily with the unconditioned body's physical response to the colonial environment, but even the standard geographic applications of the term are unnecessarily narrow and misleading. Seasoning began well before colonists, slaves, administrators, soldiers, and the like settled into life on land. It began, in all its forms, at sea. Experiences of and interactions among passengers and crew at sea left lasting impressions that shaped the earliest understanding of a colony most had yet to see firsthand. Ships served as sites of initiation to the wider French Atlantic world.

Much work has been undertaken by historians in an effort to document the experiences of African captives during the Atlantic crossing as well as to examine the impact of those experiences on identity formation and cultural cohesion among the founding generation of slaves in the Americas.[71] While historians remain engaged with the historiography of the Middle Passage, however, there has been until recently little examination of how the Atlantic crossing affected non-captives.[72] Although the circumstances surrounding the Atlantic crossing of European passengers differed greatly from those of enslaved Africans, there were common experiential elements. In 1959 Stanley Elkins described what he perceived as the shocks of enslavement and the Middle Passage as elemental to the worldview of African slaves in the Americas.[73] In the fifty years since Elkins put forth his thesis, historians have fleshed out a far more nuanced understanding of that same worldview and, in doing so, have poked a considerable number of holes in Elkins's assertion that the shocks of enslavement rendered enslaved Africans in the Americas empty vessels whose characters had been irrevocably corrupted.[74] Despite the flaws in Elkins's conclusions, however, his assertion that the experiences of captives during the Atlantic crossing shaped their later experiences on land remains valid (and uncontroversial). Clearly, the horrors of the Middle Passage were not shared or even recognized by most European passengers. But for those undertaking the transatlantic crossing for the first time, for those neophytes of the French Atlantic, shipboard experiences and encounters shaped the ways in which individuals (slave and free) came to process their future colonial environments.

In 1729 the majority of the *Durance*'s passengers were undertaking their first Atlantic sailing and so had at best only a vicarious understanding—or what Stephanie Smallwood describes as "rumor-based knowledge"—of what it might mean to be contained within a ship's confines for weeks or months on end.[75] Some had relatives, friends, or patrons who, having made the crossing, wrote letters home describing their voyage. From these letters and the handful of contemporary published accounts in circulation, passengers boarding the *Durance* likely had heard of the bouts of sickness that plagued shipmates, the outlandish rituals visited upon passengers and crew, and the sometimes brutal force used to maintain shipboard discipline.[76] But stories told of life at sea to the uninitiated did little to prepare first-time passengers for the experience of shipboard life.

Direct trade ships between Lorient and Louisiana took an average of fourteen months to complete the circuit, with the outbound leg ranging from three to six months, depending on whether the ship stopped in the Atlantic Islands (Canary, Cape Verde, and Madeira Islands) or in the West Indies and whether passengers disembarked at the Balize or the port of New Orleans.[77] During the crossing, passengers lived in close confines, regardless of their status or ration level, and faced daily reminders that life as they had known it in France had ceased. Consumed first by seasickness that propelled them to the rail, where, as Caillot put it, you could "observe a row of people all making the same music . . . until [each person] had entirely paid the tribute due to the sea," passengers then faced some of the perhaps less-anticipated aspects of life at sea.[78]

Sickness and death loomed large in contemporary travel accounts. Violent storms washed livestock overboard, water infiltrated baking stores, and worms infested water supplies. Ursuline novitiate Marie-Madeleine Hachard reported that forty-nine sheep and some chickens washed overboard during a storm before the *Gironde* reached Madeira during its 1727 sailing. Two years later, Caillot lamented the loss of many "hens, geese, turkeys, two pigs, and a donkey" in the same area.[79] And on some ships manmade ration crises prompted by captains who purposely withheld rations in order to make the voyage more profitable added to the sometimes considerable distress of those on board. In 1725 members of the Louisiana Superior Council notified company directors in Paris that "the majority of passengers" arriving from France "complain of the bad manners of the captains and of the bad food."[80] The longer the voyage and scarcer the provisions, the more likely it became that passengers and crew weakened by insufficient or unbalanced rations would succumb to fevers, intestinal illnesses, and nutritional deficiencies. But while sickness at sea often chose its victim without regard to age, sex, or standing, only first-time crossers were subjected to rites of maritime initiation.

Ritual bribery under the guise of initiation was a common and accepted practice on board company ships. Sailors' superstition and their embrace of ritual behavior often fell outside of the commissioned officers' realm of authority, in practice if not official policy. In general, officers did not interfere with time-honored maritime rituals carried out by the crew, choosing instead to keep watch over the proceedings from a distance. But though a ship's officers might be exempt—or outright barred—from direct involvement in crew members' ceremonial doings, the same could not be said of passengers. Indeed, passengers often bore the brunt of the ritualized coercion carried out by sailors and seamen.

For passengers on board the *Durance*, seamen's rituals usually ended with the lightening of passenger purses or loss of their spirits, such as wine or brandy. Boredom set in quickly during Atlantic crossings, but passengers tempted to climb to the crow's nest to break the monotony of life on deck found themselves set upon by sailors, who quickly bound the climber to the rigging. In Caillot's case, he had advised the *Durance*'s captain of his intentions, but Captain Aubin Duplessis "pretended to be ignorant of the events that were about to take place," leaving Caillot unaware of the reaction his climb would trigger. He climbed halfway up the Jacob's ladder that led from deck to nest before noticing the dozen sailors in pursuit. Thinking they were concerned for his safety, he "wore [him]self out from shouting to them that they had only to stay put." But before Caillot could convince them, the sailors caught him, shoved him through the lubber's hole, and "bound [him] fast with a rope," refusing to untie him until he pledged "to pay the tribute" due from all first-time climbers. The promise of a flagon filled with five pints of brandy secured his freedom. He later consoled himself with the knowledge that by the end of the crossing "one-half to three-fourths of the passengers succumbed to that maritime ordinance."[81]

While certain actions—typically those that found passengers leaving their proscribed portion of the ship (the main deck, e.g., or the dining area or cabins) in favor of an area under the exclusive domain of the crew—set in motion immediate chain reactions among sailors in the passenger's immediate vicinity, one maritime ritual involved the elaborate machinations of the entire noncommissioned crew. Caillot's provocative account of the Baptism of the Tropics ceremony, a variation on the more common "crossing the line" ritual practiced by seamen crossing the equator, reveals that all uninitiated adult passengers, regardless of sex or standing, were subjected to the bribe-us-or-be-drenched policy of Tropicus's "troupe of demons."[82]

The "baptism" took place as ships crossed the Tropic of Cancer and appears to have been practiced largely on board French ships. It represented a rare opportunity for sailors to subvert the ship's normally rigid hierarchy. Passengers and crew, including officers, who had never before crossed the Tropic of Cancer were subjected to baptism by Tropicus, a sort of composite sea god who shared attributes of the Greek Poseidon and Roman Neptune. Virgin ships and longboats also were subjected to a ceremonial dousing, a practice that continues today. Kenneth Banks expresses uncertainty over whether women were subjected to the baptismal ritual, but a number of contemporary descriptions make clear that both sexes endured the Baptism of the Tropics.[83] Even traveling clergy and nuns were not exempt from baptismal bribes. While traveling from Marseille to Louisiana on board the *Toulouse* in 1720, Father Laval, who had taken part in the ritual on a previous crossing, counseled his fellow clergy members to submit and not take the baptism too seriously. Seven years later, Sister Marie-Madeleine Hachard chose to keep most of the lurid details of the ceremony to herself, but in a letter home to her father she complained that "one has to pay money to be exempt from participating in it" and revealed that the crew of the *Gironde* had managed to extort two *pistoles* out of her and her fellow Ursulines.[84]

Caillot's vivid description of King Tropicus, the eldest crew member, and "his frightful entourage"—a group that included four tar-covered sailors "daubed with flour" playing makeshift instruments, two sailors dressed as pilgrims, twenty as soldiers, and two more playing the role of Tropicus's angels, who were "completely nude except for a sheepskin, the tail of which flapped between their thighs"—makes clear that the baptism was a highly ritualized ceremony, taken seriously by sailors and officers alike.[85] Of the *Durance*'s forty-eight crew members, Caillot recorded the participation of at least thirty in the ritual. As for the ship's commissioned crew, the captain took part in receiving Tropicus in his cabin, and the officers further soaked those who underwent the baptism, but their roles were secondary to those played by sailors. Passengers who failed to pay adequate homage to Tropicus through tributes of money, brandy, or other alcohol faced a thorough dousing with seawater. One unfortunate female passenger thought she had satisfied Tropicus, only to be "hit with more than fifty buckets full of water." By the end of the ceremony the crew had collected "146 livres and 11 flagons of brandy, with which they amused themselves for the rest of the day."[86] If passengers often bore the brunt of ritualized coercion carried out by sailors and seamen, crew members faced coercion of a more brutal nature at the hands of their superiors. On merchant ships, as on naval vessels, the crew operated under a strict hierarchy. At the pinnacle of the hierarchy was the captain, whose office vested in him the power to punish seamen for any breach—real or imagined—of acceptable conduct. But while the captain wielded the absolute power to maintain discipline, he was not the only authority acting to reinforce the hierarchical divisions among crew members. Power flowed from the captain down through the ranks, with each chain in the hierarchy—from the noncommissioned officers to the novices—exercising some level of control over the group beneath it. The captain at sea could not be dominated or disciplined. The crew's lowest-ranking members, shipboys, stood at the opposite end of the chain and often faced both methods of control.

Novice (also called apprentice) sailors and shipboys soon learned what Marcus Rediker refers to as the "language of punishment" that permeated verbal relations on board ship, but they were not alone in experiencing this lesson.[87] Passengers, too, bore witness to shipboard discipline, building their lexicon of words to describe instruments and processes imposed on the punished. Through personal diaries, correspondence, and memoirs, passengers carefully recorded scenes of punishment, taking time to recount in detail differences in process and effect between "wet" versus "dry" keelhauling, between lashings administered by cat-o'-nine-tails with their multiple loose cords versus *garcettes* with their braided ones.[88]

On the *Durance*, Caillot, too, recorded episodes of discipline, often with the same clinical clarity he employed when describing noteworthy marine or plant life. But what Caillot found more difficult to note objectively was the public torment and humiliation of the shipboys (whom he referred to as "poor wretches" and "poor creatures") at the hands of bored officers. "When the wind is lacking," wrote Caillot, "the officers, in order to amuse themselves, say that the wind is closed up in their breeches, and on these insinuations they are forced to pull their breeches down." The boys are then tied "to the capstan by the middle of their bodies," given whips, and forced to run round in circles, with each whipping the boy in front of him—and getting the same treatment himself from the boy behind. When the first boy struck "feels himself hit sharply, he becomes animated and does not go easy on the one who is in front of him, so when they really get going, you see them running after the other, twisting and turning, and all crying out like they are possessed." The demoralization of the *Durance*'s five shipboys aged thirteen to sixteen, who often "end up with bloody buttocks from the force used on them," struck Caillot as being somehow outside the pattern of behavior that his limited experience allowed him to process as expected, or "normal."[89] The officers' seemingly senseless abuse of shipboys did not fit neatly into his understanding of hierarchy and order, though Caillot's objections may have stemmed more from witnessing officers behave in a manner he considered beneath their station than from any inherent sympathy for the ship's lowest-ranking crew members.

How quickly shipmates overcame their boredom by playing cards, dancing, socializing, or witnessing outlandish and sometimes violent spectacles depended largely on the winds. Cooperative winds hastened a ship's entry into the Caribbean Sea, while the lack of wind or a prolonged presence in the doldrums might delay entry by days or weeks.

Either way, once a ship approached the Caribbean, passengers and crew faced fewer opportunities for diversion and were most vulnerable to food shortages, parasitic illnesses, and related complications. After spending weeks on the open waters of the Atlantic, supplies were often dangerously depleted or damaged. The time between a ship's entry into the Caribbean and its arrival at a port of call was critical in determining the overall health of those on board.

4

Stopping Over

Provisioning and Acculturation

As the *Durance* sailed through the chain of Windward Islands toward its first port of call at La Caye Saint-Louis, Saint-Domingue, provisions became a point of near daily contention. Multiple ration levels existed on board company ships, each based on passenger status and rank. Missionaries, company administrators, and individuals from the noble and merchant classes were at the top of the ration hierarchy, which entitled them to the same quality and quantity of food found at the officers' table. By the time the *Durance* entered the Caribbean, a number of passengers had begun accusing Captain Aubin Duplessis of hoarding supplies, wasting water on his orange trees, and serving "peas infested by aphids" to passengers entitled to the highest ration level while the officers "were dining on fresh food."[1]

After passengers threatened to draw up a signed memorandum to the company reporting the captain's ration irregularities—a mutinous suggestion backed up by the presence of twenty ill-fed and disgruntled soldiers from Plantin's Company—Aubin Duplessis made an attempt to ameliorate rations. His efforts were undermined days later, as the ship was passing Puerto Rico, by rats that had "bitten through" ten barrels of water, forcing him to reduce allotments to one pint per day.[2] Typical water rations stood at three pints per day, per person, with one reserved for drinking and the other two for cooking and food preparation. This reduction, combined with the water's poor quality, which Caillot described as "stinking and greenish" with "little worms wriggling in it," and the ship's dwindling provisions, weakened crew members and passengers alike.[3] At the same time, excessive heat in passengers' between-decks sleeping quarters, whose only ventilation came from portholes "the size of two hands" that often could not be opened without drenching the bunks, made the prospect of real rest impossible for the malnourished or sickened.[4] Sleeping-quarter conditions frequently forced both sick and healthy passengers to seek refuge on deck, where exposure to the elements was deemed preferable to the stifling heat below. By the time the *Durance* dropped anchor at La Caye, Caillot reported that at least twenty-two (28 percent) of the seventy-nine individuals on board showed signs of *scorbu*, or scurvy.[5]

Contraction of scurvy was not limited to sailors. Passengers and slaves on long-haul voyages also succumbed to the nutritional disorder. Manifesting itself as "red spots in the *Arms* and *Legs*," these lesions soon turned "*black* and then *blue*."[6] As the victim's vitamin C deficiency persisted, "an extraordinary *Weakness*, a *Redness*, *Itching* and *Rottenness* of the *Gums*, and a *Looseness* of the *Teeth*" marked scurvy's progression.[7] Prior to James Lind's 1754 publication of *A Treatise on Scurvy*, the malady was poorly understood, and the label "scurvy" was often applied to any number of unrelated ailments, which impeded diagnosis and treatment.[8] Not until the last decades of the eighteenth century did the addition of citrus fruits to seamen's diets become a standard method of prevention. It is likely that scurvy was not the only illness afflicting the *Durance*'s passengers.

As ships neared the Caribbean, then, shipmates often found themselves in a weakened state, ill suited to a changing landscape where heightened awareness of the environment outside the confines of their wooden world was imperative. While sightings of other vessels in the open waters of the Atlantic were rare, near the Caribbean maritime traffic grew dramatically with vessels from across Europe converging on their respective island colonies. In the confines of the Caribbean Sea, the greater presence of cargo-laden ships attracted a fair number of sloops, galleys, and other ships engaged in piracy. Merchant vessels were on high alert. Crews and passengers, including at times female passengers dressed as men, had to be at the ready to take up arms against perceived threats. Captains were under orders to throw any company correspondence into the sea (preferably in a "sack weighted down with a cannon ball") should they "find themselves in danger of being taken by pirates, or any nation [France] might be at war with."[9]

The *Durance* approached the Caribbean near the end of April, sailing into the sea between the islands of Dominica and Martinique around the twenty-sixth. As the ship sailed north by northeast, passing French-controlled Dominica and Guadeloupe, British-controlled Montserrat and St. Christophe (St. Kitts), and Spanish-controlled Puerto Rico and Santo Domingo, it came into direct contact with no fewer than ten other vessels. Two flew the Flag of No Quarter (the pirate flag), two others the English flag, and six more were company ships.[10] Among those chartered by the Company of the Indies were two ships that, like the *Durance*, were engaged in the direct carrying trade—shuttling a variety of goods, correspondence, and passengers back and forth between France and its circum-Caribbean colonies. The other four were company-outfitted slavers, plying the triangular route between France, western Africa, and the Americas.

The *Durance* dropped anchor at its first port of call in mid-May 1729. Located on the southern coast of Saint-Domingue's southern peninsula, the port at La Caye Saint-Louis (modern-day Les Cayes) served as an important way station on the France-Louisiana route. None of France's Caribbean islands were held or controlled in their entirety by the company. Its presence in Martinique and Guadeloupe was limited to the purchase of cash crops and the sale of slaves, though when necessary company ships—slavers and cargo vessels alike—anchored at both islands for provisions or to drop off sick passengers and African captives. Still, stopovers in the Caribbean took place largely in La Caye, where the company maintained a dedicated port, the only one it operated in the West Indies.

La Caye's primary function was to serve as a supply depot for all company ships on the France-Louisiana circuit, the longest in the French Atlantic. Whether inbound or out, La Caye supplied water, tafia (rum's less-refined cousin), lamb, poultry, fresh fruit, and other rations procured from neighboring plantations to Louisiana-bound crews and passengers. The port also provided sail and ship repairs and even fresh crew members to vessels in need. La Caye served a function similar to the Atlantic island ports of Madeira, the Canaries, and Cape Verde, which had all helped ensure continuous European expansion in the Atlantic world from the fifteenth through the seventeenth centuries. By the eighteenth century these ports, with their mainstays of cured and salted meats, goats for dairy, Madeira wine, fresh water, tropical fruits, chicken, beans, and yams, fueled a shape-shifting amalgam of European territories on both sides of the Atlantic.[11]

The role of provisioner-in-chief to ships bound for the Louisiana colony was not the role Louis XIV had envisioned for La Caye three decades earlier. In 1698, just one year after France's claims to the western portion of Hispaniola were confirmed via the Treaty of Ryswick, the French king granted a large undeveloped tract of mountainous land along the island's southern peninsula to the Saint-Domingue Company. This tract, known as the southern province, stretched from "Cap Tiburon to the Naybe River [now the Yaque del Sur in the Dominican Republic], including all of the area from the coast to a depth of three leagues."[12] In modern equivalents the area measured approximately 140 miles across by 7.5 miles deep (fig. 7). Marked by the interconnected Massif de La Hotte to the west and Massif de La Selle to the east, the rugged southern peninsula was fairly isolated from and, with the exception of the coastal plains and interspersed plateaus, less suited to plantation agriculture than its northern counterpart.[13]

Isolation from the western and northern provinces meant that La Caye and the surrounding area were more focused on inter-Caribbean than intra-colony trade. The south had long served as a base for marauding pirates—and in times of war legitimate privateers—and smugglers as well as buccaneers who plied smoked meat (*boucan*) to passing ships. In the late seventeenth century, French officials hoped to capitalize on the area's status as a trading crossroads by granting land and monopoly trading privileges to the Saint-Domingue Company.

Backed by a team of twelve directors, including Jérôme Pontchartrain (who was not yet minister of the Marine) and Antoine Crozat (whose failure in Louisiana was still more than a decade away), the Saint-Domingue Company's mission was threefold: encourage im-/migration to and settlement of the southern province, ensure a steady supply of African slaves to the island's nascent sugar industry, and promote trade with the Spanish empire. The last two aims were interconnected. By positioning the Saint-Domingue Company at a nexus of Caribbean trade, France hoped to procure the *assiento*, giving France exclusive rights to the African slave trade to the Spanish Americas.[14]

Despite its nonexistent tract record for the successful large-scale

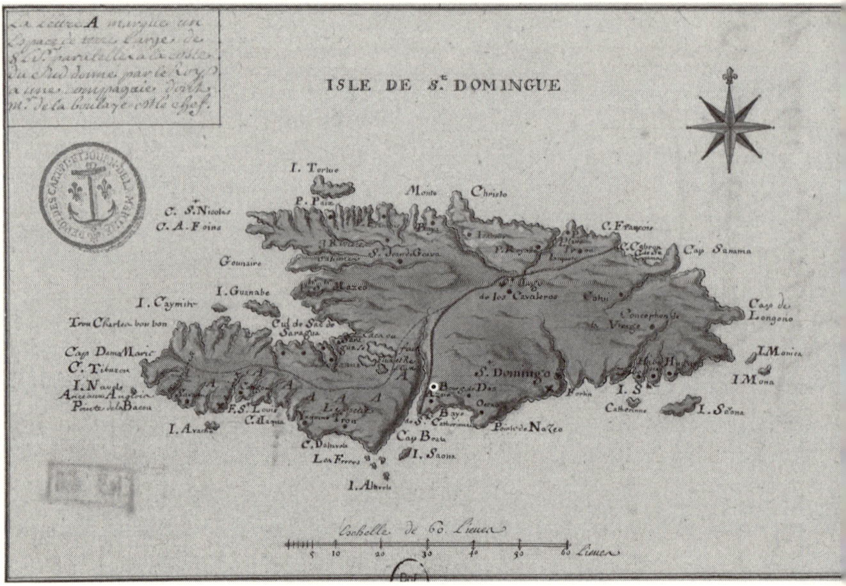

Fig. 7. Saint-Domingue, 1710. The territory ceded first to the Saint-Domingue Company and later the Company of the Indies is seen below the east-west line drawn on the southern peninsula. (Courtesy of the Bibliothèque nationale de France, Cartes et plans GE SH 18 PF.)

importation of slaves to its own colonies, France received the assiento in 1702. Thus, French merchant and trading companies, using La Caye as a provision and contraband trade base, managed to ship nearly sixteen thousand Africans to Buenos Aires, Caracas, Cartagena, Havana, Portobelo, Vera Cruz, and other Spanish ports over a ten-year period.[15] The terms of the assiento, however, required the French to import forty-eight thousand Africans—three times the number actually delivered.[16] In 1713 Spain opted not to renew its contract with the French, awarding the assiento to the British.

At the same time, the company engaged in active trade with Spanish, Dutch, and English ships and successfully attracted planters who established indigo, tobacco, cacao, and sugar plantations on company-granted concessions. Jean-Baptiste Labat, in describing how trade was carried out under the Saint-Domingue Company, maintained that the "formalities" of a mercantilist system "were observed." When ships arrived in port in search of provisions or repairs, their cargo was, according to Labat, "firmly locked up; a seal is placed on the door to the warehouse through which they carried the goods." But, he continued, "there seems to be another that is not sealed through which [the goods] disappear at night and are replaced by casks of indigo, cochineal, vanilla, silver in coin or bars, tobacco, and other goods."[17] While French officials turned a blind eye, the company turned a profit. And yet the official contraband trade was minimal in comparison to the nighttime smuggling that took place in nearly every cove and inlet along the southern peninsula's rocky coast.[18] Goods sold outside the company's closed monopoly system, in which all colonists were supposed to buy all imported goods from company stores, undermined any significant profitability the entity hoped to achieve on the island. Unable to stem the flow of smuggled goods, the company struggled, and ultimately failed, to compete.

This failure, combined with the loss of the assiento, contributed to the Saint-Domingue Company's demise. In 1720 it was absorbed by the Company of the Indies, which took control of the province. The original boundaries designated by Louis XIV's 1698 transfer of the territory remained in place, and La Caye's focus shifted from supplying slave ships bound for the Spanish Atlantic to provisioning ships bound for Louisiana.

When the Crown turned over control of the southern province to the Company of the Indies in September 1720, it also awarded the company a monopoly over the slave trade for all of France's colonies. This policy in theory allowed the company to provide a steady supply of African laborers from Senegambia to Caribbean planters, who paid for captives with the fruits of their plantations. In practice, however, the monopoly went into effect just prior to the spectacular financial collapse of John Law's system and remained in place throughout the company's reorganization. Administrators were too busy bailing water from Law's sinking ship to focus on supplying slaves to the West Indies. Father Pierre-François Xavier de Charlevoix, in his observations of the colony, wrote that the company "was prepared to furnish the islands with only 2,000 [slaves] every year," whereas "just in the neighborhoods of Cap

Français, up to three or four thousand were needed."[19] Indeed, many of the enslaved laborers living in the southern province had arrived not on French ships but, rather, on foreign vessels illegally engaged in inter-island trade.[20]

As part of its efforts to rein in extra-monopoly trade, the Crown also issued an order diminishing the value of the most widely circulated hard currency in the Antilles—the Spanish piastre, or piece of eight. Because the company was perceived as a metropolitan entity whose aims were intertwined with royal policy, much of the blame for this order fell on its shoulders. By refusing to acknowledge the money's face value, basing its value instead on weight, which devalued the coinage by roughly 20 percent, the policy outraged the island's inhabitants and caused a severe specie shortage. As a final blow, the company's exemption from paying import, export, and port duties on any and all trade goods caused income previously used to pay local government and militia salaries to plummet. Taxes, the public feared, would rise accordingly.[21]

From late November 1722 to November of the following year, the colony was in a state of revolt. Condemnation of the company and its restrictive policies prompted women-led riots in the streets of Cap Français and the burning of company warehouses in Jacmel. *Petits blancs* (indentured servants, tradesmen, hunters, buccaneers, plantation workers, and other unpropertied whites) all over the French portion of the island staged violent protests against what they perceived as company interference in their affairs. They were joined in the struggle by local Superior Council members and planters, who fanned the fires with anti-taxation and free trade rhetoric.[22] Many of the same planters also held great personal animosity toward the Company of the Indies. As creditors who had sold sugar, tobacco, cocoa, and indigo to French merchants prior to the collapse of Law's system, Saint-Domingue's planters now found themselves holding stores of near-worthless paper money. Brought on by the imposition of metropolitan policies on a local population that had grown accustomed to doing what they liked far from the gaze of French imperialists, Saint-Domingue's troubles foreshadowed not only the discontent that later ripped the colony apart but also popular protests of American colonists against British policies in the 1760s and 1770s.

In late 1723, a French naval squadron under the command of Gilles de Nos, comte de Champmeslin, arrived at Petit-Goâve with instructions to put down the rebellion and calm the populace. He carried with him orders to repeal the policy favoring specie weight over face value and the company's exemption from import, export, and port duties. These repeals, combined with Champmeslin's peaceful disbanding of rebel militia groups and reorganization of official militia units, meant the end of unrest. No one was hanged, except in effigy, sanctions were minimal, and order was restored. To further satisfy the island's inhabitants, the Crown recognized the company's inability to provide the desired volume of slave laborers and opened a portion of the trade to private merchants.[23]

The revolt and ensuing pacification of the rebels took place at the company's expense. It lost its monopoly on the slave trade and found itself forced to pay port duties like any common merchant. Worse, the rebels' success in bringing about change without facing serious punishment for their actions rendered the already unpopular trading company even weaker in terms of planter perception. The company, it seemed, could be pushed around.

By the time the *Durance* anchored at La Caye in mid-May 1729, the company's mission in Saint-Domingue was largely restricted to delivering slaves and provisioning company ships. On arrival, Captain Aubin Duplessis met with local company agents Girard and Siroux (or Cirou) to deliver packages and letters entrusted to him by administrators in France and receive any Louisiana- or France-bound communications in kind. Through these local contacts, the captain also secured the necessary provisions to sustain passengers and crew on the next leg of their voyage. Instructions issued to the captain from company headquarters named two specific provisions he was to procure from local director Sieur Chalon: *guildive*, a sugar-based distillation known more commonly as tafia; and orange juice.

Popular among Louisiana's colonists, tafia was also rationed to slaves. During his time as overseer of the company's plantation across the river from New Orleans, Le Page du Pratz found the promise of "un coup de tafia" motivated members of his enslaved workforce to work harder and longer.[24] It seems likely that liquor loaded onto the *Durance* was not only rationed to sailors but also later sold in New Orleans. Inclusion of orange juice on the captain's provisioning list—combined with his dedicated care of orange plants on board ship—suggests that Louisiana had yet to grow a number of citrus plants sufficient to slake local demand for the popular healthful beverage.[25]

Aubin Duplessis's orders prohibited him from allowing any of the *Durance*'s passengers to disembark at La Caye, but he made an exception for company employees. While the crew readied the ship and made needed repairs, Caillot and his fellow clerks met briefly with Chalon. Eager to feel land under his feet, Caillot and two others from the *Durance* went "hiking in the surrounding mountains," sampling tropical fruits in "an earthly paradise," making mental notes on his impressions, and later recording them in his memoir.[26]

When Jean-Baptiste Labat first saw La Caye nearly thirty years earlier, in 1701, he described it as "a small parcel of land measuring four to five hundred paces long by one hundred and sixty paces deep" with an elevation "just high enough not to be covered in water during high tide."[27] Caillot deemed it "more a village than a town" and was more interested in its female populace than its terrain. "There are . . . quite a number of very pretty Creole women there," whose "clothes are a dazzling white, whereas they are not, though they would seem to be."[28]

In 1720, the last year for which French enumerators separated counts by district, La Caye and its surrounding parishes were home to 797 free inhabitants and 4,818 slaves.[29] Not surprisingly, Caillot reported that the Creole women he was so enamored of "have many slaves." In La Caye, Caillot also witnessed for the first time "male and female Negroes going about naked," an act he viewed initially as "ridiculous." The clerk seems not to have considered whether slaves went about "naked" by choice or by necessity of not having been given any clothes, but after eight days on the island he "became accustomed to seeing them like that, and even to going about almost like them because of how terribly hot it is in that place."[30]

Because enumerators in the southern province distinguished only between enslaved and free, it is difficult to ascertain the racial admixture of the free population. The growing number of people of African descent who were considered *soi-disant libres* and *libres de savane*, a category reserved for individuals who were free in practice but not via an official act of manumission, further complicates how enumerators determined status.[31] Marriage records provide a clearer indication of the province's demographic. At least 17 percent of all Catholic unions in the 1720s took place between white men and women of African or Afro-European descent, and 28 percent of baptized children were listed as being "of color," code in this context for mixed race.[32] Indeed, the number of *affranchis* and free people of color of mixed racial ancestry residing in the southern province was likely far more significant than even marriage and baptismal records suggest. One observer, writing in 1734, remarked that in La Caye there were "few white persons of pure blood; they are almost all mulattoes or descendants of such," suggesting that Caillot's remarks on Creole women who were not white, "though they would seem to be," reflected the population's mixed racial heritage.[33]

Attracted as Caillot was to the town's women, local men warned him off more intimate encounters, suggesting that their beauty was not worth the inconvenient and painful consequences. The presence of "so many young men who were very afflicted because of the lack of help," wrote Caillot, "stopped me and bridled my passion."[34] The "Neapolitan disease," known as the "French disease" outside of France, generally referred to syphilis or gonorrhea, whose symptoms were often confused. Indeed, contemporary physicians did not differentiate between the two. Lacking an understanding of disease vectors, there was a general belief that women themselves were to blame for venereal diseases and their spread and that the inherent impurity of women led to the corruption of their internal organs.[35] Caillot made no mention of his personal views on disease circulation, but he seems to have heeded the local men's warnings, relying on a look-but-don't-touch policy during his visit.

After an eight-day stopover—during which time Caillot smoked tobacco, went hunting, spent money he did not have (he borrowed funds from Bussy, who had to sell some of his possessions to make the loan), shot a soldier in the arm, and managed to avoid serious punishment for having done so—the *Durance* left La Caye on May 27, 1729.[36] Within days of disembarking, Caillot and his shipmates encountered a slave ship in the Gulf of Mexico. The frigate *Galathée*, recognizable as a company vessel by its signals, was in clear distress. The previous year, on

May 27, 1728, the *Galathée* had set sail from Lorient on a transatlantic voyage that nearly did not make it. The ship left the Brittany coast for Senegambia almost a year behind schedule, after delays in staffing, outfitting, and weather had forced port officials to keep the ship anchored. The most serious difficulties stemmed from the challenge of securing a qualified team of officers to command the ship. Lorient port commander Fayet spent most of March and April 1728 scrambling to assign officers and find a replacement for Captain La Vigne, whose personal affairs prevented him from taking the helm of the *Galathée* as planned. In late April, after weeks of negotiating with administrators in Paris and Lorient, Fayet received company approval to replace La Vigne with Captain Quinet de Préville, a young officer who had served as second captain on two previous sailings.[37]

Four weeks after its tardy departure from Lorient, the *Galathée* anchored at the mouth of the Senegal River. While the crew offloaded merchandise bound for Galam, ship's carpenters set to work converting the hold into a rudimentary prison for the human cargo soon to be shuttled aboard. Quinet de Préville passed the summer overseeing delivery of captive Africans to his ship. Some 130 men, women, and children arrived at Fort Saint-Louis via a long downriver journey from the Galam slave pens; the remainder came from the collection point at Gorée Island. Once the number of slaves in the hold reached 400, the captain ordered his crew to prepare for departure.[38]

The ship left Gorée on October 21, 1728, and headed for New Orleans. Within days the dying began. The first two victims were small children, but sickness below deck spread quickly and did not discriminate by age, sex, or race. By the time the *Galathée* had reached the Caribbean in mid-November, mortality and illness among captives and crew had soared, leaving fifty-three slaves (including eleven children) and five crew members dead. First pilot Michel Beaumont filled the margins of the ship's log with day after day of loss, and conditions on board were so dreadful that Quinet de Préville overrode company orders to head straight to the Louisiana coast—orders intended to overcome some of the time lost in Lorient—and instead made an unscheduled call at La Caye Saint-Louis.[39]

During the ship's twelve-day stopover, eleven more slaves died, and poor health among a significant number of those still alive induced the captain to disembark forty-five captives, nine sailors, and a ship's officer to the company plantation for rehabilitation. All, according to Beaumont's log, suffered from scurvy. After re-embarking for Louisiana on December 12, it seemed for a time as though the precautionary measure of offloading the sick had worked. The ship's pilot recorded no further deaths for nearly three weeks, until January 1, when his mortuary notations resumed their daily frequency.[40]

The *Galathée*'s voyage was one of the most lethal company expeditions to Louisiana, resulting in the recorded deaths of 82 slaves and 11 crew members between Gorée Island and the Balize. And the deaths did not end once the ship anchored. In a letter written by Louisiana governor Étienne Périer and Director-General Jacques de La Chaise to company directors in Paris, they reported that since the arrival of Quinet de Préville at the Balize on January 18, 1729, "he has had twenty-five to thirty negroes die—although they have coats—all of scurvy."[41] In reality the loss of life was even worse than Périer and La Chaise's estimations. When the *Galathée* arrived at the Balize, the crew transferred the 273 surviving slaves to longboats intended to shuttle them upriver to the colony's capital. By the time the boats reached the company plantation across from New Orleans (in today's Algiers Point), 46 more slaves had perished. The lengthy voyage resulted in the recorded deaths of 128 slaves and 11 crew members. Those figures translate into 32 percent mortality among captives and 20 percent among crew—this at a time when the average mortality on company slavers was 7 percent.[42]

When Caillot, his fellow passengers, and the crew of the *Durance* encountered the *Galathée* off the Louisiana coast on June 9, 1729, the slaver was on its way to Léogâne, Saint-Domingue, to pick up additional supplies before returning to France. Captain Thomas Laisné, who had replaced scurvy-stricken Quinet de Préville in New Orleans, had been unable to adequately provision his ship in New Orleans, despite the needs of the remaining crew. Supplies loaded in Louisiana, according to Caillot, "were not sufficient to get them to the next port," making it necessary for Aubin Duplessis to send over the *Durance*'s longboat loaded "with brandy, flour, wine, and lard."[43] Fourteen of the *Galathée*'s original fifty-six crew members ultimately succumbed to the disease before the ship dropped anchor at Lorient in March 1730. Their deaths stretched literally across the Atlantic from Senegambia to Louisiana.

Some perished at sea, others in ports at Gorée Island, La Caye Saint-Louis, Léogâne, and the Balize. Still more languished in New Orleans.[44]

Despite the difficulties of the transatlantic crossing, the most challenging aspect of the passage from Lorient to Louisiana came not in the open waters of the Atlantic but near the journey's end, when ships reached the Mississippi River. New Orleans was a port town, but it was unlike any other Atlantic, Caribbean, or Gulf Coast ports in that it was founded not along the coast itself but, rather, thirty-five leagues up one of the world's most powerful, most sinuous rivers.

Located in a bend of the Mississippi, New Orleans was not easily accessible to deep-draft sailing ships. Mud lumps, tangles of dead trees, and sandbars at the river's mouth complicated navigation and posed a serious threat to heavily loaded ships. To minimize risk to vessels, cargoes, passengers, and slaves often were unloaded or disembarked at the Balize, a swampy, semi-fortified island outpost in the southwest pass of the river's mouth, constructed between 1722 and 1724. The Balize, which Caillot referred to as "a place swamped by the sea," served as the point of first contact for arriving cargo and passenger ships.[45] Passengers, depending on their health and the availability of small boats to bring them farther upriver, were sometimes stranded there for days or even weeks before they could embark on the final leg of their journey.

After battling "contrary winds" that pushed it off course and forced a brief return to Dauphin Island, the *Durance* finally dropped anchor five leagues off the Balize on July 2, 1729.[46] Its civilian passengers were loaded into two longboats. Six slaves rowed each vessel ashore. Passengers' trunks, furniture, mattresses, and other possessions followed. Once on soggy ground, the travelers rested briefly at the home of site commander and chief engineer Bernard Duvergé, whose duties extended to those of harbormaster and general overseer.[47] Then they faced the arduous, exhausting final leg from the coast to New Orleans. Traveling this last stretch—which took on average between six and seven days—was made more difficult by the weakened and often sickly condition of individuals who already had been at sea for months.[48]

For vessels engaged by the Company of the Indies, much of the labor required to transfer cargoes from arriving ships' holds to smaller transports was performed by the nearly four dozen adult company-owned slaves assigned to Duvergé and his enslaved African overseer Jolicoeur.[49] Eight of these slaves are identified in a 1731 inventory as matelots, or seamen, who were part of a larger group of company slaves tasked with working on the colony's waterways. Enslaved sailors made up 17 percent of the company's adult slave population, with eight stationed at the river's mouth, thirteen assigned to approximately a half-dozen small boats based in New Orleans, seven to the Natchez post upriver from the capital, and nine to Governor Périer's plantation.[50] Given the nature of maritime work at the Balize, these men likely performed a labor role similar to that of canoe men along the West African coast—a resonance that must have seemed striking to arriving African captives who found themselves shuttled both on and off slave ships from opposite sides of the Atlantic by skilled African seamen.[51]

In addition to the matelots, there were thirty-six other company-owned slaves residing at the Balize in 1731: one overseer; six skilled slaves, including two carpenters, a tailor, baker, nurse, and driver; fourteen male laborers and ten female; and six children ranging in age from three months to six years. By the mid-1720s, this labor force resided in thatched huts on a neighboring island that was accessible to and from the main island via a wooden footbridge (fig. 8).[52] The forty-four slaves residing at the Balize constituted the second largest concentration of company slaves in Louisiana, at 17 percent of the company's total slaveholdings.[53]

The *Durance*'s arrival at the river's mouth coincided with that of the slave ship *Vénus*. The *Vénus* sailed from Lorient on February 4, 1729, and reached the company's Senegambia concession three weeks later. After trading along the West African coast from Gorée Island south to Rio Nunez (in present-day Guinea), the *Vénus*'s captain, Jean-Baptiste Gaultier de La Renaudais, set sail for Louisiana on April 16 with a cargo of 150 slaves.

The ship reached the Balize two months later, after a sixty-one-day Atlantic crossing, but as was the case with the *Durance*, contrary winds prevented it from dropping anchor until early July. When the ship finally landed, it, too, was forced to anchor five leagues from its target

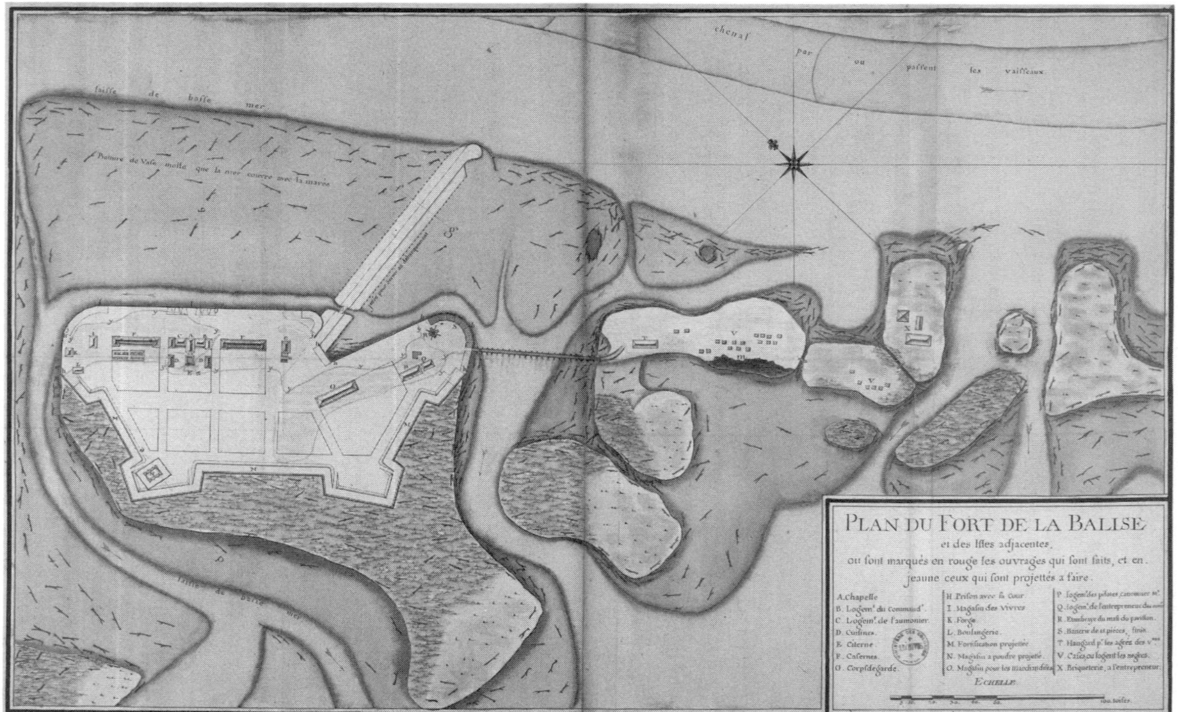

Fig. 8. The Balize, 1731. (Courtesy of the Archives nationales d'outre-mer, DFC 111B.)

and rely on smaller boats to shuttle its human cargo to land.[54] At the Balize, the number of African captives from the *Vénus* far outnumbered available crew members, many of whom were suffering from scurvy and other illnesses, prompting Duvergé to appoint several company employees from the *Durance*, including Caillot, as impromptu overseers. Each newly arrived white male passenger from the *Durance* was charged with oversight of a small boatful of captives on the journey from the Balize to New Orleans; each of these vessels was manned by a crew of six company slaves.[55]

Like those aboard the *Galathée*, many of the Africans who had boarded the *Vénus* from Senegambia some two months earlier also suffered from advanced stages of scurvy and other ailments (not to mention extreme cultural and linguistic shock). Eighty-seven captives had already succumbed before reaching the Balize.[56] Two days after setting out on their journey up the Mississippi, the fleet of lighters (*bateaux* or *chaloupes* in French) carrying passengers from the *Durance* and slaves from the *Vénus* had traveled only three leagues. Six of the slaves in Caillot's boat alone had perished. Others were sick, and all suffered from the oppressive heat, unavoidable dampness, and swarms of insects.[57]

The overwhelming presence of gnats (specifically biting midges, also known as no-see-ums) and mosquitoes on the voyage from the coast was a reoccurring complaint in mémoires from early French colonial Louisiana. Caillot swore that nothing could keep the insects away at night, when "there were so many of them that we were smashing them on our faces by the fistful."[58] Ursuline novitiate Marie-Madeleine Hachard provided a similar account of her first encounters with "Monsieurs Mosquitoes" and "frappes d'abord," the latter of which she claimed came "in such great numbers that one could cut them with a knife."[59]

As Caillot and his fellow travelers neared the comptoir's capital, they rowed past the *habitations*, or plantations, of the Canadian brothers Joseph and François Carrière and made a planned stop at the Tixerant (also Tisserand) plantation. Louis Tixerant, a Paris native and former ironmonger, had arrived in Louisiana in the early 1720s. He served first as a warehouse guard at Fort Louis in Mobile and later as storekeeper at the company warehouses in Biloxi. By 1725 an inventory scandal had unseated Tixerant from his official company post. On his arrival in

Louisiana, La Chaise recorded multiple complaints issued by colonists "against the keepers of the warehouses," including Tixerant. Those with grievances pointed to the "magnificence in which those people live" with "many slaves, good table, and good lodgings" as proof of keepers' profiteering and pilfering of company stores.[60] The company initiated criminal proceedings against Tixerant after relieving him of his duties in 1724, but the outcome remained unresolved until years after the 1731 retrocession of the colony to the Crown. Based on the nature of company claims against him, it is possible that at least some of Tixerant's wealth had been secured via personal profiteering, misappropriation of warehouse stores, and illegal personal trade with Spanish vessels stopping at Biloxi. Trade with the Spanish for the benefit of the company was permitted, but it appears some of the warehouse keepers, including Tixerant, were trading company stores on their own accounts.[61] By the late 1720s, Tixerant had accumulated enough land and slaves, including forty-five Africans (thirty-three adults and twelve children) and two Indians, to be considered one of the colony's *gros habitants*, or large-scale, settled planters.[62]

Playing hosts to the newly arrived company employees while the slaves in their charge remained at the riverbank, Tixerant, whom Caillot characterized as a "man who is a friend of pleasures and good food," and his "young and beautiful" wife, Marie, served them a midday meal "in as refined a manner as possible for the country and season." The meal lacked wine due to irregular and damaged arrivals of the staple from France, but the Tixerants compensated by serving their guests generous quantities of brandy.[63]

Well fed for the first time in weeks, the travelers returned to the river. They continued on through the night, stopping once more two leagues from New Orleans to eat, turn over the surviving slaves in their charge, rid themselves of traveling clothes plagued with "the stench of scurvy-ridden people," and switch conveyances from small sail-powered vessels to a borrowed pirogue.[64]

In contemporary accounts, travelers bore witness to the sheer torment of this last leg of the voyage. In 1727 Sister Hachard lamented to her father that "all the hardships of the *Gironde* were nothing" compared to what she and her fellow Ursulines suffered "in this little crossing, which is only thirty leagues upriver, from Belize to New Orleans." Two years later, Caillot echoed Hachard's description. "The eight days it took us for that bit of navigation," he wrote, "tired us more than the whole crossing from France."[65] By the time those who had survived this stretch of the journey arrived at their final destination, some must surely have wondered if the months-long trials of their transatlantic and riverine voyage were just a preview of difficulties ahead.

5

Louisiana

A Company Colony

Seventeen weeks after setting sail from Lorient, Caillot finally arrived at the port of New Orleans on July 13, 1729, around nine-thirty in the morning.[1] Caillot, the bookkeeper Bussy, and two more clerks—Troyes and Gontier—deposited their pirogue in front of the company warehouses and made their way on foot to the home of François Chastang, a chief inspector of the company's accounts and the newly arrived employees' superior. Considered indecisive and "old and broken" by Governor Étienne Périer and Director-General Jacques de La Chaise, Chastang had arrived from France in 1728.[2] Upon receiving the travelers, Chastang initially extended an invitation for them to dine with him but quickly reversed course when talk turned to the possibility of having their "baggage brought to his house." The prospect of living as well as working with the new recruits, if only for several days, "frightened him" and made him extremely "apprehensive."[3]

If Périer and La Chaise's characterization of Chastang was accurate, perhaps it helps explain Chastang's reticence toward the company's new recruits, or perhaps the auditor's knowledge of past employees weighed on his mind. Several scandals involving dissolute clerks had unfolded in recent years. In 1724 a bookkeeping clerk named Paulin Cadot had been found guilty of libel and slander, fined, jailed, and dismissed from his company post for writing "verses against the honor of the ladies of New Orleans."[4] The content of his dirty limericks was deemed so offensive that twenty of the objectionable verses were ordered stricken from court records. Two more New Orleans clerks—one each from the cashier and bookkeeping offices—were dismissed that year for petty theft.[5]

The year prior to Caillot's arrival brought a tidal wave of bad behavior and dismissals. In the spring, three clerks had been involved in a forgery scheme; the ringleader, a Sieur Maisonneuve, who confessed under torture to forging La Chaise's signature on promissory notes, was sentenced to "imprisonment for life in the galleys."[6] Two others were dismissed around the same time: the first, Antoine de Joye de La Goublaye, for being "lazy"; the second, Nicolas Bion, for being "absolutely incorrigible in the matter of drink."[7] Bion was not just a drunk; he was severely in debt. When he lost his post, he had no way to support himself or pay his lengthy list of creditors. He had started in 1722 as an assistant director of company accounts with a generous annual salary of 3,000 livres. The year 1724 saw Bion sharing that title with another employee and his salary cut to 1,200 livres. La Chaise then authorized an additional payout of 800 livres for Bion's help with the old accounts and recommended he be reinstated as sole assistant director of accounts if he stayed sober. Bion failed to do so and was demoted yet again, this time to a clerkship. In the summer of 1728, he was dismissed outright.[8] When he petitioned to return to France the following year, he owed a total of 2,336 livres to twenty-seven creditors, including six different bakers, a laundrywoman, the chief cashier, a seamstress, provisioners, and many others.[9]

The most violent incident involving clerks occurred on June 6, 1728, when a group of company employees gathered at a local tavern to celebrate the feast day of Claude Dubuisson, who worked as a Superior Council clerk in the New Orleans offices.[10] Among those in attendance was Sieur Bernaudat de Saint-Maur, one of Dubuisson's office mates, who had arrived in Louisiana the previous year.[11] Both clerks were held in poor regard by their superiors, who viewed them as sloppy—account books copied by Bernaudat in 1727 contained "a thousand mistakes" and had to be redone—and "very disorderly."[12] After passing the evening drinking in Dubuisson's honor, Dubuisson and Bernaudat staggered out of the tavern into the street, where they commenced to argue. Swords were drawn, and Bernaudat, "glutted with wine," dealt his friend a fatal blow.[13]

The incident was at first characterized as a duel, but a later investigation revealed it to have been no more than a drunken brawl gone wrong. La Chaise seemed thoroughly convinced that the killing of one clerk by another had been an accident, or at least he framed the story thus in order to avoid upsetting Bernaudat's patron and godfather, the duc d'Orléans. La Chaise appeared more concerned about Bernaudat's welfare than the loss of Dubuisson's life. In a letter to company directors in Paris, La Chaise recommended the company "obtain a pardon for this young man" as soon as possible. "We have put him into the fort at Mobile as the safest place while waiting for word from you," wrote La Chaise, adding that Bernaudat "seemed to us to be deeply touched by the unexpected death of his comrade," even arranging for "a service held for the repose of his soul."[14] Indeed, after facing repeated interrogations, Bernaudat had been sent from New Orleans to Fort Condé the very same day that Caillot appeared on Chastang's doorstep. The wayward clerk spent fifteen months imprisoned in Mobile awaiting a pardon that never came before he escaped to Spanish Pensacola. He later took up residence in Havana, where by all accounts he continued to await a royal pardon.[15]

Whatever the cause of Dubuisson and Bernaudat's fatal brawl, it is perhaps not surprising that François Chastang was hesitant to assume the new recruits who stood before him bedraggled and sickly after a long voyage would not soon fall prey to similarly transgressive behavior. It was common knowledge in the offices that Caillot, Troyes, and Gontier were intended as replacements for the string of clerks lost or dismissed in 1728.[16] Rather than put his own home and reputation at potential risk, Chastang led the bookkeeper and three clerks to an inn on Royal Street that was a favorite among visiting ships' officers. Its proprietor, Louis Jarry, who ran the inn with his wife, Anne, is the only inhabitant in both the 1726 and 1727 censuses listed as "innkeeper," though it seems other inns were operational by 1729. Caillot took note of "several inns and taverns where one is not very well served, but is instead well swindled." As in Lorient, other accommodations could be found in the houses of colonists who rented rooms.[17] The Jarrys' inn provided Caillot with meals and a room for most of his tenure in Louisiana.

The following day, the bookkeeper and three clerks went directly to the offices of Governor Périer to register their arrival in the colony. From there they crossed the central square, or Place d'Armes, to company headquarters, where they met with La Chaise. Company regulations required all commissioned officers and employees to be sworn in immediately on arrival by local company directors.[18] As director-general, La Chaise oversaw this procedure; introduced the new recruits to other company bureaucrats, engineers, and Superior Council members; and directed them to their assigned offices.

Most clerks, bookkeepers, and administrators in New Orleans passed their days at the company's headquarters, La Direction, in a compound of newly constructed buildings and gardens that filled the entire block bounded by Chartres, Saint-Pierre, Saint-Louis, and the river (fig. 9).[19] The handful of company clerks employed outside La Direction worked in the warehouses and at the mill. The headquarters were, according to Caillot, "very well built, both grand and spacious," with living quarters for La Chaise and his family, "a very proper meeting hall for hearings"—decked out with a tapestry as well as the requisite crucifix and portrait of the king—and "three offices."[20] The first office was occupied

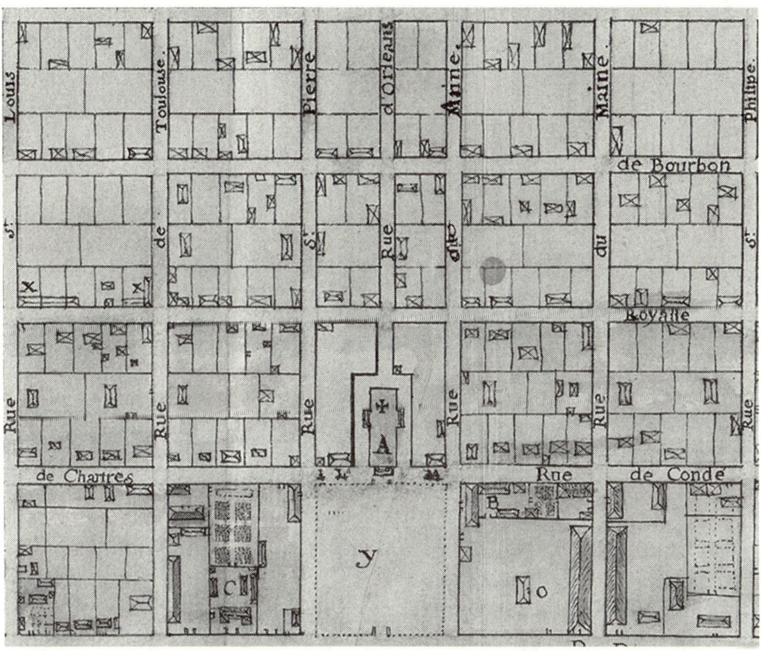

Fig. 9. Section of Caillot's map of New Orleans, dated February 14, 1731. The company's Louisiana headquarters (La Direction) are keyed to the letter C, on the riverfront next to Y, the Place d'Armes. (Courtesy of The Historic New Orleans Collection, 2005.0011.)

by Superior Council staff, namely a secretary and two assistants. Established in 1712 as French Louisiana's judicial body, the council and its members were responsible for civil and criminal matters and included the governor, company director, attorney general, notary, and between three and five councillors drawn from visiting dignitaries—such as the king's mathematician, Pierre Baron—and the local colonial population. All seats on the Superior Council were granted by a royal commission.[21] The second office housed the "special accounts" of the old *régie*. These accounts were in effect left over from the Law regime, including those established by former governor Jean-Baptiste Le Moyne de Bienville, who was recalled to France in 1723.[22] A staff of seven managed the previous administration's affairs with an eye toward merging the old accounts with the new. Last were the company's bookkeeping offices, headed by Chastang, who oversaw a staff of eight subordinate bookkeepers and clerks—Caillot, Troyes, Gontier, and Bussy now among them—in the New Orleans offices. Here clerks tracked inventory reports from the company's multiple storehouses, balanced incoming and outgoing receipts, and maintained credit and debit sheets for colonists trading with the company. Clerks stationed outside the comptoir's capital all reported to the central offices in New Orleans. Maintaining correspondence—both with outlying trading posts and company offices in Paris—represented a large portion of a clerk's daily duties.

Outside company headquarters, clustered around the Place d'Armes, were the government offices housing Périer and his staff, the parish church, prison, guard post, and Capuchin rectory. Land along the river fronting the Place d'Armes had been reserved for a public market and slaughterhouse, but no work had been undertaken on either by late 1729.[23]

Company-owned structures dominated the adjoining riverfront. Two storehouses measuring 220 feet long and 40 feet wide, one each for inbound and outbound trade goods, stretched from the docks between Sainte-Anne and Du Maine Streets nearly to Condé.[24] It was to these warehouses that goods from the *Durance* made their way, though some of the ship's cargo arrived in unsalvageable condition. The bales of Genoa paper loaded in Lorient never reached the desks of Louisiana's inhabitants. By the time it arrived, the paper was "completely spoiled and ruined by the green wood put on [the *Durance*], which sweated during the voyage," leading La Chaise to remark: "We have no paper at all. We need some of all sorts. . . . Order, if you please, gentlemen, that some be sent us by the next vessel." Casks and bottles of wine fared no better aboard the *Durance*. Nearly all company ships carried wine and brandy across the Atlantic to Louisiana, but maintaining the spirits' freshness proved tricky. Wine at sea in the summer months sometimes spoiled before reaching its destination, and storage conditions in the hold, where temperatures reached stifling levels, further undermined the wine's stability. The casks of wine transported on the *Durance* arrived spoiled from the "great heat in the hold," which, according to the ship's captain, was worsened by the placement of the cook's galleys between decks. Wine on the *Durance* had to contend not only with climate-related heat but also with heat generated by the ship's ovens.[25]

Other merchandise from the *Durance* arrived in salable condition but insufficient quantity to meet demand. The 2,657 ells of heavy Beauvais cloth sent from Picardy was not nearly sufficient to clothe Louisiana's slaves. "There is no cloth for a third of them," wrote Périer and La Chaise, asking, "How do you expect us to be able to supply some to all the inhabitants who have some?" and warning that "the inhabitants are going to complain . . . if some other vessel does not bring us more, for this part is going to be used to make coats for those who arrived this year."[26] Cloth shortages, as well as the poor quality of cloth sent to Louisiana, were chronic complaints among slaveholders, who, despite requirements that they provide annual allotments of clothing and blankets to their laborers, often found none available in company stores.[27]

Downriver from the warehouses, where Arsenal Street met the docks, a hospital stood ready to receive sick soldiers, sailors, settlers, and slaves alike, and the company bakery supplied outbound ships with bread and hardtack from its location along the wharves. Those who did not survive time spent in the hospital were interred in New Orleans's first official burial ground, Saint-Pierre's Cemetery, which was located between Saint-Pierre and Toulouse Streets at the back of the settlement.[28]

Although the town's footprint, laid out by royal engineers Adrien de Pauger and Pierre Le Blond de La Tour, comprised sixty-six blocks, only thirty-five boasted improvements by 1729.[29] With the exception of the street grid established by Pauger and La Tour, New Orleans at the time of Caillot's 1729 arrival bore little resemblance to the post that one early observer described in late 1721 as "un petit bicoq," or "a little shanty town," which had no more than "four or five scattered houses."[30] In 1729 the town was home to more than a thousand people; its population had more than doubled in the seven years since it had become the colonial capital.[31] Most residences, workshops, and businesses were clustered either along the river or within a three-block radius of Saint-Louis Church. An assortment of artisans, individuals employed in the building trades, company employees, and hospital workers lived along the quay, as did more prominent colonists, including military officers and concessionaires. The townhouses of major planters were also found along the river. Louis Tixerant maintained a home between Saint-Louis and Conti Streets for his in-town business affairs, as did the Canadian Chauvin brothers.[32] Chartres-Condé, home to two of the five members of the Superior Council, the town's notary, and the public works inspector, was the most densely populated street, followed by Royal, then Bourbon. Bourbon was the last named street running parallel to the river, but the street behind it (now Dauphine) had begun to attract poorer residents. Nineteen settlers—seven men, six women, and an equal number of children—called the unnamed street home in 1727, though its proximity to uncleared swampland must have made it rather inhospitable; only one of the families listed as residents of the "street facing the woods" in the 1727 census lived there in 1732.[33]

On opposite ends of the grid, along the outer fringes, were the munitions storehouse and powder magazine. Company troops, laborers, and craftsmen were also housed on the outskirts of the developed core in one of four barracks. Two hundred men—some from Plantin's Company, others from the king's troops—served the settlement's defense and fortification needs and also acted as New Orleans's police force. All were paid (irregularly) by the Company of the Indies, with nearly 90,000 livres per year allocated to officer and troop pay, 70,000 to rations, and 14,000 to uniform allotments. With a total allocation of 174,000 livres, the New Orleans based troops received the lion's share of a military budget that amounted to only 188,571 livres for the entire colony.[34] These troops were divided into four companies led by captains Joachim de Gauvry, Bernard Diron d'Artaguiette (also Dartaguette), Renaud d'Hauterive, and Claude Charles Dutisné, who had served as commander at the Natchez post until 1728. In New Orleans, Dutisné was head of Plantin's Company. Henry de Louboey, as garrison commander, oversaw all four companies and reported directly to the Company of the Indies.

Just upriver from the established grid, a community mill pounded corn, rice, and sometimes wheat from the Illinois country into flour. Outside of surplus shipped downriver from the Illinois country, the availability of wheat flour was limited, as stores from France often arrived damaged or rotten after months spent in ships' holds, and colonists in lower Louisiana had great difficulty coaxing newly sown wheat to full maturity. Le Page du Pratz attributed the grain's premature failure to an overabundance of acidity in the soil, but surely the high heat and humidity wrought havoc as well.[35] More typical than wheat bread were multiple varieties of corn-based bread, in which the maize was sometimes mixed with beans or rice. Indeed, maize was a staple of the colonial diet. "French Louisianans," according to anthropologist Shannon Lee Dawdy, "felt no shame in being corn eaters," and contemporary accounts are filled with recommendations—many of which derived from Indian examples—for preparing the grain, with *sagamité* (corn stew or gruel), roasted corn, and maize beer being among the most popular preparations.[36] Despite its proximity to the river, the mill, which Caillot described as "a masterpiece for this country" built at a cost to the company of eighty thousand livres, was powered by wind rather than water.[37] Horses stabled nearby powered the mill in times of insufficient wind.

Past the mill, "at a distance of a musket shot" from New Orleans, was the large tract of land owned by the Jesuits.[38] From an original frontage of twenty arpents (0.7 miles) the Jesuits had purchased in 1726, the religious order eventually expanded its holdings to thirty-two frontage arpents (1.2 miles) that stretched fifty arpents (1.8 miles) from the river toward Lake Pontchartrain.[39]

In seeking a religious order to guide Louisiana's colonial population, the French Crown had initially shunned the Society of Jesus. The Crown, following an extensive lobbying campaign by the Seminary of Foreign Missions, barred Jesuit missionaries from establishing a presence in Louisiana, despite their evangelical successes among Indian groups in New France and the Great Lakes region. A 1704 decree awarded the right to shepherd Louisiana's native and colonial souls to the Capuchin order, a move contested by the Society of Jesus and their supporters, including sometime Louisiana governor Bienville.[40] After more than a decade of inter-order infighting, company directors in Paris agreed to a compromise in 1723 that allowed the Jesuits to establish a missionary presence in the areas north of Natchez while leaving the areas to the south under Capuchin jurisdiction.

Although the compromise was intended to limit the Jesuits' sphere of influence, Jesuit superior Ignace de Beaubois convinced the company that providing him land and slaves with which he could set up a mission just outside of New Orleans would ultimately be beneficial to company interests. Known as a charismatic, wheedling character, who used his connections on both sides of the Atlantic to maintain a Jesuit foothold near New Orleans, Beaubois aimed to establish a fully self-sufficient plantation graced by provisioning and apothecary gardens as well as fields of tobacco—all of which would be worked by company-allotted slaves—that might serve as a model for other colonists.[41] In this endeavor Beaubois largely succeeded, though debts to the company in land, slaves, and supplies totaling over fifty thousand livres suggest that self-sufficiency was not achieved during the company period.[42] By 1727 he had further strengthened his order's position by convincing a group of Ursuline nuns from France to migrate to Louisiana, where they would oversee and staff the colony's hospital.[43]

In New Orleans ecclesiastic duties remained under the purview of three Capuchin priests, who carried out parish functions at Saint-Louis Church. Father Raphaël de Luxembourg, whom Caillot described as "a holy man" who "applies himself entirely" to educating the colony's youth, arrived in 1723 to assume the role of parish priest for New Orleans and as Capuchin superior for the entire colony.[44] Within three years of his arrival, Raphaël established the settlement's first educational institution in a house on Sainte-Anne Street between Royal and Chartres.[45] Intended to serve the colony's male children, including "several young Indians," the school provided instruction in reading, "Latin and the liberal arts," and catechism to day students and a handful of boarders.[46]

Caillot was less impressed by the other Capuchins, whom he claimed "secretly lead very excessive lives," going about town sporting "shirts with lacy cuffs, silk stockings, and slippers" while carrying "money, a snuffbox, a watch, and a parasol."[47] Caillot's characterization echoed concerns raised the previous year by Governor Périer.[48] Perhaps the wayward Capuchins had procured luxury goods through company employees with easy access to the storehouses along the river, or perhaps they were the beneficiaries of gifts from gracious parishioners. However they secured such items, it seems unlikely that the Capuchins purchased them with funds from the meager allowance each received from the company of six hundred livres per annum.

Another six Capuchins shepherded flocks in more remote settlements, including the Tchoupitoulas tract, the German Coast, Balize, Mobile, Natchitoches, and Natchez. Father Victorin of the Récollet order was the only non-Jesuit to maintain an evangelizing mission; he did so among the Apalache who had settled along Mobile Bay in 1704. Caillot viewed the Apalache, who had been converted to Catholicism by the Spanish during the previous century, as "Good Frenchmen and Good Christians" who "observe, with more exactitude than us, what they have been taught about our religion."[49]

Raphaël repeatedly complained to Abbé Gilles-Bernard Raguet, his superior and a company director in Paris, of the impossibility of conducting missionary work with so few Capuchins in the colony and so few funds from the company with which to support such endeavors. Lacking interpreters and "a boat to transport him by water to the villages of his mission," a Capuchin priest, wrote Raphaël, could not even begin to establish missions among Louisiana's Indians.[50] Yet the funds that underwrote the entire religious and missionary enterprise in Louisiana were not insignificant. In 1729 alone, the company disbursed nearly twenty thousand livres, or 5 percent of its Louisiana operating budget, to the Capuchins, Jesuits, and Ursulines.[51] And the company incurred additional expenses each time it granted land or slaves to the religious orders.

Raphaël ultimately failed in his attempt both to convince the company to provide greater allowances to Capuchins already in the colony and to increase the number of Capuchins. Those who made the Atlantic crossing often served only to replace those who had died or whose poor health or misconduct prompted a return to France.[52] By 1729 the number of Jesuits conducting missionary work in the colony far outnumbered the Capuchins. With missions established among the Wabash, Yazoo, Alibamon, Choctaw, Chickasaw, and other Native American groups stretching from present-day northern Louisiana to the Great Lakes region, the Jesuits were far more successful than the Capuchins in establishing a presence among the colony's native population. But the Jesuit endeavor was not exclusively an evangelical one; agricultural production also played a part. In fact the Jesuits' commitment to self-sufficiency through agriculture helps explain the company's willingness to grant land concessions and slaves to each of the Jesuit missions. Their record of successful evangelization also meant that the company allotted on average two hundred livres more per annum to the Jesuits than it did to their Capuchin brothers.[53]

Across from New Orleans, on the west bank of the Mississippi River, the company operated a nearly four-thousand-acre plantation replete with rice-processing mill, brickworks, forge, warehouse, slave quarters and hospital, and overseer's residence.[54] The plantation, which was approximately 250 arpents (9 miles) deep with 18.7 arpents (0.7 miles) of river frontage, consisted primarily of uncleared land. Some of the African captives from the slaver *Vénus*, whose summer arrival coincided with Caillot's, may have been bound for the company's west bank plantation, but most were so weakened by scurvy that they were dispatched directly to the main hospital at disembarkation. Of the 450 slaves loaded on board the *Vénus* at Gorée Island in mid-April, only 363 remained when the ship anchored off the coast of the Balize in early July. According to Périer and La Chaise, 43 of the *Vénus*'s captives were so ill by this time that they "could not go up the river or [died] along the river."[55]

Those deemed healthy enough to ascend the Mississippi met with crowds of eager purchasers at the company's plantation, but Périer and La Chaise stressed that the shipment of slaves on the *Vénus* ended in disaster for colonists, company, and slaves alike.[56] Louisiana's inhabitants were so eager to purchase slaves that they regularly "outbid each other for the scurvied, consumptive, and ulcerated" captives sold at auction, who sometimes "die half a quarter of an hour after they had been awarded" to the winning bidder.[57] The company was the only authorized importer of slaves, but it was never quite able to strike a balance between settlers' demand and slave supply. Colonists insisted that they needed more slaves to grow tobacco, but so little tobacco or other salable trade goods were actually produced that the company refused to extend the credit and invest the resources necessary to significantly increase the slave supply.[58] The cycle of anemic company investment and settler debt was a vicious one, which ultimately hindered the company's mandate to make Louisiana France's largest tobacco producer.

By August, the 320 slaves from the *Vénus* who reached New Orleans in mid-July "were so violently attacked by the scurvy that more than two-thirds of those who were sold at auction into the hands of the inhabitants have died." Périer and La Chaise attributed the slaves' high mortality to the length of time the captives had spent in slave fortresses along the Senegambian coast prior to boarding the *Vénus*, noting that company officials "must try not to leave them so long since for the greater part of the time they have only one meal there and drink nothing but brackish water."[59] Officials in Louisiana were eager to blame the poor health of newly arrived captives on substandard conditions in Senegambia. Captives held for months in Saint-Louis or Gorée while waiting for forced disembarkation across the Atlantic did suffer from exposure, poor sanitation, and insufficient rations. And those conditions were often aggravated by lengthy crossings. But the route from the Mississippi's mouth to the capital could be just as deadly, so much so in fact that after the company retroceded Louisiana to the Crown in 1731, it tried to secure permission for slave deliveries exclusively to the Balize in order to protect itself from losses. The request was denied, leading the company to back out of Louisiana trade altogether.[60]

Not all Louisiana-bound slaves were destined for service in the private sector. The colony's largest slave owner was the company itself. Split between three sites—the west bank plantation across from New Orleans, the Balize at the river's mouth, and Natchez—the company-owned enslaved population totaled 254 individuals: 157 men, 63 women, and 34 children (table 1). Their collective value, according to an inventory conducted in 1731, was 196,800 livres.[61] As in the settler population, the sex ratio among African slaves owned by the company was heavily skewed, with 2.5 men for every enslaved woman. This is higher than the 1.58 men per woman ratio that applied to Louisiana's total enslaved population for the entire French colonial period.[62] Of the 63 women, 89 percent of them were paired with African men and deemed "married," while only 36 percent of the men could make the same claim. By 1731, 40 percent of these couples had between one and three surviving children living with them in a family unit (tables 1 and 2).[63]

Table 1. Company-Owned Slave Population by Site, Sex, and Family Status

Site	Men	Women	Men with partners (%)	Women with partners (%)	Couples with 1–3 children
New Orleans Plantation	92	37	35	86	14
Balize	29	10	34	100	5
Natchez	20	12	50	83	2
Périer's Plantation	16	4	25	100	1
Total	157	63	37	92	21

Source: "Inventaire de l'habitation de la Comp. des Indes sur le fleuve St. Louis vis à vis la Nouvelle Orléans et de tous les bâtiments, marchandises, denrées et ustensils, de nègres et bestiaux à la charge de S. Le Page," September 2, 1731, Archives nationales d'outre-mer, Aix-en-Provence, France, C 2 24, ff. 183–87.

Table 2. Company-Owned Slave Children by Site and Age Group

Site	Children aged 5–8	%	Children aged 2–4	%	Children aged < 2	%	Total children	% of total
New Orleans Plantation	6	24	6	24	13	52	25	76
Balize	1	17	4	67	1	17	6	18
Natchez	0	0	1	50	1	50	2	6
Périer's Plantation	—	—	—	—	1	100	1	100
Total	7	21	11	32	16	47	34	100

Source: "Inventaire de l'habitation de la Comp. des Indes sur le fleuve St. Louis vis à vis la Nouvelle Orléans et de tous les bâtiments, marchandises, denrées et ustensils, de nègres et bestiaux à la charge de S. Le Page," September 2, 1731, Archives nationales d'outre-mer, Aix-en-Provence, France, C 2 24, ff. 183–87.

Although the Code noir and Catholic authorities in Louisiana encouraged masters to baptize their slaves, it is unclear if the company made adult baptism a prerequisite for slave marriages. Article 2 of the 1724 code required all masters to educate their slaves in preparation for baptism, but article 8 from the original 1685 code, which required all slaves to be baptized prior to entering into marriage, was stricken from the 1724 code.[64] Complaints made by Father Raphaël, who in a letter to Abbé Raguet railed against masters who permitted baptized slaves to marry "infidels," suggest that slave owners adhered unevenly to the doctrinal requirement that individuals be baptized prior to receiving the sacrament of marriage.[65] Extant sacramental records note dozens of slave baptisms performed in the 1720s—some of which involved company slaves—but there is no extant corresponding register for slave marriages.

Between the time the 1731 inventory was recorded and when it was sent to company officials in Paris on January 9 of the following year, the company sold as individual slaves four-year-olds Janneton and Marianne, six-year-old Charlot, and seven-and-a-half-year-old Isabelle. All of them had parents who were also owned by the company, making their sale a direct violation of the Code noir. During the interim, the company also sold six unmarried men and a married couple.[66] The code, originally promulgated by Louis XIV in 1685, was revised and reissued for Louisiana in 1724.[67] Article 43 of the 1724 code sought to prevent the breakup of slave families by explicitly prohibiting the sale of husbands from wives and of children under fourteen from their mothers.[68] The company's sale of prepubescent slaves away from their parents is a direct contradiction of Gwendolyn Midlo Hall's assertion that "the slave family was scrupulously protected in practice as well as in law. Mother, father, husband, wife, and children under the age of fourteen were not sold separately."[69] With regard to article 43, and others promulgated in the Code noir, colonial practice often deviated from Crown preference, especially in colonies such as Louisiana, which lacked any real enforcement mechanism.[70] Technically, the Superior Council maintained ultimate powers of oversight, but as a whole, its members tended to stay out of master-slave affairs in all but the most extreme instances of abuse.[71]

The vast majority of company-owned slaves, men and women alike, lived on the west bank plantation and worked on site or across the river in New Orleans. The 1731 inventory lists only the occupations of adult male slaves, though adult females toiled at a variety of tasks on the plantation and were just as likely as their male counterparts to be engaged in manual labor. Of the ninety-two enslaved men located in New Orleans, 61 percent were skilled workers (table 3).

One of the most labor-intensive activities company slaves engaged in was clearing the cypress forest surrounding both the plantation and the settlement across the river. In this grueling endeavor, company slaves were joined by other, privately owned slaves assigned to *corvée*, or forced labor for the settlement's public works. By Superior Council mandate, all slave owners were required to furnish each of their slaves to colonial authorities for a thirty-day term of public works labor. In Louisiana, corvéed slaves were frequently responsible for levee construction, drainage ditch digging, and land clearing. Teams of long sawyers worked to fell and prepare the tallest, strongest trees for use in shipbuilding and trade, while others felled and processed lesser trees for end uses ranging from home construction to making shingles and naval stores. Timber and its by-products were consistently listed among the items circulated in the company's trade with Saint-Domingue and Spanish settlements along the Gulf Coast, and naval stores were often used in the transatlantic trade between Louisiana and France.

On the west bank plantation, some slaves labored in the indigo works or rice fields or in the combined lumber and rice-processing mill. Others grew provisions or held skilled positions as carpenters, caulkers, hospital workers, brick- and sailmakers, carters, and blacksmiths. More than thirty slave cabins were constructed on site during the 1720s. Plantation manager Le Page du Pratz drew up the plans, and slave carpenters likely played a significant role in building the cabins.[72]

While some Africans arrived in Louisiana possessing knowledge of and tangible skills in metalworking, construction techniques, healing, shipbuilding, navigation, and agricultural cultivation of crops such as rice and indigo, others learned a trade on arrival. Across the river from the company plantation, fifteen company slaves were apprenticed to thirteen master artisans across eight different professions: blacksmithery, carpentry, cooperage, locksmithing, masonry, roofing, toolmaking, and woodworking (table 3). All slaves serving as apprentices were val-

Table 3. Occupations of Male Company-Owned Slaves

	New Orleans	Balize	Natchez	Périer's Plantation	Total
Baker	—	1	—	—	1
Blacksmith	2	—	—	1	3
Blacksmith*	1	—	—	—	1
Brickmaker	1	—	—	—	1
Carpenter	2	2	1	—	5
Carpenter*	2	—	—	—	2
Carter	2	—	—	—	2
Caulker	1	—	—	—	1
Cooper*	1	—	—	—	1
Gardener	2	—	—	—	2
Indigo worker	1	—	—	—	1
Laborer (unskilled)	36	14	11	—	61
Locksmith*	3	—	—	—	3
Longsawyer	6	—	—	2	8
Manager/driver	4	1	—	1	6
Mason*	1	—	—	—	1
Nurse/healer	1	1	—	—	2
Overseer	5	1	1	1	8
Roofer*	1	—	—	—	1
Sailmaker	1	—	—	—	1
Sailor	13	8	7	9	37
Tailor	—	1	—	—	1
Toolmaker*	2	—	—	—	2
Woodworker/joiner*	5	—	—	—	5
Total	92	29	20	16	157

* Apprenticed

Source: "Inventaire de l'habitation de la Comp. des Indes sur le fleuve St. Louis vis à vis la Nouvelle Orléans et de tous les bâtiments, marchandises, denrées et ustensils, de nègres et bestiaux à la charge de S. Le Page," September 2, 1731, Archives nationales d'outre-mer, Aix-en-Provence, France, C 2 24, ff. 183–87.

ued at twelve hundred livres each, as opposed to nine hundred for unskilled laborers, and all trained under New Orleans–based artisans.[73] The company made a concerted effort to train slaves as craftsmen in an effort to create a stable, proficient, skilled workforce, largely because it had achieved limited success in attracting the number of French artisans necessary to support the colony. And unlike French craftsmen, who were often deemed too expensive to support and who could not be counted on to remain in the colony, skilled slave labor and the initial investment in their purchase and training often paid for itself over time.

The use of skilled African labor in Louisiana was not limited to land-bound endeavors. Twenty-four percent of the company's slaves were classified as sailors. Only general, unskilled laborers made up a larger proportion of the enslaved workforce, at 39 percent. The use of slave-sailors in the Americas was not unique to Louisiana. Colonial enterprises undertaken by virtually every European power from the sixteenth through the eighteenth centuries depended on the skills of African boatmen on both sides of the Atlantic. Historian W. Jeffery Bolster, in his 1997 study of the role of African seamen in the Americas, writes, "The New World plantation system relied on canoes and pettiaugers to transport supplies and plantation products; and African boating skills kept that plantation system afloat."[74] In Louisiana, where the plantation system had barely gotten off the ground by the late 1720s, boatmen were employed in the circulation not only of agricultural products but of people and trade goods. Pilots, captains, rowers, sailors: all were roles filled by African slaves navigating Louisiana's watery landscape.

At the mouth of the Mississippi, boatmen were charged with ferrying cargo and passengers from arriving blue-water vessels to the Balize and then shuttling the same goods and passengers upriver to New Orleans. Once ships at the Balize had unburdened themselves of enough cargo to pass the bar at the river's mouth, enslaved company pilots guided them into port at New Orleans. There Balize-based sailors passed the duties to their New Orleans–based counterparts, who loaded indigo, timber, hogsheads of naval stores and sometimes tobacco, bales of pelts and skins, and chests of letters and reports into the holds of the same ships as they prepared for the return journey to Lorient. Sailors based at New Orleans and the Balize plied the waterways that snaked across lower Louisiana, just as they navigated the coastal trade between the Balize, Biloxi, Dauphin Island, Mobile, and even Pensacola. In a March 1729 letter to company directors in Paris about the colony's maritime personnel, Périer and La Chaise wrote, "We are putting in as many blacks as we can in the place of white men," suggesting that on water, as on land, the company preferred skilled slave to free white labor.[75]

A select few slave-sailors managed to translate their valuable skills in navigating the colony's waterways into service on board deep-draft sailing ships, where they joined other seasoned sailors of European descent. Service at sea tended to have a leveling effect. All seamen had a role to fill; each was dependent on the other. And crew members, regardless of race, fell within the ship's preestablished hierarchy, with each sailor subject to the same inflexible code of discipline that flowed from the captain down through the ranks. That is not to say that race disappeared entirely on board ship but, rather, that the lines between slavery and freedom blurred, sometimes creating unique opportunities for advancement or freedom.[76]

Such was the case with Scipion, a slave formerly held by the company, who sailed as a crew member aboard the transatlantic vessel *Dromadaire* between Louisiana and Lorient in 1724. Scipion was subsequently reclassified as a free black, and in the 1730s he made a living hiring out his services as a rower and bargeman to merchants and traders traveling between lower Louisiana and the Illinois country.[77] Examples such as Scipion's validate Bolster's view that African slaves and free men who filled maritime roles in the colonies often had greater access to economic opportunities—and even freedom—than their counterparts who labored in other contexts.[78]

Slaves plying the waters between Louisiana's outposts also had access to a different kind of opportunity, one marked more by the power of knowledge than by increased access to trade goods or other tangible resources. As they sailed from settlement to outpost, from the Gulf Coast to the interior, slave-sailors carried with them news of the wider world. In their travels, they became cultural and literal go-betweens, transmitting tidings at times insignificant, at times monumental. Enslaved sailors were among the key individuals who, Bolster asserts, "were at once racial go-betweens straddling black and white worlds *and* channels of communications among dispersed blacks."[79] Present among company administrators, Indian, French, and sometimes Spanish traders, Breton sailors, and religious personnel alike, African sailors played a key role in disseminating information borne upon the "common wind" to other slaves throughout the colony.[80]

As the company expanded its physical presence upriver from New Orleans, so, too, did it add to the population of company slaves assigned to waterways linking upriver outposts to the capital, particularly for the route between New Orleans and Natchez. Since 1719 the company had pinned its hope of turning Louisiana into a French version of the Chesapeake on the rich agricultural lands surrounding the settlement at Natchez. What began as a temporary trading post and storehouse in 1714 became by 1716 a permanent outpost named for Minister of Marine Pontchartrain's wife, Rosalie. Located in the midst of the Natchez chiefdom's lands, Fort Rosalie's construction during the summer of 1716 occurred as a result of negotiations to end the First Natchez War.[81] Within three years of its establishment, Natchez was considered the nexus of what John Law hoped would become the center of large-scale tobacco production in the French Atlantic world.

Tobacco cultivation began in Louisiana during the first decade of the eighteenth century as a largely private endeavor whose end product was intended for local or in-home consumption. Settlers grew their own leaf for smoking and chewing because supplies from France were virtually nonexistent. Early tobacco farmers found some profit could be made within the domestic economy by selling locally produced tobacco to sailors, soldiers, and neighbors. Indeed, so great was demand for the "stinking weed" that locally grown tobacco supplies often had to be supplemented by leaf bought from Cuba via Spanish traders along the Gulf Coast. Prior to the establishment of concessions in Natchez, local production took place in the colony's coastal reaches, where the soil was too poor to withstand large-scale cultivation, or in the vicinity of New Orleans, where farmers struggled against flooding and insect infestations to bring the crop to maturity.[82]

When Law's company took over the Louisiana monopoly from Antoine Crozat in August 1717, Law set in motion a master plan to turn the colony into France's largest and most successful commercial tobacco producer. In September 1718, he acquired France's lucrative tobacco farm, a monopoly over the commodity that guaranteed Law's company four million livres in revenue per annum. Law predicted that Louisiana would supply all eight million pounds of the tobacco then consumed under the monopoly by 1722. Within months of acquiring the tobacco monopoly, he had secured the ailing Senegal Company with the publicly declared intention of using the slave-trading company's preestablished infrastructure—ships, trading networks, personnel, and such—to bring African laborers to Louisiana. These slaves were to be taught crop-specific expertise by skilled Germans from the Rhineland and Frenchmen from Clérac (both tobacco-growing regions), who were sent to Louisiana at the company's expense in 1718–19.[83]

The proposed concessions were to be located at Natchez, long a stopover point for travelers and fur traders journeying between upper and lower Louisiana and the Illinois country. A settlement at Natchez offered distinct advantages for colonists and administrators eager to pursue plantation agriculture. Situated along the Mississippi River about ninety leagues upriver from New Orleans, Natchez benefited from the river valley's rich alluvial soils but also from its location perched atop a flood-resistant bluff, which Iberville described in 1700 as "about 150 fathoms high" and "covered with hardwood trees."[84] Yet the area was also home to the Natchez Indians. Descended from the precontact Plaquemines culture, the Natchez had continuously occupied the area for over five centuries.[85] At the time of French colonization, the Natchez occupied five settlement districts in the area—Flour, Grigra, Jenzenaque, Tiou, and White Apple—and a ceremonial center at the Grand Village.[86] The French settlement established near Fort Rosalie brought the Europeans and Natchez into close contact, a situation that produced both opportunities for frontier exchange and persistent tensions over land ownership and usage.[87] Further complications arose from preexisting Indian slave trade relationships between the northeasternmost Natchez villages and English traders from Carolina.[88] By physically occupying the area and encouraging settlement, the French hoped to cut off English encroachment from the east.

From 1721 to 1726, free French settlers migrated north to Natchez in search of greater agricultural prospects, bringing with them indentured servants and African slaves. In 1726 there were roughly 260 newcomers residing in the area, including some 140 French settlers, company administrators, representatives of absentee *concessionaires*, and soldiers; 65 African and 9 Indian slaves; and 45 indentured servants. Ten years earlier, the land had been almost exclusively inhabited by Natchez Indians. Natchez's population of white indentured servants made up a larger proportion of the population than in any of Louisiana's other settlements. While the total percentage of indentured servants residing in Louisiana was less than 7 percent, in Natchez the percentage was nearly 21 percent. They, along with the area's enslaved Africans and Indians, bore the burden of clearing, tilling, and planting lands meant for tobacco and indigo cultivation.

Unlike land agreements elsewhere in the colony, where purchases were overseen by the Superior Council, land transactions in the Natchez region took place directly between settlers and the Natchez Indians. Patricia Galloway, Jason Baird Jackson, and James Barnett suggest that the mounting tensions between French settlers and the Natchez that built over the course of the 1720s may have stemmed from different understandings of property ownership between the two groups. They posit that while the French viewed land transactions as a permanent transfer of ownership between buyer and seller, the Natchez may have perceived the conveyance as a usufruct agreement bestowing usage rights only.[89] Most colonists established small farms either along the path connecting Fort Rosalie to the Grand Village or on the outskirts of Natchez villages. The two largest land tracts were held by the Company of the Indies, administrator of the Terre Blanche (White Earth) concession established in 1718; and a group of Paris-based investors sometimes known as the Sainte-Catherine Company, which had purchased the Sainte-Catherine concession from Marc-Antoine Hubert in 1721. After the property transfer, management was overseen from France by Jean Daniel Kolly, who arrived in Louisiana in 1727 to inspect the plantation's progress in person.[90] Both the company and Kolly employed skilled tobacco workers from France to oversee and develop tobacco culture on their respective plantations. The Grand Village of the Natchez, home of a Natchez chief, temple, and ceremonial center, was located midway between the Terre Blanche and Sainte-Catherine concessions.

The company hired Sieur Montplaisir de La Guchay (Montplaisir in company records) as principal overseer of the Terre Blanche concession at an annual salary of fifteen hundred livres. Because the company had executed no plans for feeding him, the Clérac workers, and the handful of African slaves sent to clear the land, however, Montplaisir spent most of his early years in Natchez supervising the establishment of provisioning crops. By 1721 he had managed to send only five hundred pounds of tobacco to France.[91] During the company reorganization in 1723, Terre Blanche was sold to a group of investors that included Claude François Bidal, marquis de Dasfeld and comte de Belle-Isle; Girard Michel de La Jonchère, treasurer general of the Order of Saint-Louis; and Louis Claude Le Blanc, secretary of state in the war division.

Tobacco prospects beyond the company concession looked grim as well. In 1718 the company initiated efforts to encourage tobacco cultivation by small farmers in Natchez, offering twenty-five livres per quintal (one quintal equaled one hundred French livres, or 107.9 pounds) for high-quality tobacco, but within a year Bienville reported to company directors in Paris that "the lazy colonists" and "*sauvages*" preferred not to grow tobacco because there was more money to be had with less effort through trade.[92] Even Jean-Baptiste Faucon Dumanoir, who had purchased the Sainte-Catherine concession from Hubert on behalf of Paris-based partners Kolly, Jean Deucher, and Abbé Charles-Elizabeth de Coëtlogon in 1721, refused to commit all of the concession's land to tobacco cultivation. He claimed he could make more money for Sainte-Catherine's absentee owners by growing indigo and food crops. George Desfontaines, Dumanoir's counterpart at Terre Blanche (also known as the Le Blanc concession), came even more to the point when company officials pressed him to grow more tobacco. When asked to explain his unwillingness to develop additional land for tobacco cultivation, Desfontaines's response made clear that the company's expectation that farmers willingly sell tobacco to its agents for twenty-five livres per quintal, when they could fetch eight times that price in the local economy, was unrealistic.[93] Until the company increased the price it paid for tobacco—or until it established an infrastructure that brought down production costs—farmers would grow just enough to sell within the colony and would dedicate additional land to alternative crops.[94]

Prospective tobacco planters in Louisiana contended with some of the same dilemmas planters had faced some fifty years earlier, when the

French West India Company's monopsonistic policies made expanding tobacco cultivation in the West Indies untenable. Unlike in the Caribbean, however, settlers in Louisiana had few fallback options. Switching to sugar was not an option for most colonists in French Louisiana. Start-up costs were too high and the supply of slave laborers too anemic. And unlike in the Caribbean, where early contact with Europeans had decimated Native American populations nearly to the point of extinction by the seventeenth century, Louisiana's numerous Indian groups remained highly visible and relevant throughout the French colonial period, bringing their presence to bear on nearly every aspect of life in the colony, from land negotiations and trade to military and economic alliances. The presence of a well-developed frontier exchange economy in which settlers could and did sustain themselves through trade with local Indians and fellow Europeans undermined company efforts to encourage tobacco cultivation. Settlers could grow indigo, and the company could continue its limited trade with local Indians, but what company directors in France wanted was tobacco.

The quantity of trade goods destined for circulation among local Indians, whose numbers far exceeded the French, remained insufficient throughout the 1720s, even though proposed agricultural expansion required the French to maintain good relationships with polities such as the Natchez. Historian Kathleen Duval estimates that "in the mid-1720s Louisiana had some 2,500 French, plus 1,500 slaves," while the Indian population "numbered well over 35,000."[95] Inadequate supplies allowed the French to buy neutrality at best, rather than allegiance against the English and their allied polities to the east. According to Périer, the only way to succeed in Louisiana was to strengthen the relationship between the French and the Indians. To secure that alliance required a steady supply of "merchandise suitable for the Indians." Otherwise, stressed Périer, "the English who wish to penetrate into this colony" will take advantage of France's weakness, offering the Indians "as much as they wish at a better rate."[96]

Périer was not the first to make the connection between the paucity of available French trade goods and the potentially fickle loyalties of the company's Indian trading partners. As early as 1703, Nicholas de La Salle observed that the French were at a distinct disadvantage in their relationship with the Chickasaw because they could not maintain the supply of desired trade goods.[97] Nine years later, Bienville and d'Artaguiette echoed La Salle's complaints in letters to Pontchartrain, stressing that the French could not possibly prevent English raids on their Chickasaw allies without access to weapons and gunpowder for use in trade.[98]

Further complicating the company's trade relationship with local Indians—including the Natchez, Choctaw, and Chickasaw—was the price of certain trade goods, such as gunpowder and cloth, relative to their value in the peltry trade. Deer and other animal skins were among the only consistent trade goods shipped from Louisiana to France during the company's reign. To maintain trade relationships with Native Americans, the company and its agents needed access to a steady supply of powder, cloth, and other goods not subject to drastic fluctuations in price. But the company was unwilling to ensure a consistently priced supply, choosing instead to focus on developing tobacco plantations, which then undermined the bread-and-butter business of the peltry trade and eroded its standing with Indian suppliers.[99]

By the mid-1720s the company found itself in a quandary. Elsewhere in the world, it focused largely on the buying and selling of trade goods that were already available through existing supply lines. Cotton piece goods and cowrie shells from India, dozens of varieties of tea from China, spices from Southeast Asia, and even slaves from Africa were all funneled into the company's trade network by local suppliers. In Louisiana, however, company officials supported not the peltry trade, which was Louisiana's equivalent of cowries or textiles, but rather a commodity that required the creation of an entire agricultural and distribution system. Such an undertaking—one that they hoped would transform the colony from a struggling outpost on the edge of empire to a powerful player of global significance—required significant and sustained investment in land, labor, and infrastructure.

Cargo inventories for ships returning to Lorient from company comptoirs around the globe provide a useful snapshot of the types of merchandise being traded in the East Indies versus Louisiana. The 1728 inventories for three ships returning from the East Indies—the *Solide*, *Jupiter*, and *Badine*—include crates of Chinese porcelain, hundreds of bolts of silk, bricks of tea, casks of whole peppercorns, sacks of cowrie shells, and more than twelve hundred crates of "assorted merchandise from the Indies."[100] Cargo inventories from Louisiana also list goods extracted from local supply lines, including beaver and deer skins, sassafras, pitch, tar and construction wood, and items such as quinine and Campeche wood procured through coastal trade with the Spanish, but these types of goods brought in far less profit for the company than their trade equivalents from the east.[101]

Company officials in Louisiana repeatedly sought to convince their counterparts in Paris and Lorient of the worthiness of developing Louisiana's coastal trade with Pensacola, Vera Cruz, Campeche, and Cuba. Officials in Paris agreed in theory but failed to send both the variety and quantity of goods from France necessary for the development of profitable coastal trade with Spanish colonies. Throughout the 1720s Spanish ships came to call at Dauphin Island and the Balize. From the Spanish the company purchased cattle, Cuban tobacco, quinine and other apothecary stores, and an indeterminate number of slaves. In exchange, the Spanish bought "fine linens, Brittany linens, laces, and other goods."[102] On rare occasions the company also set aside African slaves for sale to the Spanish. More often than not, however, company warehouses had nothing of interest to Spanish traders, who left Louisiana's coast with cargoes of no greater value than they had when they arrived.[103]

The company tried to compensate by encouraging tobacco, and to a lesser extent indigo, production, but after years of investment it was still not unusual in the late 1720s for ships departing Louisiana to have only ballast in their holds. These ships often stopped at Saint-Domingue on their way back to France to pick up excess cargo from La Caye Saint-Louis.[104] This was the case with the *Durance*, which left Louisiana and sailed for La Caye, where the crew loaded 42 barrels of white sugar, more than 680 of unrefined sugar, 3 bales of cotton, and more than 6 barrels of indigo.[105] Yet, for all these setbacks, the company was not ready to abandon Louisiana. Administrators on both sides of the Atlantic remained hopeful that with enough support the colony would become France's primary supplier of tobacco.

This hope—as well as the company's corresponding willingness to continue pouring money into Louisiana—was primarily motivated by the potential for future profit. Because the company relied heavily on income generated from the tobacco monopoly renewed by Louis XV in 1723, company officials who might otherwise have lobbied to write off Louisiana as a hopeless cause instead rallied around the idea that tobacco might yet be cultivated there, given the right circumstances. If Louisiana could reinvent itself as a French version of the Chesapeake, the company stood to benefit not only from its role as the sole authorized seller of the narcotic within France but also from its role as the largest producer in the French Atlantic world. To that end, rather than scale back investment in the colony following the 1723 reorganization, the company renewed efforts to make Louisiana profitable.[106]

The quest to turn Louisiana into a tobacco powerhouse was not exclusively motivated by profit. It was also, in the eyes of Louis XV and his advisors, a question of national pride. A steady supply of tobacco from Louisiana would allow the company to stop purchasing the bulk of the tobacco it sold in France from the Chesapeake. Doing so required Crown subsidization to offset the higher shipping costs associated with French tobacco, but these costs would be offset in the short term by the state's satisfaction in supporting French instead of English growers.

From 1723 to 1729, the company invested millions in the Louisiana colony. Determined to make tobacco profitable, administrators increased shipments of African laborers to Louisiana from roughly eighteen hundred slaves in 1721–25 to over four thousand in 1726–30.[107] They sent additional skilled workers from France's tobacco-growing regions and even convinced three experienced Englishmen, including one from Carolina, and a Swiss-born spy named Lunel, who had spent time observing English-style cultivation (and had reportedly stolen Chesapeake seeds for Louisiana planters), to show colonists how to grow and process the crop in the Chesapeake style. They addressed some of Natchez's infrastructure needs by establishing a support operation for growers, where they could purchase provisions or newly constructed hogsheads for shipping from the new company plantation, established in 1724.[108]

Prior to this concession, one of the colonists' most persistent complaints had been the lack of coopers and therefore the lack of proper storage vessels for tobacco shipments from Natchez to New Orleans. Because there were no casks and hogsheads available, tobacco sat too long waiting for shipment and ended up rotting. To further promote tobacco cultivation, administrators reduced production costs by assigning company slaves to clear settlers' land, grow provisions, and construct flatboats (that could be broken down and sold for wood scrap in

New Orleans) for transport. They even built new drying sheds for curing privately grown tobacco and agreed to purchase and process tobacco directly in Natchez, rather than requiring colonists to foot the bill for transporting tobacco bundles downriver to New Orleans.[109]

All of these efforts, combined with an overall increase of what the company paid per quintal from twenty-five livres to between thirty and forty, helped make tobacco cultivation more attractive to prospective growers because they lowered the cost of production, processing, and transportation, thereby increasing potential profits.[110] Yet by the end of the 1728 growing season, the company had amassed perhaps 150,000 pounds of tobacco for export to France, and much of it, according to its tobacco inspector, was of very poor quality.[111] The previous two years had been even worse, with less than 100,000 pounds shipped during both years combined. Year after year, projections for Louisiana tobacco cultivation topped 300,000 pounds, but each year brought far more disappointment than tobacco. To put Louisiana's exports in perspective, the Chesapeake exported nearly 30 million pounds of tobacco per annum in the 1720s.[112]

By the time Caillot arrived in the summer of 1729, fissures of internal discord over Louisiana's value had appeared among company directors, shareholders, and syndics in France. The amount of unpaid debt colonists owed the company topped 4.4 million livres. (The Jesuits alone owed more than 50,000.)[113] Louisiana continued to produce only meager quantities of substandard tobacco, and its administration had become a significant drag on the company's overall financial well-being. At the same time, supply problems in Senegambia threatened to undermine Louisiana's access to slave laborers.[114] Abandoning Louisiana was first discussed in an annual company report in 1727, but the suggestion was seen as what Jacob Price terms "inconsistent with state objectives" that revolved around "the development of an autarkic supply of tobacco in Louisiana."[115] Just two years later, however, what had begun as scattered whispers of dissent had become a chorus of voices questioning the company's continued presence in Louisiana.

Many of those who challenged company objectives pointed to the significant disparities in profit realization between Louisiana, where the balance sheet always reflected a loss, and the East Indies and China, the company's most lucrative markets. Some backed proposals requiring the company to farm out the tobacco monopoly and let private traders handle tobacco production in Louisiana. Others supported a retrocession of the colony to the king, with the company's involvement in Louisiana limited to the purchase of all tobacco produced there. And still others pushed for a complete break with the French Atlantic, in which the company would relinquish all ties to Louisiana and the African slave and Canadian fur trades in favor of exclusive involvement with Indian Ocean markets.[116]

Early in his Louisiana residency, Caillot claimed that Natchez's inhabitants "grow good native tobacco" with "each harvest weighing up to one hundred fifty thousand pounds."[117] His estimation was an exaggeration. Conversations overheard and correspondence read at company offices in New Orleans later tempered his enthusiasm for the colony's tobacco prospects. He made no other references to the crop and certainly earned no profits from tobacco himself, choosing instead to supplement his income and provisions with goods traded through the local frontier exchange economy. In this respect, Caillot was like many other inhabitants of French colonial Louisiana who relied on local barter and trade networks to satisfy needs and wants.[118]

In early December 1729, Caillot and a band of "friends were walking together along the levee" at New Orleans when they "saw a little pirogue coming down the river . . . being rowed" and "going very fast." Thinking it might be the vessel bearing "several pieces of merchandise" he was expecting from upriver, Caillot began "to calculate to [him]self the profit [he] was going to make" in goods destined for petty trade. Instead of trade goods, however, the pirogue bore a handful of half-naked survivors of a Natchez attack on the eponymous French settlement.[119] They brought with them accounts of the bloody episode that brought the dream of creating a French version of the Chesapeake in Louisiana to a violent close.[120]

In October 1729, there were an estimated three dozen military personnel, 400 French settlers, 280 African slaves, and some 2,000 Natchez warriors and their families residing in and around Natchez.[121] The following month, on November 28, 1729, the number of colonists was reduced by more than half when Natchez Indians from the neighboring villages of White Apple, Flour, Grigra, and Jezenaque engaged in a violent campaign of protest against recent actions by French commander Sieur de Chépart (also Deschépart). Tensions between French settlers and the Natchez over land use and occupation came to a head that November, when Chépart—who was by many accounts a man of limited intellect, prone to poor judgment—ordered the decampment of the Natchez from the White Apple village. There, on a site occupied by more than eighty Natchez dwellings, Chépart planned to establish his own tobacco plantation.[122] After convincing Chépart to allow the Natchez to stay at White Apple until the fall crops could be harvested, the Natchez chiefs set in motion a plan that shattered all hope of developing the area into the center of large-scale tobacco cultivation and one that ultimately spelled a near total elimination of the Natchez polity.

On the morning of November 28, the Great Sun of the Natchez arrived at Fort Rosalie with thirty armed warriors. They bore the calumet and explained their intent to conduct a daylong hunt, to be followed by a feast that evening in honor of continued peace and mutual prosperity between the Europeans and the Natchez. The Great Sun then sang the calumet song. At its conclusion, the Natchez warriors raised their weapons and fired on Chépart and the soldiers garrisoned at the fort. The scene was repeated throughout the area, as pre-positioned Natchez Indians entered the homes of each French resident, killing nearly every white man—and some white women and children—in their path. By the end of the day, the death toll numbered 235 Europeans and 12 Natchez.[123] The hostage count stood at "54 French women and children" and between 50 and 150 African slaves.[124]

In the wake of the bloodshed, the Natchez pillaged movable goods, weaponry (including cannons), and livestock from the fort and victims' properties and seized the entire cargo of a recently arrived half-galley from New Orleans, distributing the bounty of trade goods and supplies throughout their settlements. The Natchez also captured and held two Frenchmen: a carter, who assisted them in clearing out and distributing goods taken from the galley, and a tailor, whom they set to work altering clothes taken from their victims. The final blow to the French at Natchez came in the form of fire, as warriors set the fort, warehouses, trading post, residences, and field upon field of nearly mature tobacco aflame.

6

A Colony Fit Only for a King?

Word of the Natchez attack reached the port of Lorient via the *Saint-Michel* nearly three months after the fact. Within days of the ship's arrival from Louisiana, the news had spread among company officials and bureaucrats stationed in Lorient and neighboring Port-Louis. On February 23, 1730, port commander Fayet set out for Paris to personally bring news of the disaster to Minister of Marine Maurepas.[1] Arriving in early March, Fayet delivered Governor Périer's initial account of the onslaught, which was likely based on survivor stories. Between twenty and thirty French men survived the Natchez attack, and a handful of African slaves also managed to avoid capture. Individuals from both groups made their way to plantations and settlements downriver. At least three survivors, including tobacco inspector Lunel, had arrived in Pointe Coupée on December 1. From there colonists sent word of the attack downriver to New Orleans. Other "poor wretches" who had managed to escape arrived in the capital via pirogue the first week in December.[2] The Natchez, wrote Périer, "massacred not only all the men who were in the fort in our village, but in addition attacked the concessions from which no one was able to escape," save the "women, children, and negroes" the attackers took as captives.[3]

Périer was eager to strike against the Natchez and any allied Indians but felt hamstrung by what he described as a dearth of capable troops, who were "scattered about the posts of this colony." After pleading with Maurepas to send "five to six hundred men" and warships to Louisiana "as quickly as possible," Périer signed off, making no account of the destruction of tobacco or company structures at Natchez.[4]

Focused almost entirely on retribution, Périer convinced the colony's Choctaw allies to march against the Natchez. A Choctaw contingent of between four and seven hundred warriors ambushed the Natchez on January 27, 1730, killing approximately one hundred, capturing an additional fifteen to twenty, and recovering a handful of French and some African captives. With the Choctaw mobilized, Périer sent out a combined French-Indian force under the command of Henry de Louboey from the Pointe Coupée settlement. Louboey's men joined the Choctaw outside Natchez on February 8; they spent the next two weeks engaged in near-daily skirmishes before the two camps reached an agreement to end the fighting. On February 23, the French agreed to draw back from their current position at the Grand Village to the east bank of the Mississippi River. In exchange, the Natchez agreed to release the remaining French and African captives to the Choctaws stationed at the Sainte-Catherine concession. Each side carried out its end of the bargain, but in an unexpected turn, the remaining Natchez, including more than two hundred men, women, and children, abandoned their villages and escaped into the night.

The Choctaw had succeeded in recovering fifty-four French hostages and some one hundred African slaves, but they refused to turn them over to Périer until the French paid out a bounty for each hostage recovered. After heated negotiations Choctaw demands were eventually met, but not before the surviving Natchez had fled from their villages, which led some French officers to suspect Choctaw complicity in the escape.[5] While the recovery of the French hostages could be seen as a major success of Périer's initial strike against the Natchez, the flight of the remaining members of the Natchez polity, along with a number of African captives, enraged the governor and made him look rather inept. Périer blamed the Indians' escape on the incompetence of his French troops and the collusion of the Choctaw with the enemy, but the governor had to account for more than just the absconding of the Natchez. As unconfirmed reports of the assault began to trickle into France via ships arriving at the port of Lorient, company officials and shareholders heard conflicting information on the extent of property damage in the Natchez area and sought an official account of company losses. Not until after the hostages were recovered did Périer disclose the full extent of what had been lost.

In a letter dated March 18 that likely reached company directors in Paris toward the end of May, he disclosed the grim reality: "After massacring the French," the Natchez "burnt all the houses and sheds with two hundred thousand-weight of tobacco. The galley and a boat of eighteen oars were not spared."[6] As the first loaded trade vessel to arrive from New Orleans in many months, the galley carried a cargo valued at 300,000 livres.[7] Its arrival was intended to convey the company's continued commitment to trade in the Natchez region. Without trade goods to pave the way to stable relationships with Indians in the area, settlers had little chance of successfully maintaining, and later increasing, landholdings.

Caillot provided an explicit accounting of "the booty" raided by the Natchez, which consisted "mainly of brandy and flour," with lesser quantities of "dry goods such as shoes, hats, powder, bullets, etc."[8] Intended for native and French inhabitants alike, the loss of such goods undermined company efforts to maintain stability beyond the bounds of Fort Rosalie and the Natchez villages. North and east of Natchez, the French were in constant competition with the often better-supplied English traders from Carolina, who peddled their wares among the area's Indians. If the French lost their status as active agents in the Indian trade, they lost any hope of creating an environment conducive to the establishment of plantation agriculture. There could be no settled tracts of agricultural land in a colony where Indians outnumbered the French by more than fourteen to one without stable French-Indian relations. And without agriculture—and tobacco in particular—there was no motivation for the company to continue its presence in the colony.

The loss of trade goods also made it difficult for the French to bargain with their Choctaw allies for the release of French and African captives. Without a reward for their efforts against the Natchez, the Choctaw retained the captives, preferring to plead their case for payment before the "Great French Chief" (Périer) in New Orleans, rather than risk a possible loss of bounty with an immediate, uncompensated release.[9] The paucity of available trade stores complicated an already tenuous alliance between the French and their Indian allies. When Mobile infantry captain Joseph-Christophe de Lusser scoured the Lower Mississippi Valley in early 1730 looking for French and African captives, he found one "little French boy in the band of Chickasawhays" rescued from the Natchez, who had been passed over for release because Sieur de Louboey "had been willing to give only one limburg blanket for him."[10] Like members of the Yellow Cane and other Choctaw villages, the Chickasawhays felt "very much dissatisfied because they had been promised many things when it was a question of setting out for war, but the promise to them had not been kept." Conversely, surviving members of the Natchez used pilfered trade goods and African captives in their attempts to entice other native groups to join them in attacks carried out against the French throughout the winter and spring of 1730.[11]

Fort Rosalie was not the only comptoir affected by the Natchez War. At Fort Saint-Pierre, a military and trade outpost north of Natchez along the Yazoo River, a party of Yazoo Indians who had witnessed events at Natchez stormed the fort, killing Commander du Codère, Jesuit missionary Jean-François Souel, and the entire seventeen-man garrison. In the Illinois country, events downriver at Forts Rosalie and Saint-Pierre disrupted supply lines between New Orleans and the settlements around Fort de Chartres and Kaskaskia. For the whole of 1730, settlers throughout the Mississippi Valley were on high alert.

In the capital, fear of a pan-Indian conspiracy and rumors of planned slave uprisings gripped the French populace throughout 1730. In January the capital's inhabitants "were warned that the colony's Negroes wanted to turn against [them], too. There were," wrote Caillot, "at least fifteen hundred or two thousand of them, which frightened us a great deal because they are great fighters" and are "more formidable than ten thousand Indians."[12] Word of another conspiracy leaked out later that year when an enslaved woman warned a soldier that "the French should not long insult negroes."[13] Dumont de Montigny, who documented the rumor in his mémoire, claimed that each slave planned to rise up against his or her master at night, commandeering the master's weapons and powder supplies, and moving through the capital killing on-guard soldiers and militiamen.[14] While neither of these alleged conspiracies bore fruit, perceived threats from Indians outside the capital and enslaved blacks within fed colonists' sense of insecurity and left many residents eager to board the next ship bound for France.

In the midst of the chaos, Jacques de La Chaise died on February 6, 1730. La Chaise was a colorful correspondent prone to long-winded accounts during his time as director-general. He provided far more detail about company affairs in Louisiana than his governmental counterpart Périer had. His death during the retaliatory campaign against the Natchez in the winter of 1730 meant that one of the few voices present for much of the post-1723 reorganization period was silent during an especially critical period in Louisiana's relatively brief history. La Chaise's absence also meant that company business was largely set aside as Périer channeled all able-bodied men, including company clerks, councillors, and colonists, into four newly formed militia units.

Intended to supplement the colony's existing French troops and allied Choctaw forces in protecting the settlements as well as in the retaliation campaign against the Natchez, these civilian- and bureaucrat-populated units comprised 150 men each.[15] It is difficult to determine exactly which colonists became rank-and-file militiamen, but it is likely that all available company employees were deputized. Caillot noted that the physician and botanist Louis Prat, king's prosecutor François Fleuriau, and Superior Council members Antoine Bruslé and Renaud d'Hauterive were appointed commanding officers, with colonists and company personnel divided into separate units. Out of the company employees, including perhaps any ships' officers present in the city, the "governor formed a company of cadets, which numbered 40." Because all the colony's military officers were already engaged elsewhere, the cadets "chose from among [them] a captain." They selected a storehouse guard, who conveniently advanced each cadet a "*justau corps* of red camlet," a "hat edged with silver" braid and embellished with a "white cockade," a vest and trousers "of white dimity, . . . white silk stockings," a rifle, and gloves from company stores in exchange for a steep "20-livre reduction per month" from his company wages.[16] This smartly outfitted militia company patrolled the capital throughout 1730, alternating shifts with the colonists' corps.

While company paper pushers took turns mounting the guard and parading in the Place d'Armes, bookkeeping and letter writing at company headquarters came to a near standstill. A total of just twenty letters and mémoires were received in France from the Louisiana offices in 1730, less than half the volume received in each of the two previous years. When not on guard duty, Caillot reported that he and his office mates were "bored to death."[17] La Chaise was not immediately replaced as company director in Louisiana, leaving his staff to occupy themselves for more than two months. After Laurent MacMahon was named the new company director on April 17, 1730, officials remained more focused on security in New Orleans and events unfolding in outlying comptoirs than on day-to-day company business.[18]

Official correspondence was not the only information vessel available to bureaucrats in the French Atlantic, however. Given the nature of verbal communication networks—with ships' officers and passengers bearing rumors of Louisiana's fate from abroad—it seems unlikely that company clerks such as Caillot, who fraternized frequently with maritime personnel, were unaware that the fate of the Louisiana comptoirs was a topic of much metropolitan debate.

Even before company directors and syndics in Paris understood the magnitude of the damage wrought by the Natchez in Louisiana, plans were being put forth to limit the company's losses outside the Indian Ocean trade zone. In March 1730, Director Jacques Deshayes proposed splitting the global trading company into three smaller, more self-sufficient units, so that expenses and liabilities in one sector could not drag down other, more profitable ones. Deshayes's proposal called for the creation of three relatively separate sub-companies, including "one for the East Indies, China, and all other areas past the Cape of Good Hope; one for Guinea, Senegal, the French Caribbean islands, and the Barbary Coast; and the third for Louisiana and Canada."[19] This arrangement would allow the company to isolate its losses and invest "the most funds possible" in India, where "cargoes stood at the ready to be embarked [for France] the moment company ships arrived from Europe."[20]

A scenario in which all the company had to do was send ships to pay for and pick up high-demand cargoes was completely unlike the situation faced by company officials in Louisiana. There ships waited months at the port of New Orleans to fill their holds and even then were sometimes forced to leave Louisiana with only ballast. When Deshayes penned his mémoire, it was unclear how much of Natchez's tobacco had been lost during the late-November attack, but his hesitancy to propose a complete withdrawal from Louisiana suggests that even after years of poor returns on substantial investments, directors were not ready to give up North America.

By July 1730, however, after Périer's more explicit report had revealed the instability of French-Indian relations in the colony as well as the loss of tobacco and all tobacco-related infrastructure at Natchez, directors and syndics began openly to question the company's continued presence (and long-term role) in Louisiana.[21] In a mémoire dated July 28, a Sieur Ramont recognized the utility of a French-directed global trading company, which allowed the French to bypass the Dutch and English in its trade relationships abroad, but decried the way in which the company conducted its affairs.[22] He cited two primary faults as undermining the company at every turn: the pursuit of too many lines of trade in too many areas; and the inefficient and bloated state of the company's administration. Ramont warned directors that unless something was done to address these faults, the company would "be totally lost within four to five years."[23]

After pointing explicitly to repeated losses in Africa and Louisiana, Ramont insisted that the only way for the company to remain profitable was to focus its activities on the East Indies and China. Like Deshayes, Ramont viewed the company's projects outside the Indian Ocean as an unnecessary drag on company resources. "Merchants from Marseille, Rouen, Saint-Malo, La Rochelle," and other ports, wrote Ramont, should be "charged with trade in Barbary, Senegal, Guinea, and Canada."[24] As for French holdings in the Mississippi Valley, instead of continuing to pour money, time, and bureaucrats into a colony whose value after 1729 was increasingly strategic, as a buffer against further English encroachment in North America, rather than economic, Ramont viewed it as "crucial that His Majesty take over Louisiana himself."[25]

During the second half of 1730, debates over Louisiana's future—and in the longer term the company's future—centered increasingly on a possible retrocession of the colony to the Crown. Shareholders and their syndics argued against further investment in Louisiana, urging directors to arrange a retrocession. The events of late 1729 threw additional support behind those who had pressed for a more limited company scope prior to the Natchez War. If the company's primary reason for involvement in Louisiana was tobacco cultivation, many believed that the destruction of crops and infrastructure, disruption of labor, and exposure of French-Indian fault lines in the Natchez area meant that the company's objective was no longer attainable.

Company involvement in Louisiana was not the only target of would-be reformers. As Ramont suggested, the company itself relied on too many administrators, a tendency that was costly and often ineffective. When Philibert Orry was appointed controller-general of France in March 1730, he took an active interest in the king's investment in the company and sought ways to make the entity a more profitable one. As a former company director, he was well aware of the overstretched nature of the company's global commitments and had witnessed firsthand the inefficiency with which it conducted business from Paris.

The possible retrocession of Louisiana was but one of Orry's desired reforms. Within months of becoming controller-general, he initiated a series of changes that streamlined the company's Paris operations, reducing the number of directors from twelve to six and syndics from six to two. He then eliminated the team of four inspectors general who had been appointed during the Regency as the king's representatives. The inspectors' appointments had followed the 1723 company reorganization, but Orry insisted that by 1730 their services—and accompanying salaries—were no longer necessary.[26]

Orry also sought to make existing lines of business more profitable and eliminate those, such as Louisiana, whose perpetual losses threatened the company's long-term stability. To that end, he lobbied successfully for the cessation of company involvement along the Barbary Coast and began negotiations to lease the company's tobacco monopoly to the United General Farms, a third-party entity responsible for tax collection.[27] The company reached a settlement with the Farms in July 1730. Two months later, when the contract was confirmed, the Farmers General took over purchase of tobacco from Louisiana and any other colonial or domestic producer but were no longer obliged to pay subsidies. All Farms-purchased tobacco would be paid for at rates competitive with the price of Virginia tobacco. In exchange, the company would receive 7.5 million livres per year for the first four years of the lease and 8 million annually for the last four years.[28] Like the per-slave income generated by the company's 1725 agreement, which allowed privately funded slave traders to operate between Africa and the circum-Caribbean, income generated by the tobacco lease was guaranteed to be higher than what the company had been able to reap through its own efforts.

In a summary of the arguments put forth in favor of retroceding Louisiana to the king in early December 1730, Louis Henry Brinon de

Caligny, one of the two remaining company syndics, described the untenable nature of the company's continued presence in Louisiana. The company had "in the past thirteen years invested more than 20 million livres" in Louisiana, a sum that far exceeded total company profits for the years 1725 to 1735, which amounted to just over 8.7 million livres.[29] Company funds had transported settlers to inhabit the colony and enslaved laborers to clear and tend settlers' lands. They had underwritten design and construction expenses for the establishment of New Orleans. They had provided for colonial defenses in the form of forts, munitions, and soldiers and had watched over the souls of natives and settlers alike through their investment in foreign missions. Yet in spite of all the company's contributions, stressed Brinon de Caligny, the recent destruction of the Natchez post, "where tobacco culture had shown the most promise," forced the company to reconsider its commitments.[30] Because the company in Louisiana now found itself in dire military and financial straits, he continued, "it was no longer possible to consider the colony a concession in perpetuity," as it should have been by the terms of its charter, but rather "as a valuable entity entrusted to its care" whose safety and security it could no longer guarantee.[31]

The company's focus was above all commercial. The foremost concerns of its administrators were the protection of investments and the maintenance of a fiduciary climate that allowed them to pay out guaranteed dividends to its shareholders. If France wished to keep Louisiana, and thereby prevent the spread of English settlement to the Mississippi, the king would have to find another entity to manage the colony. The only logical choice to take on an initiative of such magnitude was the Crown.

By the close of 1730, the retrocession of Louisiana was nearly complete. Writing from Versailles on December 31, Orry sought final approval from the king for new plans that would open up trade in Louisiana to private merchants. The ordinance drafted by Orry required the company to continue transporting "the provisions and merchandise necessary to the survival and well-being of its inhabitants" as well as goods to be employed in "the Indian trade."[32] Orry's plan obliged the company to send ships to the colony each year for those purposes but released it from all other obligations. No stipulation was made for future company shipments of African laborers to the colony.

The official edict transferring control of Louisiana to the king was signed in Paris on January 23, 1731.[33] Rather than require further company participation in Louisiana as specified in Orry's scheme, the terms severed all company ties to the colony, including the Illinois country. In return for such generous concessions, the company agreed to pay 1.45 million livres to the king over the course of the next ten years as compensation for any outstanding obligations.[34] Beginning July 1, the company's commercial monopoly, granted August 1717, was rescinded. Under the terms of the retrocession, trade between France and Louisiana would be thrown open to any and all interested French merchants, and ownership and responsibility for all "public squares, forts, buildings, artillery, armaments, and troops" in Louisiana was transferred from company to Crown.[35] The only right the company retained in the colony was debt collection.

By April, word of the retrocession had reached Louisiana.[36] In a letter from Maurepas, Périer learned that the promotion of commerce was to be the new "primary object" of his attention. Maurepas stressed the importance of building confidence among Louisiana's inhabitants and recommended that Périer promote the development of coastal and circum-Caribbean trade. Stronger ties with Saint-Domingue and Martinique were essential. Both could prove profitable outlets for Louisiana's nascent timber industry.[37] Left unsaid was that closer ties to the French islands would also make the colony's survival more likely. Without regular arrivals of supplies from France—which had previously been guaranteed by the company—colonists in Louisiana might find new, practical value in relationships with their West Indian counterparts.

Maurepas also charged Périer with communicating the terms of the retrocession to all inhabitants, including company employees, and with overseeing a smooth transfer of power. Within days of Périer's receipt of his orders, company and Crown officials began the process of inventorying slaves, tools, buildings, and warehouse stores to be transferred to the king. Company bureaucrats Bruslé and Bru were to remain in the colony as debt collectors, but all other personnel were to be removed from their posts and returned to Lorient via available company ships.

For Caillot, the process of attempting to leave Louisiana had begun months earlier. In early February the governor had returned to New Orleans from his most recent and final campaign against the Natchez.

With the help of soldiers, militiamen, and some two hundred additional troops who had arrived in Louisiana via the king's ship the *Somme* in September 1730, Périer and his brother Antoine-Alexis Périer de Salvert (who also arrived on the *Somme*) had defeated the Natchez and captured nearly 500 of them, including approximately 450 women and children and 45 warriors, as slaves.[38] Périer's forces brought the captives downriver to New Orleans, where nearly 45 percent died due to overcrowding and poor sanitary conditions in the jail. On May 28 the surviving 280 captives were boarded onto the *Vénus* and *Aurore* bound for Cap Français, where they were to be sold as slaves to the profit of the company. One hundred and twenty-seven additional Natchez perished en route.

As news of Périer's victory spread, inhabitants in New Orleans also learned of successful allied campaigns by the Illinois the previous fall against the Fox Indians.[39] Confident that his victory eliminated the Natchez threat to Louisiana's capital and comptoirs and buoyed by good news from the Illinois country, Périer gathered the "troops of the army, navy, and militia" in the Place d'Armes, where on February 8 troops joined civilians in singing the "Te Deum."[40] The assembled companies then fired their guns in salute, along with "324 cannon discharges." With the Natchez defeated, Périer thanked Caillot's company of cadets "on behalf of the king and the company for the fine service [they] had rendered" and discharged them from militia duty.[41]

Shortly thereafter, Caillot sought permission from local officials to leave Louisiana by way of one of the ships soon to depart for France. Unaware of the pending retrocession and hesitant to promote any outmigration from the colony, Périer "encouraged [him] to stay, with a promise of rendering [him] some service" in Louisiana. By "service," Périer likely intended to offer Caillot either a promotion or land, but the clerk remained unconvinced of the merits of remaining in New Orleans. Then a fire broke out at the Jarrys' inn, destroying his room, belongings, and "all the money, which amounted to 217 livres, that I no longer possessed."[42] Having lost his personal possessions and everything he had put aside from petty trade, Caillot appealed to members of the Superior Council, "to whom [he] explained that some very pressing affairs . . . were calling me back home to France without delay." His fabricated personal affairs, "in addition to the illness of the country, which

[he] pretended to have . . . resolved them to grant [his] request." The clerk wasted no time preparing to depart. "I left New Orleans April 1 in the year 1731," he wrote, "as happy to the same degree as I had been sad upon arriving there."[43]

Given that Périer received the official notification and terms of the retrocession in April, it is likely that Caillot had left the capital before the news arrived. His boat may even have been headed downriver to the Balize as word of the retrocession traveled upriver on another vessel to New Orleans. Or the news may have arrived in the capital while Caillot "stayed on land" at the Balize "waiting for the ships to pass a sandbar where there was shallow water, and where almost all the ships run aground very easily."[44]

Once Caillot's return vessel, the *Prince de Conty*, passed the bar, he and his fellow passengers were rowed from shore to ship in a reverse process from what he had experienced just two years earlier on the *Durance*. They set sail in early April, but after a short time at sea "a great noise arose in the ship." The *Prince de Conty* had struck a sandbar and begun to sink.[45] Passengers and crew members scrambled to board the longboat as the ship went down. "We were not two musket shots away when there was no longer any ship," wrote Caillot. "On one side you saw cattle drowning; on the other, casks, chests, planks, chairs, beds, and ten to twelve men whom we could not save, because the sea was too agitated."[46] All but one of the men ultimately survived the shipwreck, as did nearly three dozen crates of assorted peltry (beaver, deer, and squirrel) and 294 barrels of pitch.[47] The rest of the ship and its cargo were a complete loss. On April 3 the *Saint-Louis*, the last company ship to deliver slaves to Louisiana, left New Orleans, sailing downriver to the Balize. Its captain, Étienne Bréban, a former officer in the royal navy, learned of the *Prince de Conty*'s shipwreck on April 9, likely from arriving survivors.[48] In early May, after Bréban received instructions from Périer, the *Prince de Conty*'s salvaged cargo, along with its five passengers and dozens of crew members, were loaded onto the *Saint-Louis*. Caillot closed his account of his first overseas commission with the ship's departure: "We left the Balize on May 4, 1731, at five and a quarter hours in the evening, after enduring many gales while in a roadstead, which caused dreadful seas for us for five days."[49]

Epilogue

Embracing India

On May 13, 1761, twenty-three-year-old Marie-Madeleine Caillot left her home along the rue Basse-du-Rempart and made her way on foot to an imposing redbrick structure at the corner of rues Neuve des Petits Champs and Vivienne. Her husband, Claude Michel de Saint-Michel, accompanied her. They passed through the building's massive gates, crossed the gravel-strewn courtyard, and—checking the clock below the attic dormers—hurried into the Paris headquarters of the French Company of the Indies. Their destination was the office of Pierre de Mory, who, as company paymaster, oversaw the disbursal of funds from overseas' employee accounts to designated relatives in France. In the case of Marie-Madeleine, Mory had summoned her to his office to distribute more than seventeen thousand livres in cash assets from Marc-Antoine Caillot's succession. Proceeds from the sale of his property in India, valued at more than ninety five hundred *rouples arcattes* (the local silver coinage whose worth translated to nearly sixty thousand livres), might also go to Marie-Madeleine, Caillot's daughter and sole heir, assuming the British had not reduced it to rubble.[1]

Marc-Antoine Caillot died at sea in 1758. His life—his successes, failures, and fortunes—in many ways mirrored the history of the company that employed him during his thirty-year career. Caillot's departure from Louisiana in May 1731 was the earliest in what became by midsummer a steady outflux of company bureaucrats, clerks, sailors, and ships' officers. After fourteen years spent attempting to build a viable commercial presence in Louisiana, the French Company of the Indies spent less than six months dismantling operations there. By the fall of 1731, company officials had packed up their ledgers and their staff (leaving behind an unlucky few charged with debt collection) and left North America entirely.

In France, plans were under way to consolidate company operations even further. Administrators hoped that streamlining shipping, warehousing, and shipbuilding functions would allow them to extract maximum profitability from the company's most lucrative trade zone: the Indian Ocean. By the close of the 1730s, Lorient had become the central headquarters for company operations. Five of the six company directors, both syndics, and the central office staff remained in Paris, but all other operations took place exclusively in Lorient. Whereas Lorient's role in the 1720s was primarily one of outfitting the company's myriad ships, by 1734 all other support services had been relocated there. Shipbuilding, which had previously taken place in Hamburg, London, and Nantes, occurred exclusively within Lorient's domain beginning in 1730, following construction of the first of three shipyards constructed there between 1730 and 1750.[2] Then in 1733 engineers laid the first stone in what was to be a multi-million-livre merchandise complex, where the company intended to hold the annual sales of imported trade goods that had previously taken place in Nantes. Lorient's first sale, which showcased the cargoes of twelve ships recently returned from the East Indies, took place in September 1734. By moving the warehouses, sales, and associated financial and merchant services to Lorient, the company not only retained greater control over sales but, more important, eliminated transportation costs from the port of Lorient to Nantes and greatly reduced annual expenses it had incurred from goods damaged while in transport between the two towns.

In 1729 the company had outfitted two ships bound for the East Indies and four for Louisiana. The following year the number of Louisiana-bound ships remained the same, but the number of East Indies–bound ships doubled. In 1732, just one year after the company relinquished its claims in North America and eliminated its Louisiana route, it sent twelve fully outfitted ships to India and one to Île-de-France.

The company did not entirely abandon the French Atlantic. The slave and gum trades, centered at the company concession in Senegambia, continued to play important and profitable roles in company operations, but there, too, the object was trade, not colonization. And even though the company traded slaves for agricultural products, such as sugar, coffee, tobacco, and cotton, in Martinique, Saint-Domingue, and later in the eighteenth century in Guadeloupe, it did not itself play a role in the production of those agricultural products.

As officials redirected funds from aborted business sectors in the French Atlantic to the Indian Ocean, the value of cargoes arriving from India rose apace. In 1730–31, sixteen company ships hauled 4.9 million livres tournois' (l.t.) worth of trade goods from India. From January 1733 to September 1734, the number of ships returning from India was reduced by three, but the value of imported trade goods increased to 11 million l.t., with a corresponding increase in sales from 9.4 million l.t. in 1730–31 to 19.4 million l.t. in 1733–34.[3] Profits in the Indian Ocean trade zone continued to rise, reaching nearly 40 million l.t. from 1740 to 1744, before dropping precipitously during the War of Austrian Succession, when English naval vessels targeted, captured, and destroyed numerous French merchant ships. The company rebounded in the first half of the 1750s, achieving its greatest successes to date as demand for luxury goods in Europe drove profits above the 50-million mark.[4]

The results of the company's decision to refocus its attentions on the Indian Ocean trade zone after 1731 are clear. Having consolidated its operations—both in terms of personnel and support services—and jettisoned its unprofitable colony-building schemes in North America, the French Company of the Indies became for the first time since its inception a viable trading company. In abandoning Louisiana, the company relinquished its role as colony builder in favor of confirming itself as a pure trade entity. By reducing its global presence and strengthening its ties to trade networks in places such as Pondicherry, Mocha, Chandernagore, Surat, and Mahé, the company chose trade over colonization, thereby ensuring its survival into the second half of the eighteenth century.

As for Caillot, his fortunes followed those of the company. The *Saint-Louis* arrived in Lorient on June 5, 1731.[5] Just over six months later, Caillot boarded another company vessel, the *Atalante*. This time he, like the company itself, was bound for the East Indies. He arrived in Pondicherry, the site of his new clerk's commission, on August 22, 1732 (fig. 10).[6]

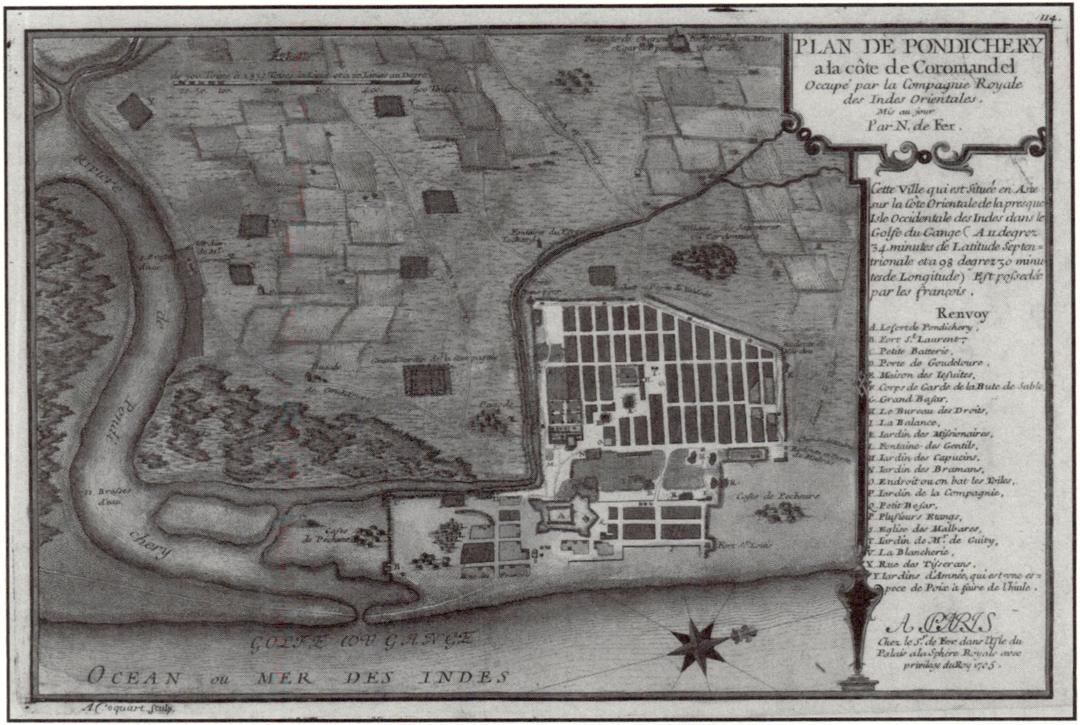

Fig. 10. Pondicherry, 1705. (Collection of the author.)

Over the next twenty-six years, Caillot moved through a series of increasingly important commissions in India. His 1736 marriage to Marie-Claire Lucas placed him on an upward trajectory within the company's Indian Ocean hierarchy.[7] Lucas—who died the year after her marriage and within days of giving birth to Marie-Madeleine, the couple's and Caillot's only child—was the great-niece of Pierre de Saintard.[8] A company syndic from 1723 to 1738 and one of six company directors from 1739 to 1759, Saintard repeatedly used his political power in Paris to secure plum positions for his niece's widower in India. A letter from Paris directors dated January 18, 1738, illuminates the weight of Saintard's power, urging the Superior Council of Pondicherry to "recognize that he [Caillot] is related to M. de Saintard, one of us."[9] Indeed, by the end of the year the council had promoted Caillot from head clerk in Pondicherry to one of four assistant merchant traders in Chandernagore, one of the most prolific textile-producing outposts in the Indian Ocean.

Caillot continued to accumulate status, power, and wealth during the 1740s and 1750s. In 1740 he remarried, this time to Marie-Anne Coquelin, daughter of a company ship captain and widow of a fellow trader.[10] Two years later, Caillot received a commission as director of the Balassor outpost, a provisioning station near the mouth of the Ganges River.[11]

By 1743 Caillot had revived his penchant for selling trade goods on the side, this time in a manner far more spectacular than when he had peddled ribbons and lace as a Louisiana clerk. In a letter from members of the Pondicherry Superior Council to their counterparts in Bengal, council members questioned how it was exactly that "sieur Caillot finds himself the owner of the brig *Cheval Marin*," which appeared to be plying the western limits of the Bay of Bengal.[12] Like many European employees in India, Caillot invested funds earned from his company position into personal ventures in the country trade. Running goods up and down the Ganges and around the Bay of Bengal on his own account increased his wealth and, as a bonus, provided a secure and nimble vessel by which the company could carry correspondence between posts.[13]

Caillot's sole journey back to France took place in December 1744, when he, then seven-year-old Marie-Madeleine, and two domestic servants boarded the six-hundred-ton *Neptune*. They disembarked in Île-de-France before boarding a second ship for Lorient.[14] His second wife did not accompany them. Caillot spent two years in France, tending to his affairs and spending time with family and friends, before returning to India alone. Marie-Madeleine, left in Paris to be raised with relatives, likely never saw her father again.

When he returned to India, the Pondicherry Superior Council acted on recommendations from directors in Paris and named Caillot a supernumerary councillor for the Chandernagore comptoir. This appointment allowed the company to expand the usual number of councillors, keeping the six fully commissioned members at the post and sending Caillot out to command French troops at Cossimbazar, a small comptoir just north of Chandernagore.[15]

In 1750 the Pondicherry council recommended Caillot be granted a permanent seat on the Chandernagore council.[16] It is unclear whether the recommendation stemmed from his effective leadership of troops in engagements against members of the Maratha Confederacy or whether friends in high places pressured administrators in India to promote him. A 1750 report on the company's employees in India, which categorized Caillot as the sort of man who should "never have been promoted above assistant merchant trader," suggests the latter, especially given the writer's assessment that "M. de Maurepas protects him without having examined his capabilities too closely."[17]

Whatever the motivation behind the recommendation, Caillot was still waiting for a permanent seat on the Chandernagore council at the end of 1751. It never came. Instead, in 1752 he ascended for a time to the ranks of the company's highest governing body in the Indian Ocean, the Pondicherry Superior Council.[18]

The Seven Years' War, declared in Europe on May 17, 1756, reached India in January of the following year, when British admiral Charles Watson arrived at the mouth of Bengal's Hugli River with a fleet of twelve ships and forty-five hundred men (twenty-five hundred British and two thousand sepoys) led by Colonel Robert Clive. The British intended to retake Calcutta, its most important trading post, from the local nawab, Siraj ud-Daulah, but soon expanded their aims to the conquest of rival French comptoirs in Bengal.[19] French forces at Chandernagore's dilapidated Fort d'Orléans were vastly outnumbered.[20] On March 23, 1757, just nine days after fighting began, French chief Pierre-

Mathieu Renault capitulated to the British. Caillot and his fellow councillors Fournier, Nicolas, and La Potière signed off on the agreement, as did Admiral Watson. French residents, with the exception of the Jesuits and company directors, for whom an exception was made, were forced to flee the settlement, leaving all of their belongings behind.[21] Governor Georges Duval de Leyrit, writing on March 28, described what took place as a "catastrophe."[22] Indeed, the successes of Clive and Watson spelled an end to the French and the dawn of British imperial presence in Bengal.[23]

Wounded during the siege, Caillot remained in Chandernagore for several months, his stay made possible by the conditions of French surrender.[24] In early 1758, he boarded his last ship, the *Nossa Segnora dos Prazeres* of Portugal. He died at sea on February 24, 1758.[25]

Notes

Abbreviations and Short Titles

ADHS	Archives départementales des Hauts-de-Seine, Nanterre, France
ADLA	Archives départementales de Loire-Atlantique, Nantes, France
ADM	Archives départementales du Morbihan, Vannes, France
ADSM	Archives départementales de Seine-Maritime, Rouen, France
AN	Archives nationales, Paris, France
ANOM	Archives nationales d'outre-mer, Aix-en-Provence, France
AVL	Archives de la ville de Lorient, Lorient, France
BA	Bibliothèque de l'Arsenal, Paris, France
BAnQ	Bibliothèque et Archives nationales de Québec, Quebec City, Canada
BnF	Bibliothèque nationale de France, Paris, France
FML	Fonds de la Marine à Lorient, Service historique de la Défense, Lorient, France
LSM-SCR	Louisiana State Museum, Superior Council Records, New Orleans, La.
MPA	*Mississippi Provincial Archives: French Dominion.* Vols. 2–3, ed. and trans. Dunbar Rowland and A. G. Sanders. Jackson: Press of the Mississippi Department of Archives, 1932. Vols. 4–5, coll., ed., and trans. Dunbar Rowland and A. G. Sanders; rev. and ed. Patricia K. Galloway. Baton Rouge: LSU Press, 1984.
SLC	Records of the Saint Louis Church/Cathedral, Archdiocese of New Orleans, New Orleans, La.
THNOC	The Historic New Orleans Collection, New Orleans, La.

Introduction

1. There are very few studies of the French Company of the Indies and even fewer of the company's role in North America. Only Philippe Haudrère's *La Compagnie française des Indes au XVIIIe siècle, 1719–1795* (Rennes: Éditions Ouest-France, 2005) situates the company in a global context, though Haudrère focuses almost exclusively on the period from 1719 to 1795. On the company in Louisiana, see Pierre Heinrich, *La Louisiane sous la Compagnie des Indes* (Paris: E. Guilmoto, 1908); Marcel Giraud, *A History of French Louisiana*, vol. 5: *The Company of the Indies, 1723–1731*, trans. Brian Pearce (Baton Rouge: LSU Press, 1991); and Cécile Vidal, "French Louisiana in the Age of the Companies, 1712–1731," in *Constructing Early Modern Empires: Proprietary Ventures in the Atlantic World, 1500–1750*, ed. L. H. Roper and B. Van Ruymbeke (Leiden, Netherlands: Brill, 2007), 133–62.

2. Marc-Antoine Caillot, "Relation du voyage de la Louisianne ou Nouv[lle] France fait par le Sr. Caillot en l'année 1730," THNOC, 2005.0011, and *A Company Man: The Remarkable French-Atlantic Journey of a Clerk for the Company of the Indies*, ed. Erin M. Greenwald, trans. Teri F. Chalmers (New Orleans: THNOC, 2013). All further citations of Caillot's memoir come from the 2013 published edition.

3. On the background of the Caillot manuscript, see Erin M. Greenwald, "Introduction," in *Company Man*, xxxiv–xxxviii; Damase Potvin, "Un Intéressant document," *L'Action Catholique*, Quebec, August 28, 1939; Bernard Weilbrenner, "Les Archives du Québec," *Revue d'histoire de l'Amérique française* 3, no. 1 (1964): 9–11; Bernard Weilbrenner to Henry Pitot, April 13, 1967, THNOC, Henry Pitot Papers, MSS 724; Lot 299, *Fine Printed Books and Manuscripts Including Americana*, Christie's New York Auction catalog, December 16, 2004, 138–41; BAnQ, "Note sur les procedures et moyens mis en oeuvre par Bibliothèque et Archives nationales du Québec pour garantir la conservation, la restitution et l'accessibilité des archives (version révisée)," issued February 2011, see esp. sec. 3 in www.banq.qc.ca/documents/a_propos_banq/acces_a_linfo/Note_ministre_2011_02.doc; and Isabelle Paré, "Des documents volés revendues aux enchères," *Le Devoir* (Quebec), November 24, 2011.

4. Laurel Thatcher Ulrich, *A Midwife's Tale: The Life of Martha Ballard, Based on Her Diary, 1785–1812* (New York: Knopf, 1990); Robert Harms, *The Diligent: A Voyage through the Worlds of the Slave Trade* (New York: Basic Books, 2002).

5. Leslie Choquette, "Proprietorships in French North America," in *Constructing Early Modern Empires: Proprietary Ventures in the Atlantic World, 1500–1750*, ed. L. H. Roper and B. Van Ruymbeke (Leiden: Brill, 2007), 130.

6. Shannon Lee Dawdy, *Building the Devil's Empire: French Colonial New Orleans* (Chicago: University of Chicago Press, 2008), 309; Greenwald, "Introduction," *Company Man*, xvi.

7. Robert Darnton, foreword to Jacques-Louis Ménétra, *Journal of My Life*, ed. Daniel Roche, trans. Arthur Goldhammer (New York: Columbia University Press, 1986), viii.

8. Antoine-Simon Le Page du Pratz, *Histoire de la Louisiane*, 3 vols. (Paris: De Bure, 1758). The most thorough survey of Louisiana *histoires* is Germain Joseph Bienvenu, "Another America, Another Literature: Narratives from Louisiana's Colonial Experience" (Ph.D. diss., Louisiana State University, 1995). Published memoirs and personal letters include Pierre-François-Xavier de Charlevoix, *Histoire et description générale de la Nouvelle France* (Paris: Rollin fils, 1744); Jean-François Benjamin Dumont de Montigny and Jean Baptiste Le Mascrier, *Mémoires historiques sur la Louisiane* (Paris: C.J.B. Bauche,

1753); Jean-François Benjamin Dumont de Montigny, *Regards sur le monde atlantique*, ed. Carla Zecher, Gordon M. Sayre, and Shannon Lee Dawdy (Sillery, Quebec: Les Éditions du Septentrion, 2008); Marie-Madeleine Hachard, *Relation du voyage des dames religieuses Ursulines de Roüen, à la Nouvelle Orleans, parties de France le 22. février 1727. & arrivez à la Louisiane le 23. juillet de la même année* (Rouen: Chez A. Le Prévost, 1728), and *Voices from an Early American Convent: Marie Madeleine Hachard and the New Orleans Ursulines, 1727–1760*, ed. Emily Clark (Baton Rouge: LSU Press, 2007); Antoine-François Laval, *Voyage de la Louisiane, fait par ordre du Roy en l'année mil sept cent vingt* (Paris: J. Mariette, 1728); André Pénicault, *Fleur de lys and Calumet: Being the Pénicault Narrative of French Adventure in Louisiana*, ed. and trans. Richebourg Gaillard McWilliams (Tuscaloosa: University of Alabama Press, 1988); Chevalier de Pradel, *Le Chevalier de Pradel: Vie d'un colon français en Louisiane au XVIIIe d'après sa correspondance et celle de sa famille*, ed. A. Baillardel and A. Prioult (Paris: Maisonneuve Frères, 1928); and Valette de Laudun, *Journal d'un voyage à la Louisiane, fait en 1720 par M. ***, capitaine de vaisseau du Roi* (La Haye: Chez Musier fils & Fournier, 1768).

9. On exoticism in colonial accounts, see Gilbert Chinard, *L'Amérique et le rêve exotique dans la littérature française au XVIIe et XVIIIe siècles* (Paris: Société d'éditions "Les Belles Lettres," 1913); and Sophie Linon-Chipon, *Gallia Orientallis: Voyages aux Indes orientales* (Paris: Université de Paris–Sorbonne, 2003).

10. Darnton, foreword to *Journal of My Life*, vii.

11. Although there is a growing historiography centered on nineteenth-century clerks and the administrative and social networks in which they operated, clerks from earlier periods have received little attention. Alexandre Dubé examines the careers of several *employés de la plume* (bureaucrats) operating in the French Atlantic, but after mentioning that an individual *was* a clerk, he focuses chiefly on their experiences in higher-level positions. Dubé, "Making a Career Out of the Atlantic: Louisiana's Plume," in *Louisiana: Crossroads of the Atlantic World*, ed. Cécile Vidal (Philadelphia: University of Pennsylvania Press, 2014), 48–67. For a delineation of the differences between copy clerks (scriviners) and administrative clerks in the Marine, see James Pritchard, *Louis XV's Navy, 1748–1762: A Study of Organization and Administration* (Montreal: Magill-Queen's University Press, 1987), 41–42. On clerks in the nineteenth century, see Thomas Augst, *The Clerk's Tale: Young Men and Moral Life in Nineteenth-Century America* (Chicago: University of Chicago Press, 2003); Michael Zakim, "The Business Clerk as Social Revolutionary; or, a Labor History of the Nonproducing Classes," *Journal of the Early Republic* 26 (2006): 563–602; and Brian Luskey, *On the Make: Clerks and the Quest for Capital in Nineteenth-Century America* (New York: New York University Press, 2010).

12. École des hautes études en sciences sociales, Bibliothèque nationale de France, Centre national de la recherche scientifique, and the Institut national d'études démographiques, eds., *Des villages de Cassini aux communes d'aujourd'hui: Territoires et population, deux siècles d'évolution*, http://cassini.ehess.fr/cassini/fr/html/index.htm (2007), last accessed March 23, 2015.

13. *The Trans-Atlantic Slave Trade: A Database on CD-ROM*, comp. and ed. David Eltis, Steven D. Behrendt, David Richardson, and Herbert S. Klein (Cambridge: Cambridge University Press, 2000), hereafter cited as Eltis, *TASTDB*. Much of the research on the post-1707 French slave trade that appears in the *TASTDB* was originally compiled by Jean Mettas and published as *Répertoire des expeditions négrières françaises au XVIIIe siècle*, vol. 1, ed. Serge Daget and Michèle Daget (Paris: Société française d'histoire d'outremer, 1978 and 1984). The online version of the *TASTDB*, "Voyages: The Trans-Atlantic

Slave Trade Database" (Emory University, 2008–9), includes an additional seven voyages that departed between 1702 and 1706 that were not included in the 2000 edition.

1. The Company in France

1. Robin Law, *The Slave Coast of West Africa, 1550–1750: The Impact of the Atlantic Trade on an African Society* (New York: Oxford University Press, 1991), 116–20.

2. On Portuguese expansion, see A.J.R. Russell-Wood, *A World on the Move: The Portuguese in Africa, Asia, and America, 1415–1808* (New York: St. Martin's Press, 1992), and "The Portuguese Atlantic, 1415–1808," in *Atlantic History: A Critical Appraisal,* ed. Jack P. Greene and Philip D. Morgan (New York: Oxford University Press, 2009), 81–109; Peter C. W. Gutkind, "Trade and Labor in Precolonial African History: The Canoemen of Southern Ghana," in *The Workers of the African Trade,* ed. Catherine Coquery-Vidrovich and Paul E. Lovejoy (London: Sage Publications, 1985), 25–28; Sanjay Subrahmanyam, *The Portuguese Empire in Asia, 1500–1700* (New York: Longman, 1993); Diogo Ramada Curto and Francisco Bethancourt, eds., *Portuguese Oceanic Expansion, 1400–1800* (Cambridge: Cambridge University Press, 2007).

3. Philip Boucher, *Les Nouvelles Frances: France in America, 1500–1815, an Imperial Perspective* (Providence, R.I.: John Carter Brown Library, 1989), 5–12. See also Boucher, *France and the American Tropics to 1700: Tropics of Discontent?* (Baltimore: Johns Hopkins University Press, 2008), 43–47, 48–51; and Jonathan Hart, *Representing the New World: The English and French Uses of the Example of Spain* (New York: Palgrave, 2001), 31–34, 38–43.

4. Choquette, "Proprietorships in French North America," 118–19.

5. The standard reference works on the Dutch and English East India companies remain C. R. Boxer, *The Dutch Seaborne Empire, 1600–1800* (New York: Knopf, 1965); and K. N. Chaudhuri, *The Trading World of Asia and the English East India Company, 1660–1760* (New York: Cambridge University Press, 1978). No comparable comprehensive overview exists for the French company, although Holden Furber's *Rival Empires of Trade in the Orient, 1600–1800* (Minneapolis: University of Minnesota Press, 1976) provides excellent comparative context for all of the major (and a few of the minor) European seventeenth- and eighteenth-century trading companies. The most expansive French-centered study, Haudrère's *La Compagnie française des Indes,* focuses almost exclusively on what Haudrère terms the "second" French Company of the Indies, which operated from 1719 to 1795.

6. Lakshmi Subramanian, editor's introduction to *The French East India Company and the Trade of the Indian Ocean: A Collection of Essays by Indrani Ray* (Calcutta: Center for Studies in Social Science, 1999), xvi.

7. Giorgio Riello, *Cotton: The Fabric That Made the Modern World* (Cambridge: Cambridge University Press, 2013), 23–30, 61–64.

8. Furber, *Rival Empires of Trade,* 38–39, 91.

9. Boucher, *France and the American Tropics,* 17.

10. Paul Cheney, *A Revolutionary Commerce: Globalization and the French Monarchy* (Cambridge: Harvard University Press, 2010), 18.

11. J. Barbier, "La Compagnie française des Indes," *Revue historique de l'Inde française* 3 (1919): 6–8; Furber, *Rival Empires of Trade,* 201–2; Carl H. Sobocinski, "Some God, Little Glory, No Gold: The French on Madagascar in the Seventeenth Century" (Ph.D. diss., University of Toledo, 2001), 39–61; Kenneth J. Banks, *Chasing Empire across the Sea: Com-*

munications and the State in the French Atlantic, 1713–1763 (Montreal: McGill-Queen's University Press, 2002), 15, 17–18, 20–22; Boucher, *France and the American Tropics.*

12. Banks, *Chasing Empire across the Sea,* 16–17. Earlier, privately funded French attempts to establish trading bases on Madagascar are discussed in Sobocinski, "Some God," 49–61.

13. Hubert Deschamps, *Histoire de Madagascar* (Paris: Berger-Levrault, 1965), 63–66.

14. Henriette de Bruyn Kops, *A Spirited Exchange: The Wine and Brandy Trade between France and the Dutch Republic in Its Atlantic Framework, 1600–1650* (Leiden: Brill, 2007).

15. Thomas J. Schaeper, *The French Council of Commerce, 1700–1715: A Study of Mercantilism after Colbert* (Columbus: Ohio State University Press, 1983), 4–5.

16. Cheney, *Revolutionary Commerce,* 28–31.

17. François Charpentier, *Discours d'un fidèle sujet du Roy touchant l'établissement d'une compagnie françoise pour le commerce des Indes Orientales, addressé à tous les François* (Paris, 1665), 26, BnF. To Charpentier's discredit he also tried to sell potential subscribers on the wonders of Madagascar and the benefits of colonizing the island (18–21).

18. Furber, *Rival Empires of Trade,* 104–5; Barbier, "La Compagnie Française," 10.

19. Inès Murat, *Colbert,* trans. Robert Francis Cook and Jeannie Van Asselt (Charlottesville: University Press of Virginia, 1984), 111–12.

20. Kenneth J. Banks, "Financiers, Factors, and French Proprietary Companies in West Africa, 1664–1713," in *Constructing Early Modern Empires: Proprietary Ventures in the Atlantic World, 1500–1750,* ed. L. H. Roper and B. Van Ruymbeke (Leiden: Brill, 2007), 87–91.

21. This remark, made by Colbert on August 3, 1664, at the first meeting of the Council of Trade, is quoted in Murat, *Colbert,* 184; see also 173–74.

22. Ibid., 173–74; Daniel Dessert, *La Royale: Vaisseaux et marins du Roi-Soleil* (Paris: Fayard, 1996); Banks, *Chasing Empire across the Sea,* 23–24; Cheney, *Revolutionary Commerce,* 35–36.

23. Claudia Schnurmann, "'Wherever Profit Leads Us, to Every Sea and Shore . . .': The VOC, the WIC, and Dutch Methods of Globalization in the Seventeenth Century," *Renaissance Studies* 17 (2003): 479–81, 486–92; Jan de Vries, "The Dutch Atlantic Economies," in *The Atlantic Economy during the Seventeenth and Eighteenth Centuries: Organization, Operation, Practice, and Personnel,* ed. Peter A. Coclanis (Columbia: University of South Carolina Press, 2005), 1–30; Henk den Heijer, "The Dutch West India Company, 1621–1791," in *Riches from Atlantic Commerce: Dutch Atlantic Trade and Shipping, 1585–1817* (Boston: Brill, 2003), 77–112; Benjamin Schmidt, "The Dutch Atlantic: From Provincialism to Globalism," in *Atlantic History: A Critical Appraisal,* ed. Jack P. Greene and Philip D. Morgan (New York: Oxford University Press, 2009), 163–87.

24. Boucher, *France and the American Tropics,* 173–85; Jacob Price, *France and the Chesapeake: A History of the French Tobacco Monopoly, 1674–1791, and of Its Relationship to the British and American Tobacco Trades* (Ann Arbor: University of Michigan Press, 1973), 1:78.

25. Boucher, *France and the American Tropics,* 179.

26. On the Dutch and the establishment of sugarcane cultivation and refining in the Caribbean, see Robert Louis Stein, *The French Sugar Business in the Eighteenth Century* (Baton Rouge: LSU Press, 1988), 6–7; and Frederick H. Smith, *Caribbean Rum: A Social and Economic History* (Gainesville: University Press of Florida, 2005), 13–15.

27. Price, *France and the Chesapeake,* 1:5, 78–80, 112–13.

28. Carl J. Ekberg, *The Failure of Louis XIV's Dutch War* (Chapel Hill: University of

North Carolina Press, 1979); John A. Lynn, *The Wars of Louis XIV, 1667–1714* (New York: Longman, 1999), 105–59. On the impact of the Dutch War on French comptoirs in the East Indies, see Glenn J. Ames, *Colbert, Mercantilism, and the French Quest for Asian Trade* (DeKalb: Northern Illinois University Press, 1996); in the West Indies, see Boucher, *France and the American Tropics*, 194–201.

29. Furber, *Rival Empires of Trade*, 105, 113–24, 203–7.

30. Lettres patentes du Roi, "Concession de la Louisiane à M. Crosat pour 10 années," September 14, 1712, in *Recueil d'arrests et autres pieces pour l'établissement de la Compagnie d'Occident* (Amsterdam: Chez Jean Frederic Bernard, 1720), 1–11, in Acts of the Royal French Administration Concerning the Company of the Indies in Louisiana, 1717–71, MSS 268, folder 14, THNOC.

31. Ibid., art. 2; Marcel Giraud, *A History of French Louisiana*, vol. 1: *The Reign of Louis XIV, 1698–1715*, trans. Joseph C. Lambert (Baton Rouge: LSU Press, 1974), 278–79.

32. Gilles Havard and Cécile Vidal, *Histoire de l'Amérique française* (Paris: Flammarion, 2003), 70–72; Boucher, *Les Nouvelles Frances*, 57–60.

33. Ibid. See also James E. Bruseth and Toni S. Turner, *From a Watery Grave: The Discovery and Excavation of La Salle's Shipwreck*, La Belle (College Station: Texas A&M University Press, 2005).

34. John C. Rule, "Jérôme Phélypeaux, Comte de Pontchartrain, and the Establishment of Louisiana, 1696–1715," in *French Men and French Ways in the Mississippi Valley*, ed. John Francis McDermott (Chicago: University of Illinois Press, 1969), 188–94.

35. On these early forts, see Pierre Le Moyne d'Iberville, *Iberville's Gulf Journals*, ed. and trans. Richebourg Gaillard McWilliams (Tuscaloosa: University of Alabama Press, 1981); Maurice Ries, "The Mississippi Fort Called Fort de La Boulaye, 1700–1715: The First French Settlement in Present-Day Louisiana," *Louisiana Historical Quarterly* 19 (October 1936): 829–99; Jay Higgenbotham, *Fort Maurepas: The Birth of Louisiana* (Mobile, Ala.: Colonial Books, 1968), and *Old Mobile: Fort Louis de la Louisiane, 1702–1711* (Tuscaloosa: University of Alabama Press, 1991).

36. Cited in Giraud, *History of French Louisiana*, 1:42.

37. Vidal, "French Louisiana in the Age of the Companies," 137–38.

38. Ibid., 131–40.

39. Bienville to Pontchartrain, August 12 and September 1, 1709, as well as October 27, 1711, ANOM, C13A, fo. 415, 567; Pénicault, *Fleur de lys and Calumet*, 80–97; Daniel Usner, *Indians, Settlers, and Slaves in a Frontier Exchange Economy: The Lower Mississippi Valley before 1783* (Chapel Hill: University of North Carolina Press, 1992), 17–18, 24–26; James F. Barnett Jr., *The Natchez Indians, A History to 1735* (Jackson: University Press of Mississippi, 2007), 51–54, 56–57; Arnaud Balvay, *La Révolte des Natchez* (Paris: Éditions du Félin, 2008), 60–64.

40. Price, *France and the Chesapeake*, 1:55–57; Daniel Dessert, *Argent, pouvoir et société au Grand Siècle* (Paris: Fayard, 1984), 82–107; Fernand Braudel, *L'Identité de la France* (Paris: Arthaud & Flammarion, 1986), 3:401–4.

41. Price, *France and the Chesapeake*, 1:57. Peter Coclanis, in a critique of what he sees as the artificial boundaries drawn by historians of Atlantic history, echoes Price's depiction of early colonial financiers as a cosmopolitan bunch. Coclanis points specifically to the Lords Proprietors of the Carolina colony, who "were nothing if not worldly, involved in financial ventures, adventures, and misadventures stretching from the Indian Ocean to West Africa to the West Indies to the Hudson Bay. Their investments included interests in Tangier, the Northwest Passage, and the Royal Africa Company, whatever and

wherever profits seemed possible." Coclanis, "Atlantic World or Atlantic/World?" *William and Mary Quarterly*, 3rd ser., 63, no. 4 (2006): 729.

42. "Concession de la Louisiane à M. Crosat pour 10 années," in *Recueil d'arrests*, 3, THNOC.

43. Giraud, *History of French Louisiana*, 1:6, 36, 48–50.

44. Ibid., 1:358–66.

45. Antoine de La Mothe de Cadillac to Minister of Marine Jérôme Phélypeaux, comte de Pontchartrain, August 14, 1712, ANOM, C13A 2, fo. 687–89. In the same series, see also Cadillac to Pontchartrain, June 29, 1712, fo. 675–76.

46. Art. 3 of Crozat's charter dealt with mining privileges; see "Concession de la Louisiane à M. Crosat pour 10 années," in *Recueil d'arrests*, THNOC.

47. Baron, *Mémoire des observations*, 1714, cited in Giraud, *History of French Louisiana*, 1:359.

48. Alan Gallay, *The Indian Slave Trade: The Rise of the English Empire in the American South, 1670–1717* (New Haven, Conn.: Yale University Press, 2002), 308–10; Usner, *Indians, Settlers, and Slaves*, 56–59; Barnett, *Natchez Indians*, 28–32; Brett Rushforth, *Bonds of Alliance: Indigenous and Atlantic Slaveries in New France* (Chapel Hill: University of North Carolina Press, 2012), 163–64, 238–41.

49. Art. 8, "Concession de la Louisiane à M. Crosat pour 10 années," in *Recueil d'arrests*, THNOC.

50. Vidal, "French Louisiana in the Age of the Companies," 139–40.

51. Giraud, *History of French Louisiana*, 1:165, 260–63, 271–73, and *A History of French Louisiana*, vol. 2: *Years of Transition, 1715–1717*, trans. Brian Pearce (Baton Rouge: LSU Press, 1993), 42–47.

52. Jean-Baptiste du Bois Duclos to Jérôme Phélypeaux, comte de Pontchartrain, October 25, 1713, ANOM, C13A, fo. 216–17.

53. Gallay, *Indian Slave Trade*, 289.

54. Art. 8, "Concession de la Louisiane à M. Crosat pour 10 années," in *Recueil d'arrests*, THNOC.

55. Price, *France and the Chesapeake*, 1:203–4.

56. "Lettres patentes sur l'arrest concernant le Commerce de la Nouvelle Colonie de la Louisiane," August 26, 1718, *Recueil d'arrests*, THNOC.

57. Claude Nières, *Histoire de Lorient* (Toulouse: Privat, 1988), 26–28.

58. Paul Kaeppelin, *La Compagnie des Indes Orientales et François Martin* (Paris: A. Challamel, 1908), 320–22; Aniruddha Ray, "Establishment of the French Factory at Patna," *Proceedings of the Indian History Congress: Millenium Session, Kolkata 2000–2001* (Kolkata: Kolkata Indian History Congress, 2001), 413–23.

59. Furber, *Rival Empires of Trade*, 116–23; Kaeppelin, *La Compagnie des Indes*, 320–22; Glenn J. Ames and Ronald S. Love, eds., *Distant Lands and Diverse Cultures: The French Experience in Asia, 1600–1700* (Westport, Conn.: Greenwood Press, 2003).

60. Idrani Ray, "The French Company and the Merchants of Bengal," *The French East India Company and the Trade of the Indian Ocean* (Calcutta: Munshiram Manoharlal, 1999), 77–87; K. N. Chaudhuri, *Trade and Civilisation in the Indian Ocean: An Economic History from the Rise of Islam to 1750* (Cambridge: Cambridge University Press, 1985), 74, 93–94.

61. Jacques Cellard, *John Law et la Régence* (Paris: Plon, 1996), 33–41; Antoin E. Murphy, *John Law: Economic Theorist and Policy Maker* (Oxford: Oxford University Press, 1997), 14–122; Harms, *The Diligent: A Voyage*, 44–46.

62. Murphy, *John Law,* 37–41.

63. Ibid., 41.

64. John Law, *Money and Trade Considered with a Proposal for Supplying the Nation with Money* (Edinburgh: Andrew Anderson, 1705); Murphy, *John Law,* 69–75; Charles W. J. Withers, *Geography, Science, and National Identity: Scotland Since 1520* (Cambridge: Cambridge University Press, 2001), 104–8.

65. For a detailed overview of France's monetary system and financial dilemmas—including the state's reliance on a handful of powerful financiers such as Crozat to keep the treasury afloat—during the reign of Louis XIV, see Dessert, *Argent, pouvoir et société.*

66. Murphy, *John Law,* 112–15.

67. Ibid., 128.

68. *Lettres patentes du Roi portant privilege en faveur du Sr. Law & sa compagnie, d'establir une banque générale,* May 2, 1716 (Paris: Imprimerie Royal, 1716), John Law Collection, MSS 606, folder 144, THNOC.

69. Price, *France and the Chesapeake,* 1:208, 304–7.

70. Art. 2, 4, 7, *Lettres patentes en forme d'édit, pourtant établissement d'une Compagnie de Commerce sous le nom de Compagnie d'Occident,* August 1717 (Paris: Chez la Veuve de François Muguet, Hubert Muguet, Premier Imprimeur du Roy, & Loüis-Denis de La Tour Libraire, 1717), Acts of the Royal French Administration Concerning the Company of the Indies in Louisiana, 1717–71, MSS 268, folder 1, THNOC.

71. Established by Louis XIV in September 1674, the tobacco farm was not a farm in the traditional sense but was instead a designation that granted monopoly holders exclusive rights to the distribution of any and all tobacco—regardless of the crop's origin—within France, plus an annual revenue of four million livres. Prior to 1718 the tobacco farm had been held by a group of prominent financiers, Antoine Crozat among them. Price, *France and the Chesapeake,* 1:21–22, 55, 245–51; "Édit concernant la ferme générale du tabac," September 1718, and "Arrest du conseil d'Estat du Roi," September 4, 1718, in *Recueil d'arrests,* THNOC.

72. Murphy, *John Law,* 185–86; Haudrère, *La Compagnie française des Indes,* 1:45.

73. See art. 2, "Arrest du Conseil d'Estat du Roy concernant la réunion des Compagnies des Indes Orientales et de la Chine à la Compagnie d'Occident," June 17, 1719, and "Édit par lequel S. M. fait fournir 25 millions de sa banque à la Compagnie d'Occident," in *Recueil d'arrests,* THNOC. Haudrère, *La Compagnie française des Indes,* 1:48–49.

74. Marcel Giraud, *Histoire de la Louisiane française,* Vol. 3: *Époque de John Law, 1717–1720* (Paris: Presse Universitaire de France, 1966), 136–53; Choquette, "Proprietorships in French North America," 127–28.

75. "Le Commerce que les Indiens du Mexique font avec les François au port de Missisipi" (Paris: François-Gérard Jollain, 1719–21), THNOC, 1952.3.

76. "Geographische Beschreibung der Provinz Louisiana in Canada von dem Fluß St. Lorenz bis an den Ausfluß des Flusses Missisipi" and "Novissima Tabula Regionis Gallice dictae La Louisiane" (Liepzig: Christoph Weigel, 1720), THNOC, 1978.211.1–2.

77. Murphy, *John Law,* 200.

78. Ibid., 214–17.

79. Ibid., 218–87.

80. Haudrère, *La Compagnie française des Indes,* 1:41–42, 52–53.

81. René Estienne, *Les Armements au long cours de la deuxième Compagnie des Indes, 1717–1773* (Lorient: Service historique de la Marine, 1996), 15–18.

82. In an arrêt dated June 3, 1720, the directors claimed to have put together a fleet

of 105 ships, not counting brigantines and frigates, but historians Marcel Giraud and Philippe Haudrère find that number implausible. Giraud, based on an inventory taken in 1724, estimates the number of ships to have been no greater than 75. See Giraud, *Histoire de la Louisiane française,* 3:104. Haudrère, *La Compagnie française des Indes,* 1:52.

83. Estienne, *Les Armements,* 18–21.

84. Haudrère, *La Compagnie française des Indes,* 1:86.

85. "Arrest du Conseil d'État du Roy, qui forme le Conseil de la Compagnie des Indes, & fixe le dividende des actions," March 24, 1723, and "Arrest du Conseil d'État du Roy, qui nomme des commissaires pour juger les demandes & contestations où la Compagnie des Indes sera partie," May 3, 1723, Dernis, *Recueil, ou Collection des titres, édits, déclarations, arrêts, réglemens et autres pièces concernant la Compagnie des Indes établie au mois d'août 1664* (Paris: Antoine Boudet, 1755–56), 3:528–32, 533–34, BnF.

86. "Arrest du Conseil d'État du Roy, pour indiquer une assemblée de la Compagnie des Indes, à l'effet de procéder à l'élection de huit syndics" and "Arrest qui regle la forme de l'administration de la Compagnie des Indes," August 30, 1723, ibid., 542–43, 544–50.

87. In the seventeenth century the building was part of the Palais Mazarin. It is now part of the Bibliothèque nationale de France's site Richelieu. Simon Balayé, *La Bibliothèque nationale des origines à 1800* (Geneva: Librairie Droz, 1988), 184–85.

88. Haudrère, *La Compagnie française des Indes,* 1:153–54, 156.

89. See "Arrest du Conseil d'État du Roy, qui ordonne que les commis & employés de la Compagnie des Indes pour l'exploitation des priviléges du tabac & du caffé, procéderont aux visites & exécutions au sujet des toiles peintes et étoffes des Indes, de la Chine & du Levant," Dernis, *Recueil ou collection,* 596–99; and Philippe Haudrère, "Le Commerce," in *L'Inde et la France: Deux siècles d'histoire commune, XVIIe–XVIIIe siècles,* ed. Philippe Le Tréguilly and Monique Morazé (Paris: CNRS éditions, 1995), 26–27.

90. Natacha Coquery, *L'Hôtel aristocratique: Le Marché du luxe à Paris au XVIIIe siècle* (Paris: Publications de la Sorbonne, 1998), 103.

91. Haudrère, *La Compagnie française des Indes,* 1:155.

92. John Thornton, *Africa and Africans in the Making of the Atlantic World, 1400–1800* (Cambridge: Cambridge University Press, 1998), 48–53; Paul E. Lovejoy, *Transformations in Slavery: A History of Slavery in Africa* (Cambridge: Cambridge University Press, 2012), 103–6; Philip D. Curtin, *Economic Change in Precolonial Africa: Senegambia in the Era of the Slave Trade* (Madison: University of Wisconsin Press, 1975), 1:237–40, 319–21.

93. "Régie du commerce à Paris" and "Tableau de la direction générale de la Comp. des Indes à Paris," ANOM, C2 284, fo. 14, 22.

94. Haudrère, *La Compagnie française des Indes,* 1:157.

95. Company directors in Paris issued orders to relocate the capital from Biloxi to New Orleans on December 23, 1721, but the directive did not arrive in Biloxi until May 1722. Lawrence N. Powell, *The Accidental City: Improvising New Orleans* (Cambridge: Harvard University Press, 2012), 57–58.

96. Caillot, "Relation du voyage."

97. All birth and death data on the Caillot family comes from ADHS, Parish registers of Meudon, Mi/MEU_7.

98. Jacqueline Boucher, "L'Évolution de la Maison du Roi: Des derniers Valois aux premiers Bourbons," *Dix-Septième siècle* 34 (1982): 359–79; Christophe Blanquie, "Dans la main du grand maître: Les Offices de la Maison du Roi," *Histoire et Mesure* 13 (1998): 243–88; Sophie de Laverny, *Les Domestiques commensaux du Roi de France au XVIIe siècle* (Paris: Presses Universitaires de Paris–Sorbonne, 2002).

99. Sharon Kettering, "Patronage and Kinship in Early Modern France," *French Historical Studies* 16 (1989): 418, and *Patrons, Brokers, and Clients in Seventeenth-Century France* (New York: Oxford University Press, 1986).

100. Laverny, *Les Domestiques commensaux*, 84–88, 105–35.

101. William Doyle, *Venality: The Sale of Offices in Eighteenth-Century France* (Oxford: Clarendon Press, 1996), 65.

102. AN, O^1 3715, fo. 154.

103. Jean-Pierre Gutton, *Domestiques et serviteurs dans la France de l'ancien régime* (Paris: Aubier Montaigne, 1981), 46; Sarah Maza, *Servants and Masters in Eighteenth-Century France: The Uses of Loyalty* (Princeton: Princeton University Press, 1983), 208–9; Kettering, *Patrons, Brokers, and Clients*, 214–24.

104. On the status of the château de Meudon between the time of the dauphin's 1711 death and Marc-Antoine's mid-1720s departure for Paris, see Paul Biver, *Histoire du château de Meudon* (Paris: Jouve & Co., 1923), 244–90.

105. ADHS, ser. 4 E, Régistres paroissiaux, Meudon and AN, Minutier central des notaires, Inventory of François Caillot, March 30, 1751, étude LXVIII, liasse 442; ARNO 1761, Quittance, Marc-Antoine Caillot, côte ET XXXV 708; and ser. O^1 Maison du Roi, carton 670, Pensions de la Maison du Roi.

2. Approaching the Atlantic World

1. James Pritchard, *In Search of Empire: The French in the Americas, 1670–1730* (New York: Cambridge University Press, 2004), 16–28; Laurent Dubois, "The French Atlantic," in *Atlantic History: A Critical Appraisal*, ed. Jack P. Greene and Philip D. Morgan (New York: Oxford University Press, 2009), 139–42; Peter N. Moogk, "Reluctant Exiles: Emigrants from France in Canada before 1760," *William and Mary Quarterly*, 3rd ser., 46 (1989): 463–505.

2. The perceived havoc wrought by the failure of both the Crown and charter companies to attract sizable numbers of stable colonists to Louisiana has been well documented in James D. Hardy Jr., "The Transportation of Convicts to Colonial Louisiana," *Louisiana History* 7 (1966): 207–20; Mathé Allain, "L'Immigration française en Louisiane," *Revue d'histoire de l'Amérique française XXVIII* (1975): 559–64, and "Manon Lescaut et Ses Consoeurs: Women in the Early French Period, 1700–1731," in *Proceedings of the Fifth Meeting of the French Colonial Historical Society*, ed. James J. Cooke (Lanham, Md.: French Colonial Historical Society, 1980), 18–26; Giraud, *Histoire de la Louisiane française*, 3:176–82; Shannon Dawdy, "La Ville Sauvage: 'Enlightened' Colonialism and Creole Improvisation in New Orleans, 1699–1769" (Ph.D. diss., University of Michigan, 2003), 33, 178–79, 203–5. On *lettres de cachet*, see Dawdy, *Building the Devil's Empire*, 151; and Brian Strayer, *Lettres de Cachet and Social Control in the Ancien Regime, 1659–1789* (New York: Peter Lang, 1992).

3. See, e.g., observations by Dumont de Montigny in *Regards sur le monde atlantique*, 83; Caillot, *Company Man*, 81; and Bienville to the Ministry of the Marine, October 20, 1719, ANOM, C13A 5, fo. 276v.

4. "État général des personnes embarquées à La Rochelle pour la Louisiane sur la *Dauphine*, le *Neptune* et la *Vigilante*," October 25, 1717; "Rôle des personnes embarquées pour la Louisiane," March 3, 1719, ANOM, F5B 57, fo. 20 and G1 464, no. 9.

5. "État des passagers embarqués sur le vaisseau la *Durance*," March 15, 1729, ANOM,

F5B 49, fo. 38; "Commission, Teneur de Livres à la Louisianne pour le Sr. de Bussy," January 27, 1729, ANOM, B43b, fo. 845.

6. Georges Livet, "La Route royale et la civilisation française de la fin du XVe au milieu du XVIIIe siècle," in *Les Routes de France: depuis les origines jusqu'à nos jours*, ed. Guy Michaud (Paris: L'Association pour la diffusion de la pensée française, 1959), 57–100; René Héron de Villefosse, *Histoire des grandes routes de France* (Paris: Librairie Académique Perrin, 1975), 17–223; Fernand Braudel, *Civilization and Capitalism, 15th–18th Century: The Structures of Everyday Life* (Berkeley: University of California Press, 1992), 424–30.

7. Murat, *Colbert*, 156–59.

8. Banks, *Chasing Empire across the Sea*, 52–56.

9. Caillot, *Company Man*, 1.

10. Ibid., 2.

11. Ibid. Caillot's hunting horn (*corps*, or *trompe de chasse*) was likely an early, valve-free example of what is generally known as a French horn.

12. Livet, "La Route royale et la civilisation française," 71.

13. Caillot, *Company Man*, 9.

14. Conversions of eighteenth-century units of measurement into their modern equivalents are derived from Russell Rowlett and the University of North Carolina at Chapel Hill's online resource, "How Many: A Dictionary of Units of Measurement," www.unc.edu/~rowlett/units/index.html (2004) (last accessed 2009–14).

15. Claude-Marin Saugrain's 1720 *Nouveau voyage de France* is one of the first descriptive travel guides to France written with business- (merchants, administrators, farmers, etc.) as well as leisure-travelers in mind. Saugrain provides distances between notable towns, villages, and cities, not in *lieues* but *postes*. See Saugrain, *Nouveau voyage de France, géographique, historique et curieux, disposé par différentes routes, à l'usage des étrangers et des François, contenant une exacte explication de tout ce qu'il y a de singulier et de rare à voir dans ce royaume* (Paris: Saugrain l'aîné, 1720), BnF.

16. Caillot, *Company Man*, 3.

17. Saugrain, *Nouveau voyage de France*, 341–42. Descriptions of the route (on land and water) found throughout this chapter benefited greatly from consultation of *La Carte générale de la France*, better known as *La Carte de Cassini*, which consists of 180 sheets of extraordinarily detailed maps of France, with each sheet acting as one quadrant in the larger map. The Cassini maps, published beginning in the mid-eighteenth century, include the standard topographical and location details, but they also identify roads by type, windmills, parishes, churches, homes of nobles, courthouses, postes, and many other notable features of a given region. The Cassini maps can be accessed online through "Des villages de Cassini aux communes d'aujourd'hui," a website developed in institutional partnership with the Bibliothèque nationale de France (where the originals are deposited), École des hautes études en sciences sociales, Centre national de la recherche scientifique, and Institut national d'études démographiques. http://cassini.ehess.fr/cassini/fr/html/index.htm.

18. The town Caillot referred to as Saint-Marc was Saint-Mars-la Brière, often abbreviated Saint-Mars (St. Mars) and less frequently Saint-Marc (St. Marc).

19. Caillot, *Company Man*, 3.

20. Even working-class Parisians, such as the journeyman-glazier Jacques-Louis Ménétra, enjoyed special treatment when traveling the French countryside by individuals eager to hear about life in Paris. Ménétra, *Journal of My Life*, 61, 74.

21. Caillot, *Company Man*, 4.

22. Ibid.

23. Ibid., 5.

24. "Filled with young people," ibid., 6; "straight, expansive" and "well-built houses," Saugrain, *Nouveau voyage de France*, 318.

25. Saugrain, *Nouveau voyage de France*, 319.

26. Saugrain, unpaginated preface, *Nouveau voyage de France* and Jean Aymar Piganiol de La Force, *Nouveau voyage de France avec un itinéraire et des cartes faites exprès qui marquent exactement les routes qu'il faut suivre pour voyager dans toutes les provinces de ce royaume* (Paris: T. Le Gras, 1724), 116, BnF.

27. Caillot, *Company Man*, 6.

28. Ibid.

29. Ibid., 6–7.

30. Thomas Kavanagh, "The Libertine's Bluff: Cards and Culture in Eighteenth-Century France," *Eighteenth Century Studies* 33 (2000): 505–8.

31. René Favier, "Jouer dans les villes de province en France au XVIIIe siècle," *Histoire urbaine* 1 (2000): 69.

32. Ibid., 72–73.

33. Dumont de Montigny, *Regards sur le monde atlantique*, 55, 348. Dumont de Montigny's much-edited account was originally published with Jean-Baptiste Le Mascrier as *Mémoires historiques sur la Louisiane* (Paris: C.J.B. Bauche, 1753). See also Dawdy, *Building the Devil's Empire*, 51–52.

34. Caillot, *Company Man*, 3. For Caillot's references to Don Quixote ("Don Guichot") and Sancho Panza, see also 2, 26, 73.

35. Olivier Grussi, *La Vie quotidienne des joueurs sous l'Ancien Régime*, 210–12; and Favier, "Jouer dans les villes," 66.

36. Caillot, *Company Man*, 7–8.

37. Ibid., 8. "Brusquembille" in Alembert, Bossut, La Lande, Condorcet, and Charles, *Encyclopédie Méthodique. Dictionnaire des jeux, faisant suite au tome III des Mathématiques* (Paris: Chez Panckoucke, 1789), 31–33.

38. Caillot, *Company Man*, 8.

39. Ibid., 9

40. Ibid., 9–11.

41. Ibid.

42. Piganiol de La Force, *Nouveau voyage*, 91–92; Gaston Martin, "Nantes et la Compagnie des Indes, 1664–1769," *Revue d'histoire économique et sociale* 15 (1927): 50.

43. Saugrain, *Nouveau voyage*, 326.

44. Martin, "Nantes et la Compagnie des Indes," 64.

45. Caillot, *Company Man*, 11.

46. Ibid., 12.

47. André Perret, "René Montaudoin, armateur et négrier nantais (1673–1731)," *Bulletin de la Société Archéologique et Historique de Nantes et de la Loire-Inférieur* 88 (1949): 86–94. Olivier Pétré-Grenouilleau provides an overview of Nantes's seventeenth-century entry into commerce with France's Caribbean colonies in *Nantes au temps de la traite des Noirs* (Paris: Hachette, 1998), 25–44. See also Gabriel Debien and Louis Merle, "Colons, marchands et engagés à Nantes au XVIIe siècle," *Revue de la Porte Océane* (December 1953): 5–8, (January 1954): 7–15.

48. Liliane Crété, *La Traite des nègres sous l'Ancien Régime* (Paris: Perrin, 1989), 48–49. On the social and economic advancement of Nantais merchants via the slave trade, see Pétré-Grenouilleau, *Nantes au temps de la traite*, 124–31. Jean-Michel Deveau provides an overview of the largest slavers in France from Nantes, Le Havre, Saint-Malo, La Rochelle, Honfleur, and Bordeaux in *La France au temps des négriers* (Paris: France-Empire, 1994), 88. The broad contours of the French transatlantic slave trade are addressed in Gaston Martin, *L'Ère des négriers (1717–1774)* (Paris: Karlatha, 1933); Crété, *La Traite des nègres;* Robert Stein, *The French Slave Trade in the Eighteenth Century: An Old Regime Business* (Madison: University of Wisconsin Press, 1979); David Geggus, "The French Atlantic Slave Trade: An Overview," *William and Mary Quarterly*, 3rd ser., 58 (2001): 119–38; and Olivier Pétré-Grenouilleau, *Les Traites négrières* (Paris: Éditions Gallimard, 2004). See also chap. 4, "Merchants and Slaves: Slavery on Saint Louis and Gorée," in James F. Searing, *West African Slavery and Atlantic Commerce: The Senegal River Valley, 1700–1860* (Cambridge: Cambridge University Press, 1993), 93–128.

49. Schaeper, *French Council of Commerce*, 55–56.

50. Harms, *The Diligent: A Voyage*, 33–35; Furber, *Rival Empires of Trade*, 203–4.

51. Harms, *The Diligent: A Voyage*, 35. Analytical data on the Nantais slave trade is based on voyage stats provided by Eltis, *TASTDB*.

52. Harms, *The Diligent: A Voyage*, 37.

53. *Lettres patentes du Roy pour la liberté du commerce de la coste de Guinée*, January 1716, ADLA, ser. C 740.

54. Pétré-Grenouilleau, *Nantes au temps de la traite*, 58–59.

55. Eltis, *TASTDB*.

56. Harms, *The Diligent: A Voyage*, 51–54, 57–61.

57. Johannes Postma, "A Monopoly Relinquished: The West India Company and the Atlantic Slave Trade," *De Halve maen* 70 (1997): 84–85.

58. Eltis, *TASTDB*.

59. Nières, *Histoire de Lorient*, 66; Léon Vignols and Henri Sée, "Les Ventes de la Compagnie des Indes à Nantes, 1723–1733," *Revue de l'histoire des colonies françaises* 13 (1925): 494, 527; Martin, "Nantes et la Compagnie des Indes," 49–50.

60. Vignols and Sée, "Les Ventes de la Compagnie," 525–26; Martin, "Nantes et la Compagnie des Indes," 45, 47.

61. Quoted in Martin, "Nantes et la Compagnie des Indes," 53.

62. Quoted in Haudrère, *La Compagnie française des Indes*, 1:176. See also Vignols and Sée, "Les Ventes de la Compagnie," 496–97.

63. Caillot, *Company Man*, 13.

64. Nières, *Histoire de Lorient*, 7–16; Gérard Le Bouëdec, "Un Chantier de construction navale," *Les Compagnies des Indes* (Rennes: Éditions Ouest-France, 2005), 20–22.

65. The elision of the town name from L'Orient to Lorient occurs throughout the eighteenth century, depending on the source, but the permanent name change took place sometime in the late eighteenth century.

66. Nières, *Histoire de Lorient*, 26–28.

67. Le Bouëdec, "Un Chantier de construction navale," 18–20.

68. Estienne, *Les Armements*, 15–24.

69. Nières, *Histoire de Lorient*, 79.

70. Ibid., 90–103; Le Bouëdec, "Du chantier à la ville nouvelle," *Les Compagnies des Indes* (Rennes: Éditions Ouest-France, 2005), 105.

71. Nières, *Histoire de Lorient,* 64–66; Commandant Vernay (Lorient) to the Marine de Ponant, 1731, AN, B3 344, fo. 166.

72. Usner, *Indians Settlers and Slaves,* 60–65, 191–214.

73. Martin, "Nantes et la Compagnie des Indes," 29–36; Marcel Giraud, *A History of French Louisiana,* vol. 5: "The Company of the Indies, 1723–1731," trans. Brian Pearce (Baton Rouge: LSU Press, 1991), 4–5; Nières, *Histoire de Lorient,* 30–31.

74. Jacques de La Chaise to the Directors of the Company of the Indies, September 6, 1723, *Mississippi Provincial Archives: French Dominion* (hereafter *MPA*), ed. and trans. Dunbar Rowland and A. G. Sanders (Jackson: Mississippi Department of Archives and History, 1929), 2:327–28.

75. Étienne Périer and Jacques de La Chaise to the Directors of the Company of the Indies, April 22, 1727, *MPA,* 2:538.

76. Ibid., November 24, 1727, *MPA,* 2:579.

77. Dawdy, *Building the Devil's Empire,* 103–7, 115–18; Giraud, *History of French Louisiana,* 5:115–18, 144–59.

78. Étienne Périer and Jacques de La Chaise to the Directors of the Company of the Indies, April 22, 1727, *MPA,* 2:538.

79. Ibid., July 31, 1728, *MPA,* 2:578–79.

80. For 1722, the year the colonial capital was physically moved from New Biloxi to New Orleans, both posts and Ship Island were included in the totals. For 1728 the numbers reflect employees assigned to New Orleans and the Balize. Minutes of the Louisiana Superior Council, April 21, 1722, *MPA,* 2:268–71; "État général des dépenses qui doivent se faire à la Louisianne pendant l'année 1728," ANOM, B43b, fo. 770.

81. "État de ce qui est dû aux employéz de la Compagnie des Indes au port de L'orient, 1729," FML 1P 250, liasse 31; "État général de la dépense annuelle pour Pondicherry, 1728," ANOM, C2 20, fo. 88; "État général des dépenses de la Compagnie des Indes à la Louisianne pour l'année 1729," ANOM, B43b, fo. 821–36.

82. Étienne Périer and Jacques de La Chaise to the Directors of the Company of the Indies, November 24, 1727, July 31 and November 3, 1728, and August 26, 1729, *MPA,* 2:578, 594–95, 665–66.

83. Quoted in Haudrère, *La Compagnie française des Indes,* 1:176.

84. Caillot, *Company Man,* 15.

85. André Bachelier, "noble homme," is listed as the inn's proprietor in "Extrait du debis et des octrois deues pour Roi par les hôtes et cabaretiers du department de Lorient pendant Mai et Juin 1740," AVL, CC Finances et contributions, 1724–92.

86. The amount of Caillot's clerk's salary is based on two sources: the average annual salary paid to bookkeeping and warehouse clerks in the Louisiana colony for the years 1728 and 1729; and a 1:2.5 ratio between the salaries paid to Caillot, a clerk, versus that paid to Bussy, a commissioned bookkeeper, whose annual salary totaled 1,500 livres. Upon arrival in Lorient, company employees bound for Louisiana received a two-month salary advance from the outfitting office. Bussy received 250 livres, Caillot 100. "État général des dépenses qui doivent se faire à la Louisianne pendant l'année 1728" and "État général des dépenses qui doivent se faire à la Louisianne pendant l'année 1729," ANOM, B43b, fo. 770 and fo. 821; "Commission, teneur de livres à la Louisianne pour le Sr. de Bussy," January 27, 1729, fo. 845; "État des passagers embarqués sur le vaisseau la *Durance,*" March 15, 1729, ANOM, F5B 49, fo. 38.

87. Father Nicole-Ignace de Beaubois to Monsieur de la Loë, November 2, 1726, *Jesuit Relations and Allied Documents: Travels and Relations of the Jesuit Missionaries in New*

France, 1610–1791, ed. Reuben Gold Thwaites (Cleveland: Burrows Brothers, 1900), 67:264.

88. Caillot, *Company Man*, 15.

3. Tropical Baptisms

1. This chapter and the technical terms employed herein benefited greatly from the use of William Falconer's classic reference work, *An Universal Dictionary of the Marine: Or, a Copious Explanation of the Technical Terms and Phrases Employed in the Construction, Equipment, Furniture, Machinery, Movements, and Military Operations of a Ship* (London: T. Cadel, 1776); and Nicolas Aubin, *Dictionnaire de marine contenant les termes de la navigation et de l'architecture navale* (Amsterdam: Chez P. Brunel, 1702).

2. *Duc de Chartres* armement, 1729, FML, 1 P 168; Comte de Volvire to the Marine de Ponant, March 18, 1729, AN, Marine, B3 330, fo. 17–20.

3. This figure is based on a survey of circuits completed by ships leaving France for the East Indies between January 1, 1725, and December 31, 1730. Of the eighteen ships surveyed, six completed the circuit in eighteen months, two each in nineteen, twenty, twenty-one, or twenty-five months, and one each in fourteen, sixteen, twenty-eight, or forty-two months. The 1729 expedition of the *Duc de Chartres* (included in the survey) took twenty-five months. Estienne, *Les Armements*, 25–30; *Duc de Chartres* disarmament, 1731, FML, 1 P 168.

4. Philippe Haudrère and Gérard Le Bouëdec, *Les Compagnies des Indes* (Rennes: Éditions Ouest-France, 2005), 35–37; Haudère, "Le Commerce," *L'Inde et la France*, 25.

5. Stanley B. Alpern, "What Africans Got for Their Slaves: A Master List of European Trade Goods," *History in Africa* 22 (1995): 5–43; Jan Hogendorn and Marion Johnson, *The Shell Money of the Slave Trade* (Cambridge: Cambridge University Press, 1986); Jeffrey P. Brain, *Tunica Treasure* (Cambridge: Peabody Museum of Archaeology and Ethnology, Harvard University, and Peabody Museum of Salem, 1979), 222; Sophie White, *Wild Frenchmen and Frenchified Indians: Material Culture and Race in Colonial Louisiana* (Philadelphia: University of Pennsylvania Press, 2012), 62–70, 193–94.

6. *Espérance* armement, 1729, FML, 1 P 168.

7. Boubacar Barry, *Senegambia and the Atlantic Slave Trade* (New York: Cambridge University Press, 1998), 46–50, 72–73; Ibrahima Seck, "The Relationship between Saint-Louis of Senegal, Its Hinterlands, and Colonial Louisiana," in *French Colonial Louisiana and the Atlantic World*, ed. Bradley Bond (Baton Rouge: LSU Press, 2005), 265–69; Philip D. Curtain, *Economic Change in Precolonial Africa: Senegambia in the Era of the Slave Trade*, (Madison: University of Wisconsin Press, 1975), 112–14; Banks, "Financiers, Factors, and French Proprietary Companies," 83–84; André Delcourt, *La France et les établissements français au Sénégal entre 1713 et 1763* (Dakar: Institut français de l'Afrique noire, 1952); Jean-Bernard Lacroix, *Les Français au Sénégal au temps de la Compagnie des Indes de 1719 à 1758* (Vincennes: Service historique de la Marine, 1986); Haudrère, *La Compagnie française des Indes*, 1:198–201; Gwendolyn Midlo Hall, *Africans in Colonial Louisiana: The Development of Afro-Creole Culture in the Eighteenth Century* (Baton Rouge: LSU Press, 1992), 32–33.

8. Estienne, *Les Armements*, 28; Eltis, *TASTDB*; Maurepas's recommendations and company responses found in "Commerce de Guinée"; "Extrait de deux mémoires presentés au nom des actionnaires sur le commerce de Guinée et des reponses des directeurs de la compagnie article par article à ces deux mémoires"; " Extrait du 1er et 2e mémoires

des actionnaires"; and "Mémoire sur la manière dont la Compagnie des Indes peut exercer son privilege en Guinée, en cas qu'elle ne continue pas à le faire en entier par elle-même," AN, M 1026, cited in Harms, *The Diligent: A Voyage*, 423 n. 5.

9. Maurepas to Robin, March 15, 1728, ANOM, C2 20, fo. 14.

10. The ordinance passed on August 8, 1725, required private merchants to pay a twenty-livre per head commission, but a revised ordinance issued July 3, 1726, lowered the sum to ten livres per head. ANOM, F2a 12, fo. 397–400 and C6 23; Haudrère, *La Compagnie française des Indes*, 1:265; Harms, *The Diligent: A Voyage*, 55–61.

11. "Armements des vaisseaux et autres bâtiments de la Compagnie des Indes," 1729, FML, 2 P 2, III.

12. Estienne, *Les Armements*, 15–28.

13. Haudrère, *La Compagnie française des Indes*, 1:193; Gerard Le Bouëdec, "Un Chantier de construction navale," *Les Compagnies des Indes* (Rennes: Éditions Ouest-France, 2005), 30–31.

14. Estienne, *Les Armements*, 28; Eltis, *TASTDB*.

15. Haudrère, *La Compagnie française des Indes*, 1:331–32.

16. Ship's passenger registers for the *Durance*, 1721 and 1725, FML, 2P 20-IV.5, 1P 166–66; "État des familles allemandes qui sont embarquées sur le vau. de la Compagnie des Indes la Durance pour passer à la Louisianne," April 23, 1721, ANOM, G1 464, no. 60; "États par vaisseaux des officiers, officiers mariniers, et matelots decedés ou noyés de 1721 à 1770," *Duc de Bourbon*, 1731, FML, 2 P 20, 1 P 45–166, 1 P 246, liasse 2; and "Extrait du Registre général des deliberations prises dans les Comitez Generaux et particuliers," June 27, 1727, ANOM, C2 277, fo. 20.

17. *Durance* armement, 1729, FML, 1 P 244.

18. Susan Read Baker, "Nautical Fare in Robert Challe's *Journal d'un voyage fait aux Indes orientales* (1690–1691)," *Cahiers du dix-septième: An Interdisciplinary Journal* 9 (2004): 22–24; Nières, *Histoire de Lorient*, 37.

19. Caillot, *Company Man*, 40

20. Étienne Périer and Jacques de La Chaise to the Directors of the Company of the Indies, August 26, 1729, ANOM, C13A 11, fo. 351–65. A French ell, or *aune*, is equal to approximately forty-five inches, a length derived from the act of stretching a piece of cloth from fingertip to shoulder.

21. "État de marchandises propres pour la traite à presens des sauvages de la province de la Louisianne à envoyer de France," 1731, ANOM, F1A 30.

22. A survey of salaries paid to commissioned officers on company ships in 1728–1729 shows that captains received 150 livres per month; first lieutenants, 120; second lieutenants, 75; ensigns/scribes, 60; surgeons, between 30 and 45; and chaplains, between 25 and 40. FML, 1 P 168, 1728–1729.

23. Haudrère, *La Compagnie française des Indes*, 1:392–93.

24. Martin, "Nantes et la Compagnie des Indes," 45–47; Pradel, *Le Chevalier de Pradel*, 51–52.

25. See, e.g., a 1728 company request for funds from the Royal Treasury to pay sixteen eligible slaver captains a total of 4,037 livres, ANOM, C2 19, fo. 97–98.

26. See, e.g., Giraud, *History of French Louisiana*, 5:148–51; Usner, *Indians, Settlers, and Slaves*, 42–43; and Dawdy, *Building the Devil's Empire*, 103–7, 115–28.

27. Gérard Pellerin to M. Soret, August 1, 1720, BA, Péllerin manuscript, MS 497, folder 54. Thank you to Dianne Guenin-Lelle for bringing this source to my attention.

28. Caillot, *Company Man*, 60. Dale Miquelon provides a detailed look at the sorts of

high-demand drygoods frequently included in Caribbean-bound cargoes. Sewing notions (*mercerie*), including lace and ribbons, were high on the list. Miquelon, *Dugard of Rouen: French Trade to Canada and the West Indies, 1729–1770* (Montreal: McGill-Queen's University Press, 1978), 55–60.

29. See, e.g., the interment record of François Guenic, a sailor who fell from his ship and drowned in the harbor at Penmanec. His body was recovered on the shore behind the company hospital in Lorient on July 9, 1729, AVL, GG5, 1727–30.

30. Caillot, *Company Man*, 17.

31. Crew data such as age, height, hair color, previous experience, and hometown comes from armament records for the *Durance*, March 16, 1729, FML, 1P168–244, 2P2–23, no. 624.

32. Personnel records of the *Dromadaire*, 1727, FML, 2 P 2 III, 1727, no. 10.

33. Jean-Baptiste Aubin, Sieur Duchesne, is listed as Le Havre's *commissaire garde de l'artillerie* in Aubin Duplessis's marriage record. Marriage of Louis-Laurent Aubin and Marie-Anne Capeau, July 8, 1739, actes d'état civil de Lorient, ADM, 4 E 121/4, 1738–41.

34. Haudrère, *La Compagnie française des Indes*, 1:173, 346.

35. Armament of the *Durance*, March 16, 1729, FML, 1P168–244, 2P2–23, no. 624.

36. Ibid.; Caillot, *Company Man*, 35.

37. Armament of the *Durance*, March 16, 1729, FML, 1P168–244, 2P2–23, no. 624.

38. Ship's passenger register for the *Durance*, March 16, 1729, ANOM, F5B 49; Commission for bookkeeper Bussy, January 27, 1729, ANOM, B43b, fo. 845.

39. The passenger register for the *Comte de Toulouse* includes a director-general, four clerks, and a tobacco inspector, November 15, 1718, ANOM, G1 464.

40. All passenger statistics in this chapter derive from a survey of passenger registers from fifty-seven ships departing from Bayonne, La Rochelle, Lorient, Nantes, and Port-Louis, France, between 1717 and 1731. ANOM, F5B 49 and G1 464. Masclary and his wife boarded the *Charente* but did not make it to Louisiana. An onboard plague epidemic forced the ship to return to Lorient. Ship's passenger register for the *Charente*, January 19, 1721, ANOM, G1 464.

41. "Mémoire au sujet de la Compagnie des Indes et de ce qu'il y a à faire pour soutenir cette établissement," July 28, 1730, ANOM, C2 23, fo. 3–8; Giraud, *History of French Louisiana*, 5:10–11.

42. There were seventy-four wives in this category who were enumerated on ships' passenger registers between 1717 and 1731, but in some cases it appears that soldiers' wives and children were simply left off the official registers. They were always the last group listed, and unlike other passengers, they were not always listed by name or by their relationship to specific individuals. Rather, they often appear as the generic categories "femmes des soldats" and "enfants des soldats," along with the number of each group present for rationing purposes. Ships' passenger registers, 1718–31, ANOM, F5B 49 and G1 464.

43. Soldiers in Plantin's Company were not soldiers of the king but, rather, members of a private security force contracted by the Company of the Indies. Giraud, *Histoire de la Louisiane*, 5:284–85, 401.

44. Haudrère, *La Compagnie française des Indes*, 2:576.

45. Unfortunately, the extant records from Plantin's Company (ANOM, ser. D) do not list soldiers' place of origin, making any geographic analysis of their labor pool difficult. "État des soldats de la Cie de Plantin envoyés à la Louisiane," March 17, 2729, ANOM, D2C, 51, fo. 71.

46. Caillot, *Company Man*, 35.

47. Capitations des villes, Le Havre, 1705, 1735, and 1750, ADSM, C 314, C 328, and C 337.

48. Usner, *Indians, Settlers, and Slaves*, 50.

49. William B. Cohen, *The French Encounter with Africans: White Responses to Blacks, 1530–1880* (Bloomington: Indiana University Press, 1980), 48–51.

50. Jennifer Spear, "Colonial Intimacies: Legislating Sex in French Louisiana," *William and Mary Quarterly*, 3rd ser., 60 (2003): 75–98; Guillaume Aubert, "'To Establish One Law and Definite Rules': Race, Religion, and the Transatlantic Origins of the Louisiana Code Noir," in *Louisiana: Crossroads of the Atlantic World*, ed. Cécile Vidal (Philadelphia: University of Pennsylvania Press, 2014), 34–43.

51. *Le Code noir, ou, Édit du Roy, servant de reglement pour le gouvernement et l'administration de la justice, police, discipline, et le commerce des esclaves nègres, dans la province et colonie de la Louisiane, donné a Versailles en mois de mars 1724* (Paris: Imprimerie Royale, 1727), 3, 14, THNOC, 82-158-RL.

52. Quotation from Father Raphaël cited in Usner, *Indians, Settlers, and Slaves*, 235.

53. See, e.g., the twelve girls taken from the sanatorium in Nantes in 1729, who were brought to Lorient and placed on board the *Mars*, a 650-ton ship that bore them to a company comptoir in China. Armament of the *Mars*, 1729, FML, 1 P 244. On earlier, seventeenth-century efforts to balance the sex ratio on Saint-Christophe and Martinique through the shipment of poor women from metropolitan sanatoriums to the Caribbean colonies, see Boucher, *France and the American Tropics*, 135.

54. Iberville, quoted in Allain, "Manon Lescaut et ses consoeurs," 18.

55. Vaughn Baker, "Cherchez les femmes: Some Glimpses of Women in Early Eighteenth-Century Louisiana" *Louisiana History* 31 (1990): 25–27.

56. Giraud, *Histoire de la Louisiane*, 3:267. Ships' passenger registers, 1717–31, ANOM, F5B 49 and G1 464. Antoine-François Prévost's fictional account (written in the 1730s, first published in its entirety in 1753) is perhaps the best-known depiction of Louisiana's female populace as thoroughly debauched, *Histoire du chevalier Des Grieux et de Manon Lescaut* (Amsterdam: Au dépense de la Compagnie, 1753).

57. Valette de Laudun, *Journal d'un Voyage*, 255–56; Marie-Madeleine Hachard, *Voices from an Early American Convent*, 82.

58. Hachard, *Voices from an Early American Convent*, 82.

59. Jacques de La Chaise to the Directors of the Company of the Indies, 6 September 1723, *MPA*, 2:315.

60. Emily Clark, "'By All the Conduct of Their Lives': A Laywomen's Confraternity in New Orleans, 1730–1744," *William and Mary Quarterly*, 3rd ser., 54 (1997), 786–90.

61. For a look at the many divergences between official French policy, which encouraged marital endogamy, and day-to-day practice, which often reflected a far more fluid reality, see chapters 1 and 2 in Jennifer Spear, *Race, Sex, and Social Order in Early New Orleans* (Baltimore: Johns Hopkins University Press, 2009), 17–78.

62. Ships' passenger registers, 1717–1731, ANOM, F5B 49 and G1 464.

63. Ship's passenger register for the *Durance*, 16 March 1729, ANOM, F5B 49.

64. Marie-Louise Le Coq appears on the ship's passenger register for the *Baleine*, December 1, 1726, ANOM, F5B 49.

65. Périer served as a witness at the marriage of Marie-Louise "Catin" Le Coq to Joseph Chaperon, May 20, 1727. SLC, Marriage Register of Saint-Louis Cathedral, bk. A, July 1, 1720, to December 4, 1730, 256.

66. See sacramental record entries for both bride and groom on November 7, 1729. SLC, Marriage Register of Saint-Louis Cathedral, bk. A, July 1, 1720 to December 4, 1730, 333; ship's passenger register for the *Durance,* March 16, 1729, ANOM, F5B 49.

67. *Déclaration du Roi, concernant les vagabons & gens sans aveu,* March 12, 1719 (Grenoble: Gaspard Giroud, 1719), THNOC, John Law Collection, MSS 606, folder 144.

68. Hardy, "The Transportation of Convicts to Colonial Louisiana," 210–11.

69. Ships' passenger registers, 1717–31, ANOM, F5B 49 and G1 464.

70. "Mémoire de la Comp^{ie} des Indes servant d'instruction pour le Sr. Aubin Duplessis Commandant le Navire la Durance destinée pour la Louisianne," February 19, 1729, ANOM, B43, fo. 840–45. The revised passenger list reflected the absence of Jacquette Mitrot, the new bride of company surgeon Jean Reytet, who was listed on the preliminary passenger list issued at the beginning of the armament process. It is not clear why Mitrot's plans to accompany her husband to Louisiana changed, only that they were changed at the last minute. *Durance,* FML, 1P244 liasse 21; "État des passagers embarqués sur le v^{au} la Durance," March 15, 1729, ANOM, F5B 49, fo. 38; marriage of Jean Reytet and Jacquette Mitrot, January 9, 1729, and marriage of Jean-Robert Chierdel and Marie Lamy de Carnaret, February 9, 1729. Reytet served as one of the seven named witnesses at the marriage of Chierdel and Lamy, AVL, GG5, 1727–30.

71. See, e.g., Stephanie Smallwood, *Saltwater Slavery: A Middle Passage from Africa to the American Diaspora* (Cambridge: Harvard University Press, 2007); and Marcus Rediker, *The Slave Ship: A Human History* (New York: Penguin Group, 2007).

72. Emma Christopher examines the shipboard experiences of captives and their captors within the confines of the Middle Passage. Emma Christopher, *Slave Ship Sailors and Their Captive Cargoes, 1730–1807* (New York: Cambridge University Press, 2006). Until Stephen R. Berry published *A Path in the Mighty Waters: Shipboard Life and Atlantic Crossings to the New World* (New Haven, Conn.: Yale University Press, 2015), the most notable exception to historians' tendency to look at the crossing purely from the perspective of the Middle Passage was David Cressy, *Coming Over: Migration and Communication between England and New England in the Seventeenth Century* (Cambridge: Cambridge University Press, 1987). Berry builds considerably on Cressy's view that the Atlantic crossing was "a vital formative part of the colonizing experience" for English settlers bound for New England in the seventeenth century. See esp. Cressy, chap. 6, "'The Vast and Furious Ocean': Shipboard Socialization and the Atlantic Passage," 144–77, and Berry, chap. 3, "Shipmates," 80–114.

73. Stanley Elkins, *Slavery: A Problem in American Institutional and Intellectual Life* (Chicago: University of Chicago Press, 1959).

74. See, e.g., John Blassingame, *The Slave Community: Plantation Life in the Antebellum South* (New York: Oxford University Press, 1979); and Richard H. King, "Domination and Fabrication: Re-Thinking Stanley Elkins' 'Slavery,'" *Slavery & Abolition* 22 (2001): 1–28.

75. Smallwood, *Saltwater Slavery,* 129–31.

76. Most of the French colonial travelers' accounts from the first half of the eighteenth century were not published until the second. One notable exception was the best-selling travel narrative written by Robert Challe describing his experiences on the *Ecueil,* a French Company of the Indies ship that sailed the circuit between France and Pondicherry in 1690–91. Robert Challe, *Journal d'un voyage fait aux Indes orientales* (Rouen: J. B. Machuel Le Jeune, 1721).

77. Estienne, *Les Armements,* 21–30; Haudrère, *La Compagnie française des Indes,* 1:438–40; Banks, *Chasing Empire across the Sea,* 84–87.

78. Caillot, *Company Man*, 18.

79. Hachard, *Voices from an Early American Convent*, 49; Caillot, *Company Man*, 22–23.

80. Superior Council of Louisiana to the General Directors of the Company of the Indies, February 27, 1725, *MPA*, 2:416.

81. Caillot, *Company Man*, 24–25.

82. The fullest exploration of the various "crossing the line" rituals remains Henning Henningsen, *Crossing the Equator: Sailors' Baptism and Other Initiation Rites* (Copenhagen: Munksgaard, 1961), though Greg Dening's contextualization of the English tradition is also useful for understanding the role of rituals in maintaining workable shipboard relations within the strict confines of maritime hierarchy. Dening, *Mr. Bligh's Bad Language: Passion, Power, and Theatre on the Bounty* (Cambridge: Cambridge University Press, 1992), 71–80. See also Berry, *A Path in the Mighty Waters*, 140–50.

83. Banks, *Chasing Empire across the Sea*, 77.

84. Valette de Laudun, *Journal d'un Voyage*, 35–38; Hachard, *Voices from an Early American Convent*, 54; Laval, *Voyage de la Louisiane*, 39. See also White, *Wild Frenchmen and Frenchified Indians*, 199–201; Banks, *Chasing Empire across the Sea*, 77; Harms, *The Diligent: A Voyage*, 105–8; and Marcus Rediker, *Between the Devil and the Deep Blue Sea: Merchant Seamen, Pirates, and the Anglo-American Maritime World, 1700–1750* (Cambridge: Cambridge University Press, 1987), 186–89.

85. Caillot, *Company Man*, 30–31.

86. Ibid., 32, 33–34. For contemporary accounts of the Baptism of the Tropics ritual, see Robert Challe, *Journal d'un voyage fait aux Indes orientales, 1690–1691* (Paris: Mercure de France, 2002), 1:303–9; and Dumont de Montigny, *Regards sur le monde atlantique*, 87–90. Dumont de Montigny wrote that French ships and crews crossing three separate planes—the Grand Banks off the coast of Terre Neuve (Newfoundland), Tropic of Cancer, and Equator—underwent the baptismal ceremony, but that any passengers and crew members who had been baptized at the Equator were exempt from the other two by default. A variation on the ceremony also took place on French ships passing through the Strait of Gibraltar, see Valette de Laudun, *Journal d'un Voyage*, 35–38.

87. Rediker, *Between the Devil and the Deep Blue Sea*, 164, 216–22. B. R. Burg looks at some of the motivations for boys to go to sea as the youngest and lowest-ranking members of a ship's crew in *Sodomy and the Perception of Evil: English Sea Rovers in the Seventeenth-Century Caribbean* (New York: New York University Press, 1983), 46–48.

88. Challe, *Journal d'un voyage*, 1:292–93; Dumont de Montigny, *Regards sur le monde atlantique*, 62–63; Caillot, *Company Man*, 26–27.

89. Caillot, *Company Man*, 27.

4. Stopping Over: Provisioning and Acculturation

1. Caillot, *Company Man*, 40–41. Londa Schiebinger recounts the experience of a Dr. Chirac, who faced a botanical quandary similar to that of Aubin Duplessis. In 1720 Chirac transported a coffee seedling—which later became the first coffee plant to bear fruit in the French Caribbean—from the Jardin du Roi in Paris to Martinique. Unlike Aubin Duplessis, who as captain could commandeer others' provisions, Chirac had no such standing. While on ship, water became so scarce that he had to "share his scant portion with the precious plant." Schiebinger, *Plants and Empire: Colonial Bioprospecting in the Atlantic World* (Cambridge: Harvard University Press, 2004), 10–11.

2. Caillot, *Company Man*, 45.

3. Ibid., 46.

4. Hachard, *Voices from an Early American Convent*, 48.

5. Caillot, *Company Man*, 46.

6. William Cockburn, MDA, *Sea Diseases: Or, A Treatise of Their Nature, Causes, and Cure* (London: G. Strahan, 1736), 11.

7. Ibid. On the history of scurvy, see Kenneth J. Carpenter, *The History of Scurvy and Vitamin C* (Cambridge: Cambridge University Press, 1986); and Stephen R. Brown, *Scurvy: How a Surgeon, a Mariner, and a Gentleman Solved the Greatest Medical Mystery in the Age of Sail* (New York: Thomas Dunne Books, 2004).

8. Richard Mead, "Dissertation sur le Scorbut," *Nouvelle method pour pomper le mauvais air des vaisseaux* (Paris: Chez Durand, 1749), 117–52; Carpenter, *History of Scurvy*, 46, 51–57; James Lind, *A Treatise on the Scurvy* (Edinburgh: A. Kinkaid & A. Donaldson, 1753), and *An Essay on the Most Effectual Means of Preserving the Health of Seamen in the Royal Navy* (Edinburgh: A. Millar, A. Kincaid, and A. Donaldson, 1757).

9. "Mémoire de la Comp[ie] des Indes servant d'instruction pour le Sr. Aubin Duplessis Commandant le Navire la Durance destinée pour la Louisianne," February 19, 1729, ANOM, B43b, 840v.

10. Marcus Rediker gives a useful overview of the types of flags flown on pirate ships in *Villains of All Nations: Atlantic Pirates in the Golden Age* (Boston: Beacon Press, 2004), 98, 201 n. 41, 202 n. 42. See also Raymond Firth, *Symbols: Public and Private* (Ithaca: Cornell University Press, 1973).

11. T. Bentley Duncan, *Atlantic Islands: Madeira, the Azores, and the Cape Verdes in Seventeenth-Century Commerce and Navigation* (Chicago: University of Chicago Press, 1972), 38–42, 158–71.

12. *Lettres patentes en forme d'édit, portant revocation de la Compagnie de Saint-Domingue* (Paris: Imprimerie du Roi, April 1720), BnF.

13. Médéric Louis Elie Moreau de Saint-Méry, *Description topographique, physique, civile, politique et historique de la partie française de l'isle Saint-Domingue* (Paris: Société de l'histoire des colonies françaises et Librarie Larose, 1958), 3:1163–65.

14. Boucher, *France and the American Tropics*, 225–26.

15. Eltis, *TASTDB*.

16. "Traité fait entre les deux roys catholique et tres chrétien, avec la compagnie royale de Guinée établie en France concernant l'introduction des nègres dans l'Amérique pendant le temps de dix années," 1701, ADLA, C738 Chambre de Commerce, Nantes.

17. Jean-Baptiste Labat, *Nouveau voyage aux isles de l'Amérique* (Paris: Pierre-François Giffart, 1724), 5:218. Labat's account is consistent with Kenneth Banks's findings on Martinique, which show that administrators there "did not merely tolerate smuggling but used their positions to foster an elaborate contraband economy within the context of existing patron/client relationships." Kenneth J. Banks, "Official Duplicity: The Illicit Slave Trade of Martinique, 1713–1763," in *The Atlantic Economy during the Seventeenth and Eighteenth Centuries: Organization, Operation, Practice, and Personnel*, ed. Peter A. Coclanis (Columbia: University of South Carolina Press, 2005), 232.

18. Labat, *Nouveau voyage aux isles de l'Amérique*, 5:219–21. See also Wim Klooster, "Inter-Imperial Smuggling in the Americas, 1600–1800," in *Soundings in Atlantic History: Latent Structures and Intellectual Currents, 1500–1830*, ed. Bernard Bailyn and Patricia L. Denault (Cambridge: Harvard University Press, 2009), 141–80.

19. Pierre-François-Xavier de Charlevoix, *Histoire de l'isle espagnole ou de S. Domingue* (Paris: J. Guérin, 1730–31), 2:393.

20. Pritchard, *In Search of Empire*, 66–67.

21. Ibid., 394–417; Joannès Tramond, "Les Troubles de Saint-Domingue en 1722–1724," *Revue de l'histoire des colonies françaises* 22 (1929): 487–512, 549–98; Charles Frostin, *Les Révoltes blanches à Saint-Domingue aux XVIIe et XVIIIe siècles* (Rennes: Presses Universitaires de Rennes, 2008), 98–99, 111–20, and "Petition des habitants de Saint-Domingue, réunis au Cul-de-Sac," December 20, 1722, ANOM, A28, fo. 105v.

22. Frostin, *Les Révoltes blanches à Saint-Domingue*, 100–103.

23. Ibid., 153–55; Haudrère, *La Compagnie française des Indes*, 1:103–4.

24. Le Page du Pratz, *Histoire de la Louisiane*, 1:347.

25. "Mémoire de la Comp[ie] des Indes servant d'instruction pour le Sr. Aubin Duplessis Commandant le Navire la Durance destinée pour la Louisianne," February 19, 1729, ANOM, B43b, fo. 840v.

26. Caillot, *Company Man*, 50–51.

27. An ordinary French *pas* (pace) measured 2.5 feet in length, while a geometric pas measured double the ordinary. It is unclear which unit Labat intended. Labat, *Nouveau voyage aux isles de l'Amérique*, 5:234–35.

28. Caillot, *Company Man*, 51. Given the ongoing debate over the meaning of *Creole*, it is interesting to note that both Caillot and Labat used the term to describe individuals born in the colonies as well as those who had effectively gone native, regardless of their race. See Labat, *Nouveaux voyages aux isles*, 5:245–46, 256.

29. John Garrigus, *Before Haiti: Race and Citizenship in French Saint-Domingue* (New York: Palgrave Macmillan, 2006), 36.

30. Caillot, *Company Man*, 53.

31. Cohen, *French Encounter with Africans*, 101.

32. Jacques Houdaille, "Trois paroisses de Saint-Domingue au XVIIIe siècle," *Population* 18 (1963): 96, 100.

33. 1734 quotation cited in Garrigus, *Before Haiti*, 47; Caillot *Company Man*, 51.

34. Caillot, *Company Man*, 53.

35. Susan P. Conner, "The Pox in Eighteenth-Century France," in *The Secret Malady: Venereal Disease in Eighteenth-Century Britain and France*, ed. Linda Evi Merians (Lexington: University Press of Kentucky, 1996), 18–19.

36. Caillot, *Company Man*, 54–62.

37. "Correspondance de la Compagnie avec M. de Fayet au sujet du Radoub et de l'armement de la Galathée pour le Senegal," June 7, 1727–June 2, 1728, ANOM, C2 19, fo. 37–38, 197–98.

38. Ship's log for the *Galathée*, May 27, 1728–March 10, 1730, AN, 4 JJ 16, 35bis.

39. Ibid.

40. Ibid.

41. Ibid.; Étienne Périer and Jacques de La Chaise to the Directors of the Company of the Indies, January 30, 1729, *MPA*, 2:690–91; no. 32905, *Galathée*, Eltis, *TASTDB*; Registres d'inventaires des morts, *Galathée*, May 27, 1728–March 10, 1730, FML, 1P240, liasse 1; Stein, *French Slave Trade in the Eighteenth Century*, 98.

42. Eltis, *TASTDB*; Stephen Behrendt, "Crew Mortality in the Transatlantic Slave Trade in the Eighteenth Century," *Slavery and Abolition* 18 (1997): 49–71; Raymond L. Cohn, "Maritime Mortality in the Eighteenth and Nineteenth Centuries: A Survey," *International Journal of Maritime History* 1 (1989): 159–91; James C. Riley, "Mortality on Long-Distance Voyages in the Eighteenth Century," *Journal of Economic History* 41 (1981): 651–56.

43. Caillot, *Company Man*, 63–64; ship's log for the *Galathée*, May 27, 1728–March 10, 1730, AN, 4 JJ 16, 35bis.

44. May 27, 1728, FML, 1P167, 2P2–23, fo. 599; no. 32905, *Galathée*, Eltis, *TASTDB*; Stein, *French Slave Trade in the Eighteenth Century*, 98; "Registres d'inventaires des morts," *La Galathée*, May 27, 1728–March 10, 1730, FML 1P240, liasse 1.

45. Caillot, *Company Man*, 84; Leblond de Latour, "Plan [et profil] des ouvrages projettés à faire à l'isle de la Balise avec les logements necessaires," September 1, 1723, ANOM, Dépôt des fortifications des colonies, 105C; Hall, *Africans in Colonial Louisiana*, 76; Giraud, *History of French Louisiana*, 5:330–42.

46. Périer and La Chaise to the Directors of the Company of the Indies, August 26, 1729, *MPA*, 2:659.

47. Hachard, *Voices from an Early American Convent*, 68.

48. Hall, *Africans in Colonial Louisiana*, 79–80, 83.

49. Giraud, *History of French Louisiana*, 5:230, 332–39.

50. "État général des dépenses de la Comp. des Indes à la Louisiane pour l'année 1729," ANOM, B43; "Inventaire de l'habitation de la Comp. des Indes sur le fleuve St. Louis vis à vis la Nouvelle Orléans et de tous les bâtiments, marchandises, denrées et ustensils, de nègres et bestiaux à la charge de S. Le Page," September 2, 1731, ANOM, C2 24, fo. 183–87.

51. Gutkind, "Trade and Labor in Early Precolonial African History," *Workers of the African Trade*, 25–49, and "The Boatmen of Ghana: The Possibilities of a Pre-Colonial African Labor History," *Confrontation, Class Consciousness and the Labor Process*, ed. Michael Hanagan (New York: Greenwood Press, 1986), 123–66; Robin Law, "Between the Sea and the Lagoons," *Cahiers d'études africaines* 29 (1989): 224–29; Randy Sparks, *The Two Princes of Calabar: An Eighteenth-Century Atlantic Odyssey* (Cambridge: Harvard University Press, 2004), 10, 41, 49–51; Christopher, *Slave Ship Sailors*, 147–51.

52. See keyed letter V in "Plan du fort de la Balise et des isles adjacentes," July 1731, ANOM, 4 Dépôt des fortifications des colonies, 111B (fig. 8).

53. Of the other 210 individuals owned by the company in Louisiana, 155 resided at the company plantation located across the river from New Orleans (in present-day Algiers, La.), 34 were based at the Natchez post, and 21 at Governor Périer's plantation. "Inventaire de l'habitation," September 2, 1731, ANOM, C2 24, fo. 183–87.

54. Ship's log for the *Vénus*, AN, 4JJ 63, no. 32; armament records for the *Vénus*, February 4, 1729, FML, 1P168–244, 2P2–23, no. 622; and no. 32909, Eltis, *TASTDB*.

55. Caillot, *Company Man*, 70.

56. Périer and La Chaise to the Directors of the Company of the Indies, August 26, 1729, *MPA*, 2:659–60; and no. 32909, *Vénus*, Eltis, *TASTDB*.

57. Caillot, *Company Man*, 70. On slave ships and sickness of captives and crew on disembarkation, see Hall, *Africans in Colonial Louisiana*, 84–86; Christopher, *Slave Ship Sailors*, 205–8; Rediker, *Slave Ship*, 273–76; and Usner, *Indians, Settlers, and Slaves*, 37–41.

58. Caillot, *Company Man*, 71.

59. Hachard, *Voices from an Early American Convent*, 56, 68. See also Dumont de Montigny, *Regards sur le monde atlantique*, 111, 137.

60. Jacques de La Chaise to the Directors of the Company of the Indies, March 8, 1724, *MPA*, 2:303.

61. Ibid., 336. The only references in the Superior Council records to Tixerant's condemnation appear in 1741 and 1743. Both involved Jean-Baptiste Prevost, one of the company's agents who remained in Louisiana after the 1731 retrocession to collect outstand-

ing debts. On March 4, 1741, Tixerant was ordered by the Superior Council to pay 26,834 livres to the company, 15,445 of which he owed for inventory missing from the time he had served as warehouse keeper in Biloxi in 1721–22. Two years later, in a petition filed November 20, 1743, Prevost was still trying to collect on the debt. See entries on March 3 and 4, 1741, and November 20, 1743, LSM-SCR and La Chaise to the Directors of the Company of the Indies, March 8, 1724, *MPA,* 2:300, 303, 336.

62. Jacques de La Chaise to the Directors of the Company of the Indies, March 8, 1724, 303, 326, 336; Charles R. Maduell, ed. and trans., "Census of the Inhabitants along the River Mississippi Dated 1731," *The Census Tables for the French Colony of Louisiana from 1699 through 1732* (Baltimore: Genealogical Publishing Co., 1972), 114; Caillot, *Company Man,* 72; Giraud, *History of French Louisiana,* 5:21.

63. Caillot, *Company Man,* 73.

64. Ibid., 74. Those afflicted with scurvy, even in its early stages, often emit a putrefied stench from their mouths. As scurvy progresses, ulcers appear on the body and gums rot, worsening the smell of decay.

65. Hachard, *Voices from an Early American Convent,* 67; Caillot, *Company Man,* 68. On the difficulty of the voyage between the Balize and New Orleans, see also Banks, *Chasing Empire across the Sea,* 85–86.

5. Louisiana: A Company Colony

1. Étienne Périer and Jacques de La Chaise to the Directors of the Company of the Indies, August 26, 1729, *MPA,* 2:659–60.

2. Passenger list for the *Aurore,* 1728, ANOM, F5B 49, no. 27; Étienne Périer and Jacques de La Chaise to the Directors of the Company of the Indies, August 26, 1729, *MPA,* 2:665–66.

3. Caillot, *Company Man,* 74.

4. Petition to sue Paulin Cadot, February 5 and 7, 1724; and decision and sentencing in case vs. Paulin Cadot, March 28, 1724, LSM-SCR.

5. "Employés revoqués," in "Employés actuellement au service de la Comp[ie]," 1724, ANOM, B43, fo. 378.

6. Étienne Périer and Jacques de La Chaise to the Directors of the Company of the Indies, July 31, 1728, *MPA,* 2:578–79.

7. Ibid., November 3, 1728, 594; "État des appointemens accordés aux directeurs et employés à la Louisiane à commencer du premier janvier 1722," ANOM, B43, fo. 41.

8. "État des appointemens accordés aux directeurs et employés à la Louisianne," 1722; "État général des dépenses que la Comp. des Indes a ordonné être faites à la Louisianne," 1724, ANOM, B43, fo. 41, 376; Étienne Périer and Jacques de La Chaise to the Directors of the Company of the Indies, July 31, 1728, *MPA,* 2:578–79.

9. List of creditors and petition of Nicolas Bion, January 9 and 25, 1729, LSM-SCR.

10. Father Raphaël to Abbé Raguet, May 18, 1726, ANOM, C13A 10, fo. 43.

11. Passenger list for the *Baleine,* November 30, 1726, F5B 49, no. 21

12. Étienne Périer and Jacques de La Chaise to the Directors of the Company of the Indies, November 2, 1727, and November 3, 1728, *MPA,* 2:551, 594.

13. Ibid., August 26, 1729, 670–71.

14. Ibid.

15. Sieur Bernaudat de Saint-Maur to Maurepas, April 4, 1731, and Syndics and Direc-

tors of the Company of the Indies to Maurepas, July 26, 1731, ANOM, Col E28, fo. 286–90 and C2 24, fo. 43.

16. Étienne Périer and Jacques de La Chaise to the Directors of the Company of the Indies, August 26, 1729, *MPA*, 2:664.

17. Maduell, "General Census of All Inhabitants of the Colony of Louisiana Dated January 1, 1726," and "Census of New Orleans as Reported by M. Périer, Commandant General of Louisiana, July 1, 1727," *Census Tables*, 71, 87; Caillot, *Company Man*, 100, 106.

18. "Ordonnance pour les appointemens des officiers et employés de la Louisianne," September 30, 1726, ANOM, B43b, fo. 652–53.

19. Caillot, "Plan de la Nouvelle Orléans," February 14, 1731, in *Company Man*, pl. 19; Pierre Baron, Étienne de Périer, and Laurent MacMahon, "Plan des bâtimens de la Direction," July 22, 1730, ANOM, 4 Dépôt des fortifications des colonies, fo. 87c.

20. Caillot, *Company Man*, 78; Étienne Périer and Jacques de La Chaise to the Directors of the Company of the Indies, March 25, 1729, *MPA*, 2:631.

21. Haudrère, *La Compagnie française des Indes*, 1:231–37; James D. Hardy Jr., "The Superior Council in Colonial Louisiana," in *Frenchmen and French Ways in the Mississippi Valley*, ed. John Francis McDermott (Urbana: University of Illinois Press, 1969), 87–101.

22. Louis XV issued the order to recall Bienville October 15, 1723, but Bienville lingered in Louisiana until June 1725. Giraud, *History of French Louisiana*, 5:32–37.

23. Étienne Périer and Jacques de La Chaise to the Directors of the Company of the Indies, November 3, 1728, *MPA*, 2:603.

24. Condé Street was a continuation of Chartres. Chartres was on the upriver side of the Place d'Armes, while Condé was on the downriver side.

25. Étienne Périer and Jacques de La Chaise to the Directors of the Company of the Indies, August 26, 1729, ANOM, C13A 11, fo. 351–65.

26. Ibid.

27. Louis Sala-Molins, *Le Code Noir, ou le Calvaire de Canaan* (Paris: Presses Universitaires de France, 2003), 135, 143; Périer and La Chaise to the Directors of the Company of the Indies, November 3, 1728, *MPA*, 2:599.

28. Caillot, *Company Man*, 102 and pl. 19; Dawdy, *Building the Devil's Empire*, 139–40; Shannon Lee Dawdy and Christopher N. Matthews, "Colonial and Antebellum New Orleans," in *Archaeology of Louisiana*, ed. Mark A. Rees (Baton Rouge: LSU Press, 2010), 278; Douglas W. Owsley, Charles E. Orser Jr., Robert Montgomery, and Claudia C. Holland, "An Archaeological and Physical Anthropological Study of the First Cemetery in New Orleans" (Baton Rouge: Louisiana Division of Archaeology, 1985).

29. On the role of engineers and contemporary urban development theories in laying out New Orleans, see Gilles-Antoine Langlois, *Des villes pour le Louisiane française* (Paris: Harmattan, 2003), 332–39.

30. Dumont de Montigny, *Regards sur le monde atlantique*, 147.

31. Maduell, "General Census of All Inhabitants of New Orleans and Environs Dated November 24, 1721, as Reported by Sieur Diron" and "Census of New Orleans as Reported by M. Périer, Commandant General of Louisiana, July 1, 1727," *Census Tables*, 17–21, 82 95.

32. Dawdy, *Building the Devil's Empire*, 158–62.

33. Maduell, "Census of New Orleans as Reported by M. Périer, Commandant General of Louisiana, July 1, 1727," and "Census of the Inhabitants and Property Owners of New Orleans as of January 1732," *Census Tables*, 82–95, 124–41.

34. "État général des dépenses de la Compagnie des Indes à la Louisiane pour l'année 1729," ANOM, B43b, fo. 821–25.

35. Le Page du Pratz, *History of Louisiana*, 227–28.

36. Shannon Lee Dawdy, "'A Wild Taste': Food and Colonialism in Eighteenth-Century Louisiana," *Ethnohistory* 57 (2010): 393–94; Charles Hudson, *The Southeastern Indians* (Knoxville: University of Tennessee Press, 1976), 302–7.

37. Caillot, *Company Man*, 98.

38. Ibid., 80; Giraud, *History of French Louisiana*, 5:237–39.

39. Richard Campanella, *Time and Place in New Orleans: Past Geographies in the Present Day* (New Orleans: Pelican Publishing, 2002), 88.

40. Giraud, *History of French Louisiana*, 5:26–30, 53.

41. Ibid., 72–76.

42. "Mémoire sur la situation des Missions Jesuites à la Louisianne," December 31, 1729, ANOM, C2 25, fo. 93.

43. On state-sponsored religion and religious orders in French colonial Louisiana, see Charles Edwards O'Neill, *Church and State in French Colonial Louisiana: Policy and Politics to 1732* (New Haven, Conn.: Yale University Press, 1966); Jane Frances Heaney, *A Century of Pioneering: A History of the Ursuline Nuns in New Orleans, 1727–1827* (New Orleans: Ursuline Sisters of New Orleans, 1993); and Emily Clark, *Masterless Mistresses: The New Orleans Ursulines and the Development of a New World Society, 1727–1834* (Chapel Hill: University of North Carolina Press, 2007).

44. Caillot, *Company Man*, 81.

45. Samuel Wilson Jr., *The Capuchin School in New Orleans, 1725: The First School in Louisiana* (New Orleans: Archdiocesan School Board, 1961), 9.

46. Father Raphaël to Abbé Raguet, September 15, 1725, and May 18, 1726, *MPA*, 2:507–10, 519–20.

47. Caillot, *Company Man*, 81. George Edward Milne suggests that Caillot's criticisms were aimed at Jesuit Father Beaubois, but Caillot arrived in Louisiana after Beaubois's recall to France forced his departure. Milne, *Natchez Country: Indians, Colonists, and the Landscapes of Race in French Louisiana* (Athens: University of Georgia Press, 2015), 147.

48. Étienne Périer to Abbé Raguet, October 15, 1728, C13A 11, fo. 239–39v.

49. Caillot, *Company Man*, 104; "État général des dépenses de la Comp. des Indes à la Louisiane pour l'année 1729," ANOM, B43b, fo. 825–26; Usner, *Indians, Settlers, and Slaves*, 61; Gallay, *Indian Slave Trade*, 144–49.

50. Father Raphaël to Abbé Raguet, May 15, 1725, *MPA*, 2:484–85.

51. "État général des dépenses," 1729, ANOM, B 43b, fo. 825–26.

52. Giraud, *History of French Louisiana*, 5:61–63.

53. "État général des dépenses," 1729, ANOM, B 43b, fo. 826.

54. "Inventaire de l'habitation de la Comp. des Indes sur le fleuve Saint- Louis vis à vis la Nouvelle Orléans," October 15, 1731, ANOM, C2 24, fo. 184–87; Alexandre de Batz and Ignace-François de Broutin, January 13, 1732, "Plan du bâtiment de l'Hôpital des nègres construit sur l'habitation de la Compagnie"; "Plan du rez de chaussée et premier étage du bâtiment servant de magazin construit sur l'habitation de la Compagnie" and "Plan des moulins à pilons et à tonnelle construit sur l'habitation de la Compagnie," January 14, 1732, ANOM, F3 290, nos. 36–38.

55. Étienne Périer and Jacques de La Chaise to the Directors of the Company of the Indies, August 26, 1729, *MPA*, 2:659–60.

56. Section, elevation, and floor plans submitted by engineering corps member

Chambellan Graton to the company in September 1729 show plans to build a structure along the east bank of the Mississippi River at New Orleans, where arriving slaves could be housed prior to sale or auction. There is no evidence that the building was ever constructed. ANOM, 4 Dépôt des fortifications des colonies, nos. 80c, 81b, and 82c.

57. Étienne Périer and Jacques de La Chaise to the Directors of the Company of the Indies, August 26, 1729, *MPA*, 2:668.

58. Price, *France and the Chesapeake*, 1:316–17.

59. Étienne Périer and Jacques de La Chaise to the Directors of the Company of the Indies, August 26, 1729, *MPA*, 2:660.

60. "Proposition de la Compagnie des Indes à la Marine du Roy," December 16, 1732; "Reponse à la proposition de la Compagnie des Indes sur l'Introduction des nègres à la Louisianne," December 1732; and Maurepas to Company Directors, December 31, 1732, ANOM, C2 25, fo. 95, 98, 92.

61. "Inventaire," September 2, 1731, ANOM, C2 24, fo. 183–87.

62. Gwendolyn Midlo Hall, "African Women in French and Spanish Louisiana," in *The Devil's Lane: Sex and Race in the Early South*, ed. Catherine Clinton and Michele Gillespie (New York: Oxford University Press, 1997), 248.

63. "Inventaire," ANOM, C2 24, fo. 183–87.

64. Sala-Molins, *Le Code noir*, 95, 106–7; *Le Code noir*, 28–29.

65. Father Raphaël to Abbé Raguet, April 18, 1727, ANOM, C13A 10, fo. 326v; Spear, *Race Sex and Social Order*, 71; Clark, *Masterless Mistresses*, 170–71.

66. All slaves sold in the interim are included in tables throughout this chapter. "Inventaire," ANOM, C2 24, fo. 183–87.

67. For a detailed discussion of the differences between the 1685 and 1724 codes, see Sala-Molins, *Le Code noir;* and Spear, *Race Sex and Social Order*, 59–68.

68. Sala-Molins, *Le Code noir*, 184–85.

69. Hall, *Africans in Colonial Louisiana*, 168; "African Women in French and Spanish Louisiana," 251–52.

70. Spear, *Race, Sex, and Social Order*, 68–75.

71. See, e.g., the case of Joseph Chaperon discussed ibid., 52–53.

72. Le Page du Pratz, *History of Louisiana*, 382–83; Alexandre de Batz, "Plan du camp des nègres," January 9, 1732, ANOM, 4 Dépôt des fortifications des colonies, 91B. See also Patricia Galloway, "Rhetoric of Difference: Le Page du Pratz on African Slave Management in Eighteenth-Century Louisiana," *French Colonial History* 3 (2003): 6; and Dawdy, *Building the Devil's Empire*, 147–48.

73. "Inventaire," ANOM, C2 24, fo. 183–87.

74. W. Jeffrey Bolster, *Black Jacks: African American Seamen in the Age of Sail* (Cambridge: Harvard University Press, 1997), 45. Although Bolster's study primarily focuses on the British Atlantic after 1740, his findings on the translation of skills from Africa to the Americas and the opportunities available to seamen in the colonial context are useful for understanding African seamen in the Atlantic world writ large. See also David S. Cecelski, *The Waterman's Song: Slavery and Freedom in Maritime North Carolina* (Chapel Hill: University of North Carolina Press, 2001); and Thomas C. Buchanan, *Black Life on the Mississippi: Slaves, Free Blacks, and the Western Steamboat World* (Chapel Hill: University of North Carolina Press, 2004).

75. Étienne Périer and Jacques de La Chaise to the Directors of the Company of the Indies, March 25, 1729, *MPA*, 2:634.

76. Bolster, *Black Jacks*, 68–69; Christopher, *Slave Ship Sailors*, 52–55.

77. Hall, *Africans in Colonial Louisiana*, 130.

78. Bolster, *Black Jacks*, 131–34.

79. W. Jeffrey Bolster, "An Inner Diaspora: Black Sailors Making Selves," in *Through a Glass Darkly: Reflections on Personal Identity in Early America*, ed. Ronald Hoffman, Mechal Sobel, and Frederika Teute (Chapel Hill: University of North Carolina Press, 1997), 421. On sailors as go-betweens, see also Alida C. Metcalf, *Go-Betweens and the Colonization of Brazil, 1500–1600* (Austin: University of Texas Press, 2005), 50–53.

80. On the role of African and African American seamen in the transmission of news throughout the Atlantic world, see Julius Sherrard Scott III, "The Common Wind: Currents of Afro-American Communication in the Era of the Haitian Revolution" (Ph.D. diss., Duke University, 1986), 59–60, 67–68.

81. Usner, *Indians, Settlers and Slaves*, 28–29; Barnett, *Natchez Indians*, 57–60, 70–71; Balvay, *La Révolte des Natchez*, 68–76; Milne, *Natchez Country*, 60–78.

82. Price, *France and the Chesapeake*, 1:302–8.

83. Ibid.

84. Iberville, *Iberville's Gulf Journals*, 125.

85. Ian W. Brown and Vincas P. Steponaitis, "The Grand Village of the Natchez Indians Was Indeed Grand: A Reconsideration of the Fatherland Site Landscape," in *Forging Southeastern Identities: Social Archaeology and Ethnohistory of the Mississippian to Early Historic South*, ed. Gregory A. Waselkov and Marvin T. Smith (Tuscaloosa: University of Alabama Press, forthcoming).

86. The settlement districts are identified in Ignace-François Broutin, "Carte des environs du Fort Rosalie aux Natchez," 1723, BnF, département des cartes et plans, Ge DD 2987 (8834 B). See also Barnett, *Natchez Indians*, 40–48.

87. Usner, *Indians, Settlers, and Slaves*, 65–70.

88. Gallay, *Indian Slave Trade*, 296–97; Barnett, *Natchez Indians*, 28–32; Patricia Galloway and Jason Baird Jackson, "Natchez and Neighboring Groups," *Handbook of North American Indians, Southeast*, ed. Raymond D. Fogelson (Washington, D.C.: Smithsonian Institution, 2004), 14:608.

89. Galloway and Jackson, "Natchez and Neighboring Groups," 609; Barnett, *Natchez Indians*, 78–79.

90. "Extrait de l'acte de Société entre la Cie des Indes et les associés en la Concession de Ste. Catherine," September 4, 1719, ANOM, G1, 465.

91. Price, *France and the Chesapeake*, 307–8.

92. Bienville to Company Directors, April 15, 1719, ANOM, C13A 5, fo. 208v.

93. Company Directors to Louisiana Council, August 26, 1723, and January 4, 1724; Jean Baptiste Faucon Dumanoir to Company Directors, January 1724; and George Desfontaines to Company Directors, January 4, 1724, ANOM, G1, 465.

94. On privately held farms and concessions in the Natchez area, including those owned by absentee owners and French conglomerates, see Giraud, *History of French Louisiana*, 5:160–73; Price, *France and the Chesapeake*, 1:309–14; Barnett, *Natchez Indians*, 78–82, 99–100; Balvay, *La Révolte des Natchez*, 82–84, 89–92.

95. Kathleen Duval, "Interconnectedness and Diversity in 'French Louisiana,'" in *Powhatan's Mantle: Indians in the Colonial Southeast*, ed. Gregory A. Waselkov, Peter H. Wood, and Tom Hatley (Lincoln: University of Nebraska Press, 2006), 138.

96. Étienne Périer to Abbé Raguet, April 25, 1727, *MPA*, 2:542. See also the letter of August 14, 1728, 585–86.

97. Gallay, *Indian Slave Trade,* 143.

98. Ibid., 289–90.

99. Étienne Périer and Jacques de La Chaise to the Directors of the Company of the Indies, April 22, 1727 and November 2, 1727, *MPA,* 2:537, 549–50.

100. Comte de Volvire, Marine commander at Port-Louis, to Minister of Marine, December 12, 1729, AN, B3 322, fo. 177.

101. On typical Louisiana cargo inventories, see Comte de Volvire, marine commander at Port-Louis, to Minister of Marine, January 30 and August 2, 1728; January 24, 1729, AN, B3 322, fo. 134, 171.

102. Étienne Périer and Jacques de La Chaise to the Directors of the Company of the Indies, November 3, 1728, *MPA,* 2:604.

103. On trade with the Spanish, see also in *MPA* letters from Périer and La Chaise dated November 2, 1727, 2:549–50; November 24, 1727, 2:560–62; November 3, 1728, 2:593, 603–5; and June 22, 1729, 2:614.

104. Comte de Volvire, Marine commander at Port-Louis, to Minister of Marine, AN, B3 329, fo. 118; B3 330, fo. 58.

105. Comte de Volvire, Marine commander at Port-Louis, to Minister of Marine, AN, B3 337, fo. 83.

106. Price, *France and the Chesapeake,* 1:289–90.

107. Of the 5,680 slaves shipped to the colony from 1720 to 1730, approximately 4,999 reached the Gulf Coast. Among those who disembarked, countless numbers perished soon after their arrival in Louisiana, as they succumbed to scurvy, the yaws, and other nutritional and infectious diseases contracted during the journey. Eltis, *TASTDB.*

108. Price, *France and the Chesapeake,* 1:308, 311–12, 315, 320–21.

109. "Memoir on Tobacco at Natchez," October 1724; Committee of Louisiana to Company Directors, November 8, 1724; Étienne Périer and Jacques de La Chaise to the Directors of the Company of the Indies, April 22, 1727, *MPA,* 2:396–97, 398–99, 532–35.

110. The company paid thirty livres per quintal as a standard, unless the purchase price was applied to old debt, in which case they credited tobacco farmers with forty livres per quintal. Price, *France and the Chesapeake,* 316.

111. Ibid., 320–23; Sieur Lunel to the Directors of the Company of the Indies, January 30, 1729, ANOM, C2 22, fo. 326–29.

112. Jack P. Greene, *Pursuits of Happiness: The Social Development of Early Modern British Colonies and the Formation of American Culture* (Chapel Hill: University of North Carolina Press, 1988), 85–86.

113. "Mémoire sur la situation des Missions Jesuites à la Louisianne," December 31, 1729, ANOM, C2 25, fo. 93.

114. Hall, *Africans in Colonial Louisiana,* 92–94.

115. Price, *France and the Chesapeake,* 325.

116. Ibid., 325–27.

117. Caillot, *Company Man,* 89.

118. Usner, *Indians, Settlers, and Slaves;* Sophie K. White, "'A Baser Commerce': Retailing, Class, and Gender in French Colonial New Orleans," *William and Mary Quarterly,* 3rd ser., 63, no. 3 (2006): 517–50.

119. Caillot, *Company Man,* 123.

120. No eyewitness accounts of the initial Natchez attack have survived, but several contemporary secondary accounts informed by survivors' tales, including those penned

by Caillot, Charlevoix, Diron d'Artaguiette, Dumont de Montigny, Le Page du Pratz, and Périer, provide a basic outline of events. See Caillot, *Company Man*, 123–30; Diron d'Artaguiette to Minister of Marine Maurepas, February 9 and March 20, 1730, *MPA*, 1:56–61, 76–81; Dumont de Montigny (who provides a scathing indictment of the company), *Regards sur le monde atlantique*, 235–58; Le Page du Pratz, *History of Louisiana*, 79–95; and Étienne Périer to Minister of Marine Maurepas, December 5, 1729, and March 18, 1730, *MPA* 1:54–56, 61–70. More detailed recent interpretations can be found in Barnett, *Natchez Indians;* Balvay, *La Révolte des Natchez;* George Edward Milne, "Picking Up the Pieces: Natchez Coalescence in the Shatter Zone," in *Mapping the Mississippian Shatter Zone: The Colonial Indian Slave Trade and Regional Instability in the American South*, ed. Robbie Ethridge and Sheri M. Shuck-Hall (Lincoln: University of Nebraska Press, 2009), 388–417; and Gordon Sayre, "Plotting the Natchez Massacre: Le Page du Pratz, Dumont de Montigny, Chateaubriand," *Early American Literature* 37 (2002): 381–413.

121. Diron d'Artaguiette to Minister of Marine Maurepas, March 20, 1730, *MPA* 2:76; Galloway and Jackson, "Natchez and Neighboring Groups," 610.

122. Le Page du Pratz, *Histoire de La Louisiane*, 3:235.

123. Father Philibert, the Capuchin priest charged with shepherding colonists in Natchez, was in New Orleans at the time of the attack. In 1730 he recorded the names of 235 French victims, including 144 men, 35 women, and 56 children. Father Philibert, June 9, 1730, *MPA*, 1:122–26.

124. Diron d'Artaguiette to Minister of Marine Maurepas, February 10, 1730; March 18, 1730; and March 20, 1730, *MPA* 1:61, 68, 78. The wide range of the number of African slaves taken hostage reflects an uncertainty over how many slaves were forcibly taken versus how many fled willingly to the Natchez in hopes of bettering their situations.

6. A Colony Fit Only for a King?

1. Comte de Volvire to Minister of the Marine, February 24, 1730, AN, B3 337, fo. 19.

2. Caillot, *Company Man*, 124.

3. It is not clear that all of the Africans were taken as hostages. Some may have willingly fled to the Natchez in hopes of escaping slavery. Étienne Périer to Minister of Marine Maurepas, December 5, 1729, *MPA*, 1:54; Balvay, *La Révolte des Natchez*, 133–37.

4. Étienne Périer to Minister of Marine Maurepas, December 5, 1729, *MPA*, 1:55.

5. Diron d'Artaguiette to Minister of Marine Maurepas, February 10 and March 20, 1730, *MPA* 1:61, 78; Étienne Périer to Minister of Marine Maurepas, March 18, 1730, *MPA* 1:68; Barnett, *Natchez Indians*, 116–18; Milne, *Natchez Country*, 195–96.

6. Étienne Périer to Minister of Marine Maurepas, March 18, 1730, *MPA* 1:71.

7. Caillot, *Company Man*, 126.

8. Ibid.

9. Joseph-Christophe de Lusser to Minister of Marine Maurepas from journal entries dated March 1–16, 1730, *MPA* 1:101 and 97–113. See also Usner, *Indians, Settlers, and Slaves*, 73–74.

10. Joseph-Christophe de Lusser to Minister of Marine Maurepas from journal entries dated March 1–16, 1730, *MPA*, 1:107–8.

11. Ibid., 105–6, 109.

12. Caillot, *Company Man*, 127.

13. Dumont de Montigny, quoted in Usner, *Indians, Settlers, and Slaves*, 75.

14. In 1731 Périer caught word of another conspiracy through an enslaved domestic servant, who warned of a pending Bambara-led revolt led by one of the company's enslaved overseers, Samba Bambara. The domestic servant claimed that Bambara slaves would set fire to New Orleans while its inhabitants were at Mass. Whatever the actual plan of attack, Périer quashed the reputed rebellion before it began, sending Samba Bambara and several other alleged coconspirators to the Place d'Armes to be broken on the wheel. Dan Usner conflates the conspiracy reported by Dumont de Montigny with the later 1731 plot (ibid., 74–75). For more on the 1731 conspiracy, see reports dated July 21 and 28, 1731, ANOM, C13A 13, fo. 85.

15. Étienne Périer to Minister of Marine Maurepas, March 18, 1730, *MPA* 1:71; Dumont de Montigny, *Regards sur le monde atlantique*, 260.

16. Caillot, *Company Man*, 132.

17. Ibid., 134.

18. On the transfer of powers to MacMahon, a known smuggler, see Dawdy, *Building the Devil's Empire*, 123–25.

19. Mémoire by Jacques Deshayes, March 1730, ANOM, C2 23, fo. 9v.

20. Ibid., fo. 10v.

21. Étienne Périer to Minister of Marine Maurepas, March 18, 1730, *MPA* 1:71–76.

22. "Mémoire au sujet de la Compagnie des Indes et de ce qu'il y a à faire pour soutenir cet établissement," July 28, 1730, ANOM, C2 23, fo. 3–8. Ramont's role in company affairs is unclear. His mémoire is filed as a company document, suggesting that he was likely a syndic, director, or investor.

23. Ibid., fo. 3.

24. Ibid., fo. 4v–5.

25. Ibid., fo. 5.

26. Haudrère, *La Compagnie française des Indes*, 1:106–8.

27. Ibid., 108–9; Paul Masson, *Histoire des établissements et du commerce français dans l'Afrique barbaresque, 1560–1793* (Paris: Librairie Hachette, 1903), 282–91; Roland Mousnier, *The Institutions of France under the Absolute Monarchy, 1598–1789*, vol. 2: *The Organs of State and Society*, trans. Arthur Goldhammer (Chicago: University of Chicago Press, 1984), 421–66.

28. Although the initial lease was for an eight-year term, the United General Farms retained the monopoly until 1791. Both the United General Farms and the Company of the Indies profited from the arrangement. Price, *France and the Chesapeake*, 1:292–93, 327–28.

29. Louis Henry Brinon de Caligny, "Estrait du registre général des déliberations prises dans les Assemblées Générales d'Administration," December 6, 1730, ANOM, C2 24, fo. 28–32; Haudrère, *La Compagnie française des Indes*, 2:321.

30. Ibid., fo. 29v.

31. Ibid., fo. 30.

32. Philibert Orry to Louis XV, December 31, 1730, AN, B3, fo. 180–81.

33. *Arrêt du conseil d'état du Roy, concernant la retrocession faite à sa Majesté par la Compagnie des Indes de la Louisiane et du pays d'Illinois*, January 23, 1731 (Paris: Imprimerie royale, 1731), THNOC, MSS 268, folder 18.

34. "Procès-verbal de l'assemblée des syndics et directeurs de la Compagnie des Indes autorisant ceux-ci à traiter de la retrocession de la Louisiane et du pays des Illinois au Roi, sur le pied de l'indemnité de 1.450.000 livres fixée par le contrôler général Orry," January 24, 1731, ANOM, C13A 13, fo. 254.

35. *Arrêt du conseil d'état du Roy, concernant la retrocession.*

36. Details of the retrocession were sent to Governor Périer in a letter from Maurepas dated January 30, 1731, ANOM, B55, fo. 583–86.

37. Ibid., fo. 585v.

38. Balvay, *La Révolte des Natchez,* 144–48, 169.

39. Caillot, *Company Man,* 154–55; Étienne Périer to Philibert Orry, "Mémoire sur la défaite des Natchez," March 25, 1731, ANOM, C13A 13, fo. 33. On French presence and Euro-Indian relations in the Illinois country, see Richard White, *The Middle Ground: Indians, Empires, and Republics in the Great Lakes Region, 1650–1815* (Cambridge: Cambridge University Press, 1991); R. David Edmunds and Joseph L. Peyser, *The Fox Wars: The Mesquakie Challenge to New France* (Norman: University of Oklahoma Press, 1993); Giraud, *History of French Louisiana,* 5:440–94; W. J. Eccles, *The French in North America, 1500–1783* (East Lansing: Michigan State University Press, 1998); and M. J. Morgan, *Land of Big Rivers: French and Indian Illinois, 1699–1778* (Carbondale: Southern Illinois University Press, 2010).

40. Caillot, *Company Man,* 155. The "Te Deum," according to historian Daniel Roche, served three primary functions in ancien régime France. "First, it called attention to major events, distinguished by the king's presence; it marked historical commemorations which confirmed the importance of military and dynastic aims; and it played a diplomatic role by speaking to allies and enemies as well as Frenchmen. Second, it indicated the king's intention to dominate all of French territory from the palace of Versailles to the most remote diocese. Finally, the ceremony ritualized magnificence in a brief burst of consumption (of food, wood, candles, and fireworks), as if pressing a claim against nature and scarcity while at the same time upholding the established order." For more on the use of the "Te Deum," see Roche, *France in the Enlightenment,* trans. Arthur Goldhammer (Cambridge: Harvard University Press, 1998), 269–71.

41. Caillot, *Company Man,* 155.

42. Ibid.

43. Ibid., 156.

44. Ibid.

45. Ibid.; Étienne Périer to Minister of Marine Maurepas and Sieur Laye to Philibert Orry, April 16, 1731, ANOM, C13A 13, fo. 55, 212. A 1733 watercolor drawn by Sieur Callot (no relation to Marc-Antoine Caillot) clearly shows the wreckage of the ship; see "Plan et veuë du Fort de la Balize," ANOM, 4 Dépôt des fortifications des colonies 115A.

46. Caillot, *Company Man,* 156.

47. "États par vaisseaux des officiers, officiers mariniers, et matelots decedés ou noyés de 1721–1770," FML, I P 246, liasse 2; inventory of cargo taken on board the *Saint-Louis* from the shipwrecked *Prince de Conty,* ADM, 9 B 208.

48. Because the shipwreck of the *Prince de Conty* resulted in not only material losses to the company in the form of cargo but also financial losses on the part of all of the ship's crew members, whether from loss of salary or personal possessions, many of the ship's records were placed on deposit with Brittany's admiralty court in Vannes, France. See esp. Étienne Bréban, "Journal du navire le *Saint-Louis,*" which chronicles the ship's journey from the Senegambian coast in 1729 to its departure from Louisiana in 1731, ADM, 9 B, art. 99. Also useful is the ship's log, with observations recorded by the *Saint-Louis*'s ensign, AN, 4 JJ 17, 50.

49. Caillot, *Company Man,* 157.

Epilogue: Embracing India

1. Marc-Antoine Caillot Quittance, May 13, 1761, AN, Minutes des notaires de Paris, ARNO 1761, côte 1761 ET XXX 708; Marc-Antoine Caillot and Pierre Denoual, Inventory of property and associated values in Chandernagore, January 13, 1757, ANOM, C2 93, fo. 41v.

2. Haudrère, *La Compagnie française des Indes,* 1:171–76; Geneviève Beauchesne, *Historique de la construction navale à Lorient de 1666 à 1770* (Vincennes: Service historique de la Marine, 1980); Pierre Thomas-LaCroix, "Les Constructions et les ventes de navires dans les admirautés de Vannes et de Lorient au XVIIIe siècle," *Mémoires de la société d'histoire et d'archéologie de Bretagne* 49 (1969): 71–107.

3. These figures relate to sales generated in Nantes. There is no available data for sales out of the Lorient warehouses prior to 1758. Vignols and Sée, "Les Ventes de la Compagnie des Indes à Nantes," 492.

4. Haudrère, *La Compagnie française des Indes,* 1:289; Cheney, *Revolutionary Commerce,* 22; Gérard Le Bouëdec and Brigitte Nicolas, eds., *Le Goût de l'Inde* (Rennes: Presses Universitaires de Rennes, 2008).

5. Disarmament of the *Saint-Louis,* June 5, 1731, FML, 1 P 168, no. 123.

6. Armament of the *Atalante,* January 14, 1732, FML, 2 P 3, no. 25; disarmament of the *Atalante,* May 4, 1733, FML, 2 P 25, no. 7.

7. Marriage of Marc-Antoine Caillot and Marie-Claire Lucas, January 23, 1736, AN, registres de l'état civil, Outre-mer, Pondichéry, 85 Miom 1218.

8. Baptism of Marie-Madeleine Caillot, June 12, 1737; and internment of Marie-Claire Lucas, June 15, 1737, ibid.

9. Company directors to the Pondicherry Superior Council, January 18, 1738, *Correspondance du Conseil Supérieur de Pondichéry et de la Compagnie,* ed. Alfred Martineau (Pondicherry: Société de l'histoire de l'Inde française, 1927), 2:254.

10. Marriage of Marc-Antoine Caillot and Marie-Anne Coquelin, November 1, 1740, AN, registres de l'état civil, Outre-mer, Chandernagor, 85 Miom 1209.

11. Pondicherry Superior Council to Chandernagore Superior Council, March 16, 1742, *Correspondance du Conseil Supérieur de Pondichéry avec le Conseil de Chandernagor,* 2:209.

12. Ibid., April 4, 1743, 2:272.

13. Ibid., March 4, 1744, 2:311.

14. Ship's register for the *Neptune,* 1743–46, FML, 2 P 33-II.6.

15. Pondicherry Superior Council to Chandernagore Superior Council, July 11 and November 28, 1748, *Correspondance du Conseil Supérieur de Pondichéry avec le Conseil de Chandernagor,* 3:25, 36–37.

16. Ibid., October 17, 1750, 3:124.

17. "État général des employés au service de la Compagnie existans en janvier 1750," ANOM, C2 284, fo. 40.

18. "Nomination de la Compagnie des Indes en faveur du Sr. Caillot pour remplir l'office du Conseiller au Conseil Supérieur de Pondichéry," 1752, ANOM, Personnel E 59 (241Miom 66); Marc-Antoine Caillot Quittance, May 13, 1761, AN, Minutes des notaires de Paris, ARNO 1761, côte 1761 ET XXX 708.

19. Robert Travers, *Ideology and Empire in Eighteenth-Century India: The British in Bengal* (New York: Cambridge University Press, 2007), 32–34; Sushil Chaudhury, "The Im-

peratives of Empire: Private Trade, Sub-Imperialism and the British Attack on Chandernagore, March 1757," *Studies in History* 8, no. 1 (1992): 1–12; S. C. Hill, *Three Frenchmen in Bengal, or the Ruin of the French Settlements in 1757* (London: Longmans, Green, 1903).

20. Hill, *Three Frenchmen in Bengal*, 38.

21. Voltaire, *Fragments sur l'Inde, sur le général Lalli et sur le comte de Morangiès* (1773), 89.

22. Pierre-Mathieu Renault to Georges Duval de Leyrit, March 28, 1757, ANOM, C2 93, fo. 69.

23. Robert Travers, *Ideology and Empire*, 31–66.

24. Ibid.; Hill, *Three Frenchmen in Bengal*, 53.

25. Marc-Antoine Caillot Quittance, May 13, 1761, AN, Minutes des notaires de Paris, ARNO 1761, côte 1761 ET XXX 708.

Bibliography

Primary Sources

MANUSCRIPTS

France

Archives de la ville de Lorient, Lorient

CC Finances et contributions, 1724–92

GG5 Baptêmes, mariages et sépultures de la paroisse Saint-Louis, 1727–30

Archives départementales de Loire-Atlantique, Nantes

C 738 and 740 Répertoire du fonds de la Chambre de commerce de Nantes

Archives départementales du Morbihan, Vannes

9 B Amirauté de Vannes

4 E 121/4 Baptêmes, mariages et sépultures, Lorient, 1738–41

Archives départementales des Hauts-de-Seine, Nanterre

4 E Régistres parroissaux, Meudon

Archives départementales de Seine-Maritime, Rouen

C Administration provinciales, capitations des villes, Le Havre

Archives nationales, Paris

Archives des notaires

Fonds de la Marine

B3 Lettres reçues

4 JJ Journaux de bord

M Mélanges

O[1] Maison du Roi

Registres de l'état civil, Outre-mer, Pondichéry and Chandernagor (microfilm 85 Miom)

Archives nationales d'outre-mer, Aix-en-Provence

Dépôt des Fortifications des Colonies

80c Plan des fondations du bâtiment à faire construire, sur le bord du fleuve de Mississipy, 1729
81b Plan et élévation du bâtiment à faire construire sur le bord du fleuve Mississipy, 1729
82c Coupe et profil du bâtiment à faire construire, sur le bord du fleuve du Mississipy, 1729
87c Plan des bâtiments de la Direction, 1730
91b Plan du Camp des Nègres, 1732
105c Plan [et profil] des ouvrages projettés à faire à l'isle de la Balise avec les logements necessaires, 1723
111b Plan du fort de la Balise et des isles adjacentes, 1731
115a Plan et veuë général du Fort de la Balize, 1733
Fonds Ministériels
C2 Compagnie des Indes et Inde Française
C6 Sénégal et Côtes d'Afrique
E Personnel colonial ancien
F1A Comptes et états financiers, Louisiane
F2A Compagnies de commerce
F3 Collection Moreau de Saint-Méry
F5B Passagers
G1 Dépôt des papiers publics des colonies: Recensements, rôles et états des réfugiés, fois et hommages, titre de concessions
Secrétariat d'état à la Marine
A Bureau des Colonies: arrêts, déclarations, édits et ordonnances
B Correspondance au départ avec les colonies
C13A Correspondance à l'arrivée de la Louisiane
D2C Troupes et personnel civil
D2D Personnels militaire et civil, listes
Bibliothèque de l'Arsenal, Paris
Pellerin manuscript, MSS 497, folder 54
Bibliothèque nationale de France, Département des cartes et plans, Ge DD 2987 (8834 B)
Service historique de la Défense, Fonds de la Marine, Lorient
1P, 2P Fonds de la Compagnie des Indes

United States

Louisiana State Museum, New Orleans
Records of the Superior Council of Louisiana
Archdiocese of New Orleans, New Orleans
Records of the Saint Louis Church/Cathedral

The Historic New Orleans Collection, New Orleans

Acts of the Royal French Administration Concerning the Company of the Indies in Louisiana, MSS 268

Caillot, Marc-Antoine. "Relation du voyage de la Louisianne ou Nouv[lle] France fait par le Sr. Caillot en l'année 1730," 2005.0011

John Law Collection, MSS 606

PUBLISHED WORKS

Arrêt du Conseil d'État du Roy, concernant la retrocession faite à sa Majesté par la Compagnie des Indes de la Louisiane et du pays d'Illinois. Paris: Imprimerie Royale, 1731.

Bellin, Nicolas. *Le Petit atlas maritime: Recueil de cartes et plans des quatres parties du monde.* 5 vols. Paris: Imprimerie Royale, 1764.

Bibliothèque nationale de France, École des hautes études en sciences sociales, Centre national de la recherche scientifique, and Institut national d'études démographiques. "Des villages de Cassini aux communes d'aujourd'hui." Last modified 2007. http://cassini.ehess.fr/cassini/fr/html/index.htm.

Bossu, Jean-Bernard. *Nouveaux voyages aux indes occidentales.* Paris: Le Jay, 1768.

Caillot, Marc-Antoine. *A Company Man: The Remarkable French-Atlantic Voyage of a Clerk for the Company of the Indies, a Memoir by Marc-Antoine Caillot.* Edited by Erin M. Greenwald. Translated by Teri F. Chalmers. New Orleans: THNOC, 2013.

Cassini de Thury, César-François. *Carte générale de France.* 181 sheets. 1756–1815.

Challe, Robert. *Journal d'un voyage fait aux Indes Orientales, 1690–1691.* 1721. Reprint. Paris: Mercure de France, 2002.

Charlevoix, Pierre-François-Xavier de. *Charlevoix's Louisiana: Selections from the History and the Journal.* Edited by Charles E. O'Neill. Baton Rouge: LSU Press, 1977.

———. *Histoire de l'Îsle espagnole ou de S. Domingue.* 2 vols. Paris: J. Guérin, 1730–31.

———. *Histoire et description générale de la Nouvelle France.* Paris: Rollin fils, 1744.

Charpentier, François. *Discours d'un fidèle sujet du Roy touchant l'établissement d'une compagnie françoise pour le commerce des Indes Orientales, addressé à tous les François.* Paris, 1665.

Cockburn, William. *Sea Diseases: Or, a Treatise of Their Nature, Causes, and Cure.* London: G. Strahan, 1706 and 1736.

Le Code noir, ou, Édit du Roy, servant de réglement pour le gouvernement et l'administration de la justice, police, discipline, et le commerce des esclaves nègres, dans la province et colonie de la Louisiane, donné a Versailles en mois de mars 1724. Paris: Imprimerie Royale, 1727.

Daudet, Louis-Pierre. *Nouveau guide des chemins du royaume de France, contenant toutes les routes, tant générales que particulières dédié au Roy, par le sieur Daudet de Nismes, ingenieur-géographe de Sa Majesté*. Paris: E. Ganeau, 1724.

Déclaration du Roi, concernant les vagabons & gens sans aveu. Grenoble: Gaspard Giroud, 1719.

Dernis. *Recueil, ou Collection des titres, édits, déclarations, arrêts, réglemens et autres pièces concernant la Compagnie des Indes établie au mois d'août 1664*. 4 vols. Paris: Antoine Boudet, 1755–56.

Dumont de Montigny, Jean-François Benjamin, and Jean Baptiste Le Mascrier. *Mémoires historiques sur la Louisiane*. Paris: C.J.B. Bauche, 1753.

Dumont de Montigny, Jean-François Benjamin. *Regards sur le monde atlantique, 1715–1747*. Edited by C. Zecher, Shannon Dawdy, and Gordon Sayre. Quebec: Septentrion, 2008.

Eltis, David, Stephen D. Behrendt, David Richardson, and Herbert S. Klein, eds. and comps. *The Trans-Atlantic Slave Trade: A Database on CD-ROM*. Cambridge: Cambridge University Press, 1999.

Emory University. "Voyages: The Trans-Atlantic Slave Trade Database." Last modified 2009. www.slavevoyages.org/tast/index.faces.

Estienne, René, ed. *Les Armements au long cours de la deuxième Compagnie des Indes, 1717–1773*. Lorient: Service historique de la Marine, Archives du port de Lorient, 1996.

"Geographische Beschreibung der Provinz Louisiana in Canada von dem Fluß St. Lorenz bis an den Ausfluß des Flusses Missisipi." Liepzig: Christoph Weigel, 1720.

Hachard, Marie-Madeleine. *Relation du voyage des dames religieuses Ursulines de Roüen, à la Nouvelle Orleans, parties de France le 22 février 1727. & arrivez à la Louisiane le 23. Juillet de la même année*. Rouen: Chez A. Prevost, 1728.

———. *Voices from an Early American Convent: Marie Madeleine Hachard and the New Orleans Ursulines, 1727–1760*. Edited by Emily Clark. Baton Rouge: LSU Press, 2007.

Iberville, Pierre Le Moyne d'. *Iberville's Gulf Journals*. Edited and translated by Richebourg Gaillard McWilliams. Baton Rouge: LSU Press, 1981.

Labat, Jean-Baptiste. *Nouveau voyage aux isles de l'Amérique*. 6 vols. La Haye: P. Husson, 1724.

Laval, Antoine François. *Voyage de la Louisiane, fait par ordre du Roy en l'année mil sept cent vingt*. Paris: J. Mariette, 1728.

Law, John. *Money and Trade Considered with a Proposal for Supplying the Nation with Money.* Edinburgh: Andrew Anderson, 1705.

"Le Commerce que les Indiens du Mexique font avec les François au port de Missisipi." Paris: François-Gérard Jollain, 1719–21.

Le Page du Pratz, Antoine Simon. *Histoire de la Louisiane.* 3 vols. Paris: De Bure, 1758.

———. *The History of Louisiana.* Edited by Joseph G. Tregle Jr. Baton Rouge: LSU Press, 1975.

Lettres patentes du Roi portant privilège en faveur du Sr. Law & sa compagnie, d'establir une banque générale. Paris: Imprimerie Royal, 1716.

Lettres patentes en forme d'édit, portant établissement d'une compagnie de commerce sous le nom de Compagnie d'Occident. Paris: Chez la Veuve de François Muguet, Hubert Muguet, premier imprimeur du Roy, & Loüis-Denis de La Tour Libraire, 1717.

Lettres patentes en forme d'édit, portant revocation de la Compagnie de Saint-Domingue. Paris: Imprimerie du Roi, April 1720.

Lind, James. *An Essay on the Most Effectual Means of Preserving the Health of Seamen in the Royal Navy.* Edinburgh: A. Millar, A. Kincaid, and A. Donaldson, 1757.

———. *A Treatise on the Scurvy.* Edinburgh: A. Kinkaid and A. Donaldson, 1753.

Liste générale des postes de France. Paris: Jaillot, 1721.

Maduell, Charles, Jr., ed. and trans. *The Census Tables for the French Colony of Louisiana from 1699 through 1732.* Baltimore: Genealogical Publishing Co., 1972.

Martineau, Alfred, ed. *Correspondance du Conseil supérieur de Pondichéry avec le Conseil de Chandernagor.* 3 vols. Pondichéry: Société de l'histoire de l'Inde, 1915–27.

Mead, Richard. "Dissertation sur le Scorbut." *Nouvelle méthode pour pomper le mauvais air des vaisseaux.* Paris: Chez Durand, 1749.

Ménétra, Jacques-Louis. *Journal of My Life.* Edited by Daniel Roche and translated by Arthur Goldhammer. New York: Columbia University Press, 1986.

Mettas, Jean. *Répertoire des expéditions négrières françaises au XVIIIe siècle.* Vol. 1. Edited by Serge Daget and Michèle Daget. Paris: Société française d'histoire d'outre mer, 1978.

Mississippi Provincial Archives: French Dominion. Vols. 2–3. Edited and translated by Dunbar Rowland and A. G. Sanders. Jackson: Press of the Mississippi Department of Archives, 1932. Vols. 4–5. Collected, edited, and translated by Dunbar Rowland and A. G. Sanders; revised and edited by Patricia K. Galloway. Baton Rouge: LSU Press, 1984.

Moreau de Saint-Méry, Médéric Louis Elie. *Description topographique, physique, civile, politique et historique de la partie française de l'îsle Saint-Domingue*. 3 vols. Paris: Société de l'histoire des colonies françaises & Librarie Larose, 1958.

"Novissima Tabula Regionis Gallice dictae La Louisiane." Liepzig: Christoph Weigel, 1720.

Pénicault, André. *Fleur de lys and Calumet: Being the Pénicault Narrative of French Adventure in Louisiana*. Edited and translated by Richebourg Gaillard McWilliams. Tuscaloosa: University of Alabama Press, 1988.

Piganiol de La Force, Jean Aymar. *Nouveau voyage de France avec un itinéraire et des cartes faites exprès qui marquent exactement les routes qu'il faut suivre pour voyager dans toutes les provinces de ce royaume*. Rev. ed. Paris: T. Le Gras, 1740.

Pradel. *Le Chevalier de Pradel: Vie d'un colon français en Louisiane au XVIIIe d'après sa correspondance et celle de sa famille*. Edited by A. Baillardel and A. Prioult. Paris, 1928.

Recueil d'arrests et autres pièces pour l'établissement de la Compagnie d'Occident. Amsterdam: Chez Jean Frederic Bernard, 1720.

Saugrain, Claude-Marin. *Nouveau voyage de France, géographique, historique et curieux, disposé par différentes routes, à l'usage des étrangers et des François, contenant une exacte explication de tout ce qu'il y a de singulier et de rare à voir dans ce royaume, avec les adresses pour trouver facilement les routes, les voitures et autres utilitez nécessaires aux voyageurs*. Paris: Saugrain l'aîné, 1720.

Thwaites, Reuben Gold, ed. *Jesuit Relations and Allied Documents: Travels and Relations of the Jesuit Missionaries in New France, 1610–1791*. Vols. 67–68. Cleveland: Burrows Brothers, 1900.

Valette de Laudun, M. *Journal d'un voyage à la Louisiane, fait en 1720 par M.***, capitaine de vaisseau du Roi*. La Haye: Chez Musier fils & Fournier, 1768.

Vallée, M. G., ed. *Au service de la Compagnie des Indes: Lettres inédites d'une famille du Poitou au XVIIIe siècle, les Renault de Saint-Germain*. Paris: Maisonneuve & Larose, 2001.

Technical References

Alembert, Bossut, La Lande, Condorcet, and Charles. *Encyclopédie méthodique. Dictionnaire des jeux, faisant suite au tome III des Mathématiques*. Paris: Chez Panckoucke, 1789.

Aubin, Nicolas. *Dictionnaire de Marine*. Amsterdam: Brunel, 1702.

Beawes, Wyndham, and Joseph Chitty. *Lex mercatoria, or, A complete code of commercial law being a general guide to all men in business . . . with an account of our mercantile companies, of our colonies and factories abroad, of our com-*

mercial treaties with foreign powers, of the duty of consuls, and of the laws concerning aliens, naturalization, and denization: to which is added an account of the commerce of the whole world describing the manufactures and products of each country, with tables of the correspondence and agreement of their respective coins, weights and measures. London: F. C. and J. Rivington, 1813.

Falconer, William. *An Universal Dictionary of the Marine: Or, a Copious Explanation of the Technical Terms and Phrases Employed in the Construction, Equipment, Furniture, Machinery, Movements, and Military Operations of a Ship . . . To Which Is Annexed, a Translation of the French Sea-Terms and Phrases, Collected from the Works of Mess. du Hamel, Aubin, Saverien, &c.* London: T. Cadel, 1776.

Guiffrey, Jules. *Comptes des bâtiments du Rois sous le règne de Louis XIV.* Vols. 4–5. Paris: Imprimerie nationale, 1881–1901.

Guyot. *Traité des droits, fonctions, franchises, exemptions, prérogatives et privilèges annexés en France à chaque dignité. . . .* 4 vols. Paris: Visse, 1786–88.

Marion, Marcel. *Dictionnaire des institutions de la France au XVIIe et XVIIIe siècles.* Paris: A. Picard, 1923.

O'Neill, E. Wesley, Jr. "French Coinage in History and Literature." *French Review* 39, no. 1 (1965): 1–14.

Parlett, David. *The Oxford Dictionary of Card Games.* New York: Oxford University Press, 1996.

Rowlett, Russell, and the University of North Carolina at Chapel Hill. "How Many: A Dictionary of Units of Measurement." www.unc.edu/~rowlett/units/index.html (accessed 2009–15).

Secondary Sources

Allain, Mathé. "L'Immigration française en Louisiane." *Revue d'histoire de l'Amérique française* 28 (1975): 555–64.

———. "Manon Lescaut et Ses Consoeurs: Women in the Early French Period, 1700–1731." In *Proceedings of the Fifth Meeting of the French Colonial Historical Society*, edited by James J. Cooke, 18–26. Lanham, Md.: French Colonial Historical Society, 1980.

Alpern, Stanley B. "What Africans Got for Their Slaves: A Master List of European Trade Goods." *History in Africa* 22 (1995): 5–43.

Ames, Glenn J. *Colbert, Mercantilism, and the French Quest for Asian Trade.* DeKalb: Northern Illinois University Press, 1996.

Ames, Glenn J., and Ronald S. Love, eds. *Distant Lands and Diverse Cultures: The French Experience in Asia, 1600–1700.* Westport, Conn.: Greenwood Press, 2003.

Aubert, Guillaume. "'To Establish One Law and Definite Rules': Race, Religion, and the Transatlantic Origins of the Louisiana Code Noir." In *Louisiana: Crossroads of the Atlantic World*, edited by Cécile Vidal, 21–43. Philadelphia: University of Pennsylvania Press, 2014.

Augst, Thomas. *The Clerk's Tale: Young Men and Moral Life in Nineteenth-Century America*. Chicago: University of Chicago Press, 2003.

Baker, Susan Read. "Nautical Fare in Robert Challe's *Journal d'un voyage fait aux Indes orientales* (1690–1691)." *Cahiers du dix-septième: An Interdisciplinary Journal* 9 (2004): 21–32.

Baker, Vaughn. "*Cherchez les femmes:* Some Glimpses of Women in Early Eighteenth-Century Louisiana." *Louisiana History* 31 (1990): 21–37.

Balayé, Simon. *La Bibliothèque nationale des origines à 1800*. Geneva: Librairie Droz, 1988.

Balvay, Arnaud. *La Révolte des Natchez*. Paris: Éditions le Félin, 2008.

Banks, Kenneth J. *Chasing Empire across the Sea: Communications and the State in the French Atlantic, 1713–1763*. Montreal: McGill-Queen's University Press, 2002.

———. "Financiers, Factors, and French Proprietary Companies in West Africa, 1664–1713." In *Constructing Early Modern Empires: Proprietary Ventures in the Atlantic World, 1500–1750*, edited by L. H. Roper and B. Van Ruymbeke, 79–116. Leiden: Brill, 2007.

———. "Official Duplicity: The Illicit Slave Trade of Martinique, 1713–1763." In *The Atlantic Economy during the Seventeenth and Eighteenth Centuries: Organization, Operation, Practice, and Personnel*, edited by Peter A. Coclanis, 229–51. Columbia: University of South Carolina Press, 2005.

Barbier, J. "La Compagnie Française des Indes." *Revue historique de l'Inde Française* 3 (1919): 5–96.

Barnett, James F., Jr. *The Natchez Indians: A History to 1735*. Jackson: University Press of Mississippi, 2007.

Barry, Boubacar. *Senegambia and the Atlantic Slave Trade*. New York: Cambridge University Press, 1998.

Beauchesne, Geneviève. *Historique de la construction navale à Lorient de 1666 à 1770*. Vincennes: Service historique de la Marine, 1980.

Behrendt, Stephen. "Crew Mortality in the Transatlantic Slave Trade in the Eighteenth Century." *Slavery and Abolition* 18 (1997): 49–71.

Berry, Stephen R. *A Path in the Mighty Waters: Shipboard Life and Atlantic Crossings to the New World*. New Haven, Conn.: Yale University Press, 2015.

Bienvenu, Germain Joseph. "Another America, Another Literature: Narratives from Louisiana's Colonial Experience." Ph.D. diss., Louisiana State University, 1995.

Biver, Paul. *Histoire du Château de Meudon*. Paris: Jouve & Co., 1923.

Blanquie, Christophe. "Dans la main du grand maître: Les Offices de la Maison du Roi, 1643–1720." *Histoire & mesure* 8 (1998): 243–88.

Blassingame, John. *The Slave Community: Plantation Life in the Antebellum South*. New York: Oxford University Press, 1979.

Bolster, Jeffrey W. *Black Jacks: African American Seamen in the Age of Sail*. Cambridge: Harvard University Press, 1997.

———. "An Inner Diaspora: Black Sailors Making Selves." In *Through a Glass Darkly: Reflections on Personal Identity in Early America*, edited by Ronald Hoffman, Mechal Sobel, and Frederika Teute, 419–62. Chapel Hill: University of North Carolina Press, 1997.

Bond, Bradley, ed. *French Colonial Louisiana and the Atlantic World*. Baton Rouge: LSU Press, 2005.

Boucher, Jacqueline. "L'Évolution de la Maison du Roi des derniers Valois aux premiers Bourbons." *Dix-septième siècle* 34 (1982): 359–79.

Boucher, Philip. *France and the American Tropics to 1700: Tropics of Discontent?* Baltimore: Johns Hopkins University Press, 2008.

———. *Les Nouvelles Frances: France in America, 1500–1815, an Imperial Perspective*. Providence, R.I.: John Carter Brown Library, 1989.

Bourquin, Laurent. *La Noblesse dans la France moderne (XVIe–XVIIIe siècles)*. Paris: Belin, 2002.

Boxer, C. R. *The Dutch Seaborne Empire, 1600–1800*. New York: Knopf, 1965.

Brain, Jeffrey P. *Tunica Treasure*. Cambridge: Peabody Museum of Archaeology and Ethnology, Harvard University, and Peabody Museum of Salem, 1979.

Braudel, Fernand. *Civilization and Capitalism, 15th–18th Century: The Structures of Everyday Life*. Berkeley: University of California Press, 1992.

———. *L'Identité de la France*. Paris: Arthaud & Flammarion, 1986.

Brown, Ian W., and Vincas P. Steponaitis. "The Grand Village of the Natchez Indians Was Indeed Grand: A Reconsideration of the Fatherland Site Landscape." In *Forging Southeastern Identities: Social Archaeology and Ethnohistory of the Mississippian to Early Historic South*, edited by Gregory A. Waselkov and Marvin T. Smith. Tuscaloosa: University of Alabama Press, forthcoming.

Brown, Stephen R. *Scurvy: How a Surgeon, a Mariner, and a Gentleman Solved the Greatest Medical Mystery in the Age of Sail*. New York: Thomas Dunne Books, 2004.

Bruseth, James E., and Toni S. Turner. *From a Watery Grave: The Discovery and Excavation of La Salle's Shipwreck,* La Belle. College Station: Texas A&M University Press, 2005.

Buchanan, Thomas C. *Black Life on the Mississippi: Slaves, Free Blacks, and the*

Western Steamboat World. Chapel Hill: University of North Carolina Press, 2004.

Burg, B. R. *Sodomy and the Perception of Evil: English Sea Rovers in the Seventeenth-Century Caribbean.* New York: New York University Press, 1983.

Campanella, Richard. *Time and Place in New Orleans: Past Geographies in the Present Day.* New Orleans: Pelican Publishing, 2002.

Carpenter, Kenneth J. *The History of Scurvy and Vitamin C.* Cambridge: Cambridge University Press, 1986.

Cecelski, David S. *The Waterman's Song: Slavery and Freedom in Maritime North Carolina.* Chapel Hill: University of North Carolina Press, 2001.

Cellard, Jacques. *John Law et la Régence.* Paris: Plon, 1996.

Chaudhuri, K. N. *Trade and Civilisation in the Indian Ocean: An Economic History from the Rise of Islam to 1750.* Cambridge: Cambridge University Press, 1985.

———. *The Trading World of Asia and the English East India Company, 1660–1760.* New York: Cambridge University Press, 1978.

Chaudhury, Sushil. "The Imperatives of the Empire: Private Trade, Sub-Imperialism and the British Attack on Chandernagore, March 1757." *Studies in History* 8 (1992): 1–12.

Cheney, Paul. *Revolutionary Commerce: Globalization and the French Monarchy.* Cambridge: Harvard University Press, 2010.

Chinard, Gilbert. *L'Amérique et le rêve exotique dans la littérature française au XVIIe et au XVIIIe siècles.* Paris: Société d'éditions "Les Belles Lettres," 1913.

Choquette, Leslie. "Proprietorships in French North America." In *Constructing Early Modern Empire: Proprietary Ventures in the Atlantic World, 1500–1750,* edited by L. H. Roper and B. Van Ruymbeke, 117–32. Leiden: Brill, 2007.

Christopher, Emma. *Slave Ship Sailors and Their Captive Cargoes, 1730–1807.* New York: Cambridge University Press, 2006.

Clark, Emily. "'By All the Conduct of Their Lives': A Laywomen's Confraternity in New Orleans, 1730–1744." *William and Mary Quarterly,* 3rd ser., 54 (1997): 769–94.

———. *Masterless Mistresses: The New Orleans Ursulines and the Development of a New World Society, 1727–1834.* Chapel Hill: University of North Carolina Press, 2007.

Coclanis, Peter A. "Atlantic World or Atlantic/World?" *William and Mary Quarterly,* 3rd ser., 63, no. 4 (2006): 725–42.

Cohen, William. *The French Encounter with Africans: White Response to Blacks, 1530–1880.* Bloomington: Indiana University Press, 1980.

Cohn, Raymond L. "Maritime Mortality in the Eighteenth and Nineteenth Centuries: A Survey." *International Journal of Maritime History* 1 (1989): 159–91.

Conner, Susan P. "The Pox in Eighteenth-Century France." In *The Secret Mal-*

ady: *Venereal Disease in Eighteenth-Century Britain and France*, edited by Linda Evi Merians, 15–33. Lexington: University Press of Kentucky, 1996.

Coquery, Natacha. *L'Hôtel aristocratique: Le marché du luxe à Paris au XVIIIe siècle*. Paris: Publications de la Sorbonne, 1998.

Cressy, David. *Coming Over: Migration and Communication between England and New England in the Seventeenth Century*. Cambridge: Cambridge University Press, 1987.

Crété, Liliane. *La Traite des Nègres sous l'Ancien Régime*. Paris: Perrin, 1998.

Curtin, Philip D. *Economic Change in Precolonial Africa: Senegambia in the Era of the Slave Trade*. 2 vols. Madison: University of Wisconsin Press, 1975.

Curto, Diogo Ramada, and Francisco Bethancourt, eds. *Portuguese Oceanic Expansion, 1400–1800*. Cambridge: Cambridge University Press, 2007.

Davis, Natalie Z. *Society and Culture in Early Modern France*. Stanford: Stanford University Press, 1975.

Dawdy, Shannon Lee. *Building the Devil's Empire: French Colonial New Orleans*. Chicago: University of Chicago Press, 2008.

———. "La Ville Sauvage: 'Enlightened' Colonialism and Creole Improvisation in New Orleans, 1699–1769." Ph.D. diss., University of Michigan, 2003.

———. "'A Wild Taste': Food and Colonialism in 18th-century Louisiana." *Ethnohistory* 57 (2010): 389–413.

Dawdy, Shannon Lee, and Christopher N. Matthews. "Colonial and Antebellum New Orleans." In *Archaeology of Louisiana*, edited by Mark A. Rees, 273–90. Baton Rouge: LSU Press, 2010.

Debien, Gabriel, and Louis Merle. "Colons, marchands et engagés à Nantes au XVIIe siècle." *Revue de la Porte Océane* (December 1953): 5–8 and (January 1954): 7–15.

Delcourt, André. *La France et les établissements français au Sénégal entre 1713 et 1763*. Dakar: Institut français d'Afrique Noire, 1952.

Dening, Greg. *Mr. Bligh's Bad Language: Passion, Power, and Theatre on the Bounty*. Cambridge: Cambridge University Press, 1992.

Dermigny, Louis. *La Chine et l'Occident: le commerce à Canton au XVIIIe siècle, 1719–1833*. 3 vols. Paris: SEVPEN, 1964.

Deschamps, Hubert. *Histoire de Madagascar*. Paris: Berger-Levrault, 1965.

Dessert, Daniel. *Argent, pouvoir et société au Grand Siècle*. Paris: Fayard, 1984.

———. *La Royale: Vaisseaux et marins du Roi-Soleil*. Paris: Fayard, 1996.

———. *Le Royaume de Monsieur Colbert, 1661–1683*. Paris: Perrin, 2007.

Deveau, Jean-Michel. *La France au temps des négriers*. Paris: France-Empire, 1994.

Doyle, William. *Venality: The Sale of Offices in Eighteenth-Century France*. Oxford: Clarendon Press, 1996.

Dubé, Alexandre. "Making a Career out of the Atlantic: Louisiana's Plume." In

Louisiana: Crossroads of the Atlantic World, edited by Cécile Vidal, 44–67. Philadelphia: University of Pennsylvania Press, 2014.

Dubois, Laurent. "The French Atlantic." In *Atlantic History: A Critical Appraisal*, edited by Jack P. Greene and Philip D. Morgan, 137–62. New York: Oxford University Press, 2009.

Duncan, T. Bentley. *Atlantic Islands: Madeira, the Azores, and the Cape Verdes in Seventeenth-Century Commerce and Navigation*. Chicago: University of Chicago Press, 1972.

Duval, Kathleen. "Interconnectedness and Diversity in French Louisiana." In *Powhatan's Mantle: Indians in the Colonial Southeast*, edited by Gregory A. Waselkov, Peter H. Wood, and Tom Hatley, 133–62. Lincoln: University of Nebraska Press, 2006.

Eccles, W. J. *The French in North America, 1500–1783*. East Lansing: Michigan State University Press, 1998.

Edmunds, R. David, and Joseph L. Peyser. *The Fox Wars: The Mesquakie Challenge to New France*. Norman: University of Oklahoma Press, 1993.

Ekberg, Carl J. *The Failure of Louis XIV's Dutch War*. Chapel Hill: University of North Carolina Press, 1979.

Elkins, Stanley. *Slavery: A Problem in American Institutional and Intellectual Life*. Chicago: University of Chicago Press, 1959.

Favier, René. "Jouer dans les villes de province en France au XVIIIe siècle." *Histoire Urbaine* 1 (2000): 65–85.

Firth, Raymond. *Symbols: Public and Private*. Ithaca: Cornell University Press, 1973.

Frostin, Charles. *Les Révoltes blanches à Saint-Domingue aux XVIIe et XVIIIe siècles*. Rennes: Presses universitaires de Rennes, 2008.

Furber, Holden. *Rival Empires of Trade in the Orient, 1600–1800*. Minneapolis: University of Minnesota Press, 1976.

Gallay, Alan. *The Indian Slave Trade: The Rise of the English Empire in the American South, 1670–1717*. New Haven, Conn.: Yale University Press, 2003.

Galloway, Patricia. "Rhetoric of Difference: Le Page du Pratz on African Slave Management in Eighteenth-Century Louisiana." *French Colonial History* 3 (2003): 1–16.

Galloway, Patricia and Jason Baird Jackson. "Natchez and Neighboring Groups." *Handbook of North American Indians, Southeast*. Vol. 14. Edited by Raymond Fogelson, 598–615. Washington, D.C.: Smithsonian Institution, 2004.

Garrigus, John. *Before Haiti: Race and Citizenship in French Saint-Domingue*. New York: Palgrave Macmillan, 2006.

Geggus, David. "The French Slave Trade: An Overview." *William and Mary Quarterly*, 3rd ser., 58 (2001): 119–38.

Giraud, Marcel. *Histoire de la Louisiane française*. Vol. 3: *Époque de John Law, 1717–1720*. Paris: Presse universitaire de France, 1966.

———. *Histoire de la Louisiane française*. Vol. 4: *La Louisiane après le système de Law, 1721–1723*. Paris: Presse universitaire de France, 1974.

———. *A History of French Louisiana*. Vol. 1: *The Reign of Louis XIV, 1698–1715*. Translated by Joseph C. Lambert. Baton Rouge: LSU Press, 1974.

———. *A History of French Louisiana*: Vol. 2: *Years of Transition, 1715–1717*. Translated by Brian Pearce. Baton Rouge: LSU Press, 1993.

———. *A History of French Louisiana*. Vol. 5: *The Company of the Indies, 1723–1731*. Translated by Brian Pearce. Baton Rouge: LSU Press, 1991.

Greene, Jack P. *Pursuits of Happiness: The Social Development of Early Modern British Colonies and the Formation of American Culture*. Chapel Hill: University of North Carolina Press, 1988.

Grussi, Olivier. *La Vie quotidienne des joueurs sous l'Ancien Régime à Paris et à la Cour*. Paris: Hachette, 1985.

Gutkind, Peter C. W. "The Boatmen of Ghana: The Possibilities of a Pre-Colonial African Labor History." In *Confrontation, Class Consciousness, and the Labor Process*, edited by Michael Hanagan and Charles Stephenson, 123–66. New York: Greenwood Press, 1986.

———. "Trade and Labor in Early Precolonial African History: The Canoemen of Southern Ghana." In *The Workers of the African Trade*, edited by Catherine Coquery-Vidrovitch and Paul E. Lovejoy, 25–50. London: Sage Publications, 1985.

Gutton, Jean-Pierre. *Domestiques et serviteurs dans la France de l'Ancien Régime*. Paris: Aubier Montaigne, 1981.

Hall, Gwendolyn Midlo. "African Women in French and Spanish Louisiana: Origins, Roles, Family, Work, Treatment." In *The Devil's Lane: Sex and Race in the Early South*, edited by Catherine Clinton and Michele Gillespie, 247–62. New York: Oxford University Press, 1997.

———. *Africans in Colonial Louisiana: The Development of Afro-Creole Culture in the Eighteenth Century*. Baton Rouge: LSU Press, 1992.

Hardy, James D., Jr. "The Superior Council in Colonial Louisiana." In *Frenchmen and French Ways in the Mississippi Valley*, edited by John Francis McDermott, 87–101. Urbana: University of Illinois Press, 1969.

———. "The Transportation of Convicts to Colonial Louisiana." *Louisiana History* 7 (1966): 207 20.

Harms, Robert. *The Diligent: A Voyage through the Worlds of the Slave Trade*. New York: Basic Books, 2002.

Hart, Jonathan. *Representing the New World: The English and French Uses of the Example of Spain*. New York: Palgrave, 2001.

Haudrère, Philippe. *La Compagnie française des Indes au XVIIIe siècle, 1719–1795.* 2 vols. Paris: Les Indes savantes, 2005.

———. "Le Commerce." In *L'Inde et la France: Deux siècles d'histoire commune, XVIIe–XVIIIe siècles,* edited by Philippe Le Tréguilly and Monique Morazé, 23–31. Paris: CNRS éditions, 1995.

Haudrère, Philippe, and Gérard Le Bouëdec. *Les Compagnies des Indes.* Rennes: Éditions Ouest-France, 2005.

Havard, Gilles, and Cécile Vidal. *Histoire de l'Amérique française.* Paris: Flammarion, 2003.

Heaney, Jane Frances. *A Century of Pioneering: A History of the Ursuline Nuns in New Orleans, 1727–1827.* New Orleans: Ursuline Sisters of New Orleans, 1993.

Heijer, Henk den. "The Dutch West India Company, 1621–1791." In *Riches from Atlantic Commerce: Dutch Atlantic Trade and Shipping, 1585–1817,* edited by Johannes Postma and V. Enthoven, 77–112. Boston: Brill, 2003.

Heinrich, Pierre. *La Louisiane sous la Compagnie des Indes.* Paris: E. Guilmoto, 1908.

Henningsen, Henning. *Crossing the Equator: Sailors' Baptism and Other Initiation Rites.* Copenhagen: Munksgaard, 1961.

Higgenbotham, Jay. *Fort Maurepas: The Birth of Louisiana.* Mobile, Ala.: Colonial Books, 1968.

———. *Old Mobile: Fort Louis de la Louisiane, 1702–1711.* Tuscaloosa: University of Alabama Press, 1991.

Hill, Samuel C. *Three Frenchmen in Bengal, or the Commercial Ruin of the French Settlement in 1757.* London: Longmans, Green, 1903.

Hogendorn, Jan, and Marion Johnson. *The Shell Money of the Slave Trade.* Cambridge: Cambridge University Press, 1986.

Houdaille, Jacques. "Trois paroisses de Saint-Domingue au XVIIIe siècle." *Population* 18 (1963): 93–110.

Hudson, Charles. *The Southeastern Indians.* Knoxville: University of Tennessee Press, 1976.

Kaeppelin, Paul. *La Compagnie des Indes Orientales et François Martin.* Paris: A. Challamel, 1908.

Kavanagh, Thomas. "The Libertine's Bluff: Cards and Culture in Eighteenth-Century France." *Eighteenth-Century Studies* 33 (2000): 505–21.

Kettering, Sharon. "Patronage and Kinship in Early Modern France." *French Historical Studies* 16 (1989): 408–35.

———. *Patrons, Brokers, and Clients in Seventeenth-Century France.* Oxford: Oxford University Press, 1986.

King, Richard H. "Domination and Fabrication: Re-Thinking Stanley Elkins' 'Slavery.'" *Slavery & Abolition* 22 (2001): 1–28.

Klooster, Wim. "Inter-Imperial Smuggling in the Americas, 1600–1800." In *Soundings in Atlantic History: Latent Structures and Intellectual Currents, 1500–1830*, edited by Bernard Bailyn and Patricia L. Denault, 141–80. Cambridge: Harvard University Press, 2009.

Kops, Henriette de Bruyn. *A Spirited Exchange: The Wine and Brandy Trade between France and the Dutch Republic in Its Atlantic Framework, 1600–1650*. Leiden: Brill, 2007.

Lacroix, Jean-Bernard. *Les Français au Sénégal au temps de la Compagnie des Indes de 1719 à 1758*. Vincennes: Service historique de la Marine, 1986.

Langlois, Gilles-Antoine. *Des Villes pour la Louisiane française: Théorie et pratique de l'urbanistique coloniale au 18e siècle*. Paris: Harmattan, 2003.

Laverny, Sophie de. *Les domestiques commensaux du Roi de France au XVIIe siècle*. Paris: Presses de l'université de Paris–Sorbonne, 2002.

Law, Robin. "Between the Sea and the Lagoons." *Cahiers d'études africaines* 29 (1989): 209–37.

———. *The Slave Coast of West Africa, 1550–1750: The Impact of the Atlantic Trade on an African Society*. New York: Oxford University Press, 1991.

Le Bouëdec, Gérard. "Un Chantier de construction navale" and "Du chantier à la ville nouvelle." *Les Compagnies des Indes*, 19–31. Rennes: Éditions Ouest-France, 2005.

Le Bouëdec, Gérard, and Brigitte Nicolas, eds. *Le Goût de l'Inde*. Rennes: Presses universitaires de Rennes, 2008.

Le Tréguilly, Philippe, and Monique Morazé, eds. *L'Inde et la France: Deux siècles d'histoire commune, XVIIe–XVIII siècles*. Paris: CNRS éditions, 1995.

Linon-Chipon, Sophie. *Gallia Orientalis: Voyages aux Indes orientales, 1529–1722*. Paris: l'Université de Paris–Sorbonne, 2003.

Livet, Georges. "La Route royale et la civilisation française de la fin du XVe au milieu du XVIIIe siècle." In *Les Routes de France: depuis les origines jusqu'à nos jours*, edited by Guy Michaud, 57–100. Paris: L'Association pour la diffusion de la pensée française, 1959.

Lovejoy, Paul E. *Transformations in Slavery: A History of Slavery in Africa*. Cambridge: Cambridge University Press, 2012.

Luskey, Brian. *On the Make: Clerks and the Quest for Capital in Nineteenth-Century America*. New York: New York University Press, 2010.

Lynn, John A. *The Wars of Louis XIV, 1667–1714*. New York: Longman, 1999.

Martin, Gaston. *L'Ère des négriers (1717–1774)*. Paris: Karlatha, 1933.

———. "Nantes et la Compagnie des Indes (1664–1769)." *Revue d'histoire économique et sociale* 15 (1927): 231–53.

Masson, Paul. *Histoire des établissements et du commerce français dans l'Afrique barbaresque, 1560–1793*. Paris: Librairie Hachette, 1903.

Maza, Sarah. *Servants and Masters in Eighteenth-Century France: The Uses of Loyalty.* Princeton: Princeton University Press, 1983.

Metcalf, Alida. *Go-Betweens and the Colonization of Brazil.* Austin: University of Texas Press, 2005.

Milne, George Edward. *Natchez Country: Indians, Colonists, and the Landscapes of Race in French Louisiana.* Athens: University of Georgia Press, 2015.

———. "Picking Up the Pieces: Natchez Coalescence in the Shatter Zone." In *Mapping the Mississippian Shatter Zone: The Colonial Indian Slave Trade and Regional Instability in the American South,* edited by Robbie Ethridge and Sheri M. Shuck-Hall, 388–418. Lincoln: University of Nebraska Press, 2009.

Miquelon, Dale. *Dugard of Rouen: French Trade to Canada and the West Indies, 1729–1770.* Montreal: McGill-Queen's University Press, 1978.

Moogk, Peter N. "Reluctant Exiles: Emigrants from France in Canada before 1760." *William and Mary Quarterly,* 3rd ser., 46 (1989): 463–505.

Morgan, M. J. *Land of Big Rivers: French and Indian Illinois, 1699–1778.* Carbondale: Southern Illinois University Press, 2010.

Mousnier, Roland. *The Institutions of France under Absolute Monarchy, 1598–1789.* 2 vols. Translated by Brian Pearce and Arthur Goldhammer. Chicago: University of Chicago Press, 1979.

Murat, Inès. *Colbert.* Translated by Robert Francis Cook and Jeannie Van Asselt. Charlottesville: University Press of Virginia, 1984.

Murphy, Antoin E. *John Law: Economic Theorist and Policy Maker.* Oxford: Oxford University Press, 1997.

Musée de la Compagnie des Indes. *La mer et la navigation: Lorient au temps de la Compagnie des Indes.* Port-Louis: Musée de la Compagnie des Indes, 1998.

Nières, Claude. *Histoire de Lorient.* Toulouse: Privat, 1988.

O'Neill, Charles Edwards. *Church and State in French Colonial Louisiana: Policy and Politics to 1732.* New Haven, Conn.: Yale University Press, 1966.

Owsley, Douglas W., Charles E. Orser Jr., Robert Montgomery, and Claudia C. Holland. "An Archaeological and Physical Anthropological Study of the First Cemetery in New Orleans." Baton Rouge: Louisiana Division of Archaeology, 1985.

Perret, André. "René Montaudoin, armateur et négrier nantais (1673–1731)." *Bulletin de la Société archéologique et historique de Nantes et de la Loire-Inférieure Nantes* 88 (1949): 78–94.

Pétré-Grenouilleau, Olivier. *Nantes au temps de la traite des Noirs.* Paris: Hachette, 1998.

———. *Les Traites négrières.* Paris: Èditions Gallimard, 2004.

Postma, Johannes. "A Monopoly Relinquished: The West India Company and the Atlantic Slave Trade." *De Halve maen* 70 (1997): 84–85.

Prévost, Antoine-François. *Histoire de chevalier Des Grieux et de Manon Lescaut.* Amsterdam: Au dépense de la Compagnie, 1753.

Price, Jacob M. *France and the Chesapeake: A History of the French Tobacco Monopoly, 1674–1791, and of Its Relationship to the British and American Tobacco Trades.* 2 vols. Ann Arbor: University of Michigan Press, 1973.

Pritchard, James. *In Search of Empire: The French in the Americas.* Cambridge: Cambridge University Press, 2004.

———. *Louis XV's Navy, 1748–1762: A Study of Organization and Administration.* Montreal: Magill-Queen's University Press, 1987.

Ray, Aniruddha. "Establishment of the French Factory at Patna." *Proceedings of the Indian History Congress: Millenium Session, Kolkata 2000–2001,* 413–23. Kolkata: Kolkata Indian History Congress, 2001.

Ray, Indrani. *The French East India Company and the Trade of the Indian Ocean: A Collection of Essays.* Edited by Lakshami Subramanian. New Delhi: Munshiram Manoharlal Publishers, 1999.

Rediker, Marcus. *Between the Devil and the Deep Blue Sea: Merchant Seamen, Pirates, and the Anglo-American Maritime World.* Cambridge: Cambridge University Press, 1987.

———. *Villains of All Nations: Atlantic Pirates in the Golden Age.* Boston: Beacon Press, 2004.

———. *The Slave Ship: A Human History.* New York: Viking, 2007.

Riello, Giorgio. *Cotton: The Fabric That Made the Modern World.* Cambridge: Cambridge University Press, 2013.

Ries, Maurice. "The Mississippi Fort Called Fort de La Boulaye, 1700–1715: The First French Settlement in Present-Day Louisiana." *Louisiana Historical Quarterly* 19 (October 1936): 829–99.

Riley, James C. "Mortality on Long-Distance Voyages in the Eighteenth Century." *Journal of Economic History* 41 (1981): 651–56.

———. *The Seven Years War and the Old Regime in France.* Princeton: Princeton University Press, 1986.

Roche, Daniel. *France in the Enlightenment.* Translated by Arthur Goldhammer. Cambridge: Harvard University Press, 1998.

Rule, John C. "Jérome Phélypeaux, Comte de Pontchartrain, and the Establishment of Louisiana, 1686–1715." In *Frenchmen and French Ways in the Mississippi Valley,* edited by John Francis McDermott, 179–97. Urbana: University of Illinois Press, 1969.

Rushforth, Brett. *Bonds of Alliance: Indigenous and Atlantic Slaveries in New France.* Chapel Hill: University of North Carolina Press, 2012.

Russell-Wood, A.J.R. "The Portuguese Atlantic, 1415–1808." In *Atlantic History:*

A Critical Appraisal, edited by Jack P. Greene and Philip D. Morgan, 81–109. New York: Oxford University Press, 2009.

———. *A World on the Move: The Portuguese in Africa, Asia, and America, 1415–1808*. New York: St. Martin's Press, 1992.

Sala-Molins, Louis. *Le Code Noir, ou, le Calvaire de Canaan*. Paris: Presses universitaires de France, 2003.

Sayre, Gordon. "Plotting the Natchez Massacre: Le Page du Pratz, Dumont de Montigny, Chateaubriand." *Early American Literature* 37 (2002): 381–412.

Schaeper, Thomas J. *The French Council of Commerce, 1700–1715: A Study of Mercantilism after Colbert*. Columbus: Ohio State University Press, 1983.

Schiebinger, Londa. *Plants and Empire: Colonial Bioprospecting in the Atlantic World*. Cambridge: Harvard University Press, 2004.

Schmidt, Benjamin. "The Dutch Atlantic: From Provincialism to Globalism." In *Atlantic History: A Critical Appraisal*, edited by Jack P. Greene and Philip D. Morgan, 163–87. New York: Oxford University Press, 2009.

Schnurmann, Claudia. "'Wherever profit leads us, to every sea and shore . . .': The VOC, the WIC, and Dutch Methods of Globalization in the Seventeenth Century." *Renaissance Studies* 17 (2003): 474–93.

Scott, Julius Sherrard, III. "The Common Wind: Currents of Afro-American Communication in the Era of the Haitian Revolution." Ph.D. diss., Duke University, 1986.

Searing, James F. *West African Slavery and Atlantic Commerce: The Senegal River Valley, 1700–1860*. Cambridge: Cambridge University Press, 1993.

Seck, Ibrahima. "The Relationships between St. Louis of Senegal, Its Hinterlands, and Colonial Louisiana." In *French Colonial Louisiana and the Atlantic World*, edited by Bradley G. Bond, 265–90. Baton Rouge: LSU Press, 2005.

Smallwood, Stephanie. *Saltwater Slavery: A Middle Passage from Africa to the American Diaspora*. Cambridge: Harvard University Press, 2007.

Smith, Frederick H. *Caribbean Rum: A Social and Economic History*. Gainesville: University Press of Florida, 2005.

Sobocinski, Carl. "Some God, Little Glory, No Gold: The French on Madagascar in the Seventeenth Century." Ph.D. diss., University of Toledo, 2001.

Sparks, Randy. *The Two Princes of Calabar: An Eighteenth-Century Atlantic Odyssey*. Cambridge: Harvard University Press, 2004.

Spear, Jennifer. "Colonial Intimacies: Legislating Sex in French Louisiana." *William and Mary Quarterly*, 3rd ser., 60 (2003): 75–98.

———. *Race, Sex, and Social Order in Early New Orleans*. Baltimore: Johns Hopkins University Press, 2009.

Stein, Robert Louis. *The French Slave Trade in the Eighteenth Century: An Old Regime Business*. Madison: University of Wisconsin Press, 1979.

———. *The French Sugar Business in the Eighteenth Century.* Baton Rouge: LSU Press, 1988.

Strayer, Brian. *Lettres de Cachet and Social Control in the Ancien Régime, 1659–1789.* New York: Peter Lang, 1992.

Subramanian, Lakshmi, ed. *The French East India Company and the Trade of the Indian Ocean: A Collection of Essays by Idrani Ray.* Calcutta: Center for Studies in Social Science, 1999.

Subrahmanyam, Sanjay. *The Portuguese Empire in Asia, 1500–1700: A Political and Economic History.* New York: Longman, 1993.

Terjanian, Anoush Fraser. *Commerce and Its Discontents in Eighteenth-Century French Political Thought.* Cambridge: Cambridge University Press, 2013.

Thomas-Lacroix, Pierre. "Les Constructions et les ventes de navires dans les amirautés de Vannes et de Lorient au XVIIIe siècle." *Mémoires de la Société d'Histoire et d'Archéologie de Bretagne* 49 (1969): 71–107.

Thornton, John. *Africa and Africans in the Making of the Atlantic World, 1400–1800.* Cambridge: Cambridge University Press, 1998.

Tramond, Joannès. "Les Troubles de Saint-Domingue en 1722–1724." *Revue de l'histoire des colonies françaises* 22 (1929): 487–512 and 549–98.

Travers, Robert. *Ideology and Empire in Eighteenth-Century India: The British in Bengal.* New York: Cambridge University Press, 2007.

Ulrich, Laurel Thatcher. *A Midwife's Tale: The Life of Martha Ballard, Based on Her Diary, 1785–1812.* New York: Knopf, 1990.

Usner, Daniel H., Jr. *Indians, Settlers, and Slaves in a Frontier Exchange Economy: The Lower Mississippi Valley before 1783.* Chapel Hill: University of North Carolina Press, 1992.

Vidal, Cécile. "French Louisiana in the Age of the Companies, 1712–1731." In *Constructing Early Modern Empires: Proprietary Ventures in the Atlantic World, 1500–1750,* edited by L. H. Roper and B. Van Ruymbeke, 133–62. Leiden, Netherlands: Brill, 2007.

Vignols, Léon, and Henri Sée. "Les Ventes de la Compagnie des Indes à Nantes, 1723–1733." *Revue de l'histoire des colonies françaises* 13 (1925): 489–534.

Villefosse, René Héron de. *Histoire des grandes routes de France.* Paris: Librairie Académique Perrin, 1975.

Vinha, Matieu da. "Les Nyert, exemple d'une ascension sociale dans la Maison du Roi au XIIe siècle." *Dix-Septième Siècle* 54 (2002): 15–34.

Vries, Jan de. "The Dutch Atlantic Economics." In *The Atlantic Economy during the Seventeenth and Eighteenth Centuries: Organization, Operation, Practice, and Personnel,* edited by Peter A. Coclanis, 1–29. Columbia: University of South Carolina Press, 2005.

Waselkov, Gregory A., Peter H. Wood, and Tom Hatley, eds. *Powhatan's Mantle:*

Indians in the Colonial Southeast. Lincoln: University of Nebraska Press, 2006.

Weber, Jacques. *Compagnies et comptoirs: L'Inde des français, XVIIe–XXe siècles.* Paris: Société française d'histoire d'outre-mer, 1991.

White, Richard. *The Middle Ground: Indians, Empires, and Republics in the Great Lakes Region, 1650–1815.* Cambridge: Cambridge University Press, 1991.

White, Sophie. "'A Baser Commerce': Retailing, Class, and Gender in French Colonial New Orleans." *William and Mary Quarterly,* 3rd ser., 63, no. 3 (2006): 517–50.

———. *Wild Frenchmen and Frenchified Indians: Material Culture and Race in Colonial Louisiana.* Philadelphia: University of Pennsylvania Press, 2012.

Wilson, Samuel, Jr. *The Capuchin School in New Orleans, 1725: The First School in Louisiana.* New Orleans: Archdiocesan School Board, 1961.

Withers, Charles W. J. *Geography, Science, and National Identity: Scotland since 1520.* Cambridge: Cambridge University Press, 2001.

Zakim, Michael. "The Business Clerk as Social Revolutionary; or, a Labor History of the Nonproducing Classes." *Journal of the Early Republic* 26 (2006): 563–602.

Index

Note: Italics indicate pages with illustrations.

affranchis, 102–103
Africans: as apprentices, 126–28; at the Balize, 106–107, *108*, 124, 127; and baptism, 125; and *captiveries*, 71, 104, 123; and clothing, 12, 117; and *Code noir*, 8, 82, 125; on company plantation, 122–23, 125–27; and *corvée*, 126; enslaved, 24, 98–99, 109–110, 122–30, 134, 137; families of, 124–25; health of, 104–105, 109, 122–23, 183n57; as hostages in Natchez War, 140, 141–142, 143–44; marriage in Louisiana, 124–25; Middle Passage, 5, 86–87, 104–105, 179n72; in Natchez, 124, 127, 131–32, 137–38; in New Orleans, 124, 126–28; and opportunities for freedom, 129; as sailors, 106–107, 128–30; in Saint-Domingue, 82, 97, 99–100; and sex ratio, 82, 123–24; skills, 106–107, 126–30, 131; slave conspiracies, 144, 190–91n14. *See also* slave trade, African
agriculture and agricultural products
—indigo, 18, 20, 55, 56, 69, 98–99, 100, 126, 127, 132–34, 136
—provisioning crops: 96, 133; rice, 66, 69, 122, 126; wheat, 47, 52, 53, 60, 62, 119
—sugar: 56, 97, 98, 134, 136; distribution, 100, 155; and Dutch influence, 18, 165n26; processing, 19–20
—tobacco: and company monopoly, 30, 130–31, 136–37, 138–39, 148; consumption of, 103, 130; Cuban, 136; cultivation, 19, 24, 30, 120, 123, 131–34, 136–38, 147; demand in France, 2, 59, 131, 136–37; demand in Louisiana, 130; *en carotte*, 19–20; in Natchez, 86, 130–34, 137, 139, 140, 149; pricing, 19–20, 133, 138; processing in Chesapeake style, 19; shipments, 18, 128, 133, 136, 138; and skilled workers, 80, 131–33, 137; subsidies, 148
alcohol and drinking: 91, 113; beer, 119; brandy, 69, 75, 89–90, 91, 105, 110, 117; liqueur, 35, 49–50; tafia (*guildive*), 96, 101–102; trade in alcohol, 11, 51, 69, 143; wine, 16, 49–50, 69, 75, 89, 97, 105, 110, 113, 117
Ancenis, 9, 53
Angers, 9, 51–52, 53
Angola, 72
Apalache, 121
Artaguiette, Bernard Diron d', 23, 118, 135, 189–90n120
Artaguiette, Jean-Baptiste d', 31
artisans and craftsmen: 5, 62, 118; and Plantin's Company, 79, 80–81; slaves as, 107, 126–28
assiento, 55, 97–99
Atlantic Islands (Canary, Cape Verde, Madeira), 11, 63, 70, 88, 96–97
Aubin, Jean-Baptiste, Sieur Duchesne, 78, 177n33
Aubin, Louis-Laurent, Sieur du Plessis, 78, 86, 89, 94, 101–102, 105, 177n33, 180n1
Auray, 60

Bachelier, André, 67, 174n85
Balassor, 26, 27, 157
Balize, 66, 86, 88, 105–109, 121, 122–29, 136, 152
Balligant, Marc-Antoine, 40
Banks, Kenneth, 90, 181n17

Banque Générale, 29–30
Banque Royale, 30, 32, 34, 36
Baptism of the Tropics. *See* maritime rituals
Barbary Coast, 146, 147–48
Barnett, James, 132
Baron, Pierre, 116
Bay of Bengal, 1, 26–27, 157–58
Beaubois, Father Nicole-Ignace, 68, 120, 186n47
Beauce, 46–47
Beaumont, Michel, 104–106
Bengal: 1, 17, 26–27, 157–58; textile industry in, 27
Bernaudat de Saint-Maur, 113–14
Bidal, Claude François, marquis de Dasfeld and comte de Belle-Isle, 133
Bienvenu, André-Jacques, 78
Bigot, Paul, 22
Biloxi, 39, 64, 109–10, 129, 169n95, 174n80, 183–84n61
Bion, Nicolas, 113
Blanche, Jean-Mary, 79
Blanche, Marie-Catherine, 40
Blavet River, 60–61, 68
Bolster, W. Jeffrey, 128–29, 187n74
Bonelle, 45
Bourbon, island of (Réunion), 31, 35
Bréban, Etienne, 152
Brest, 21, 35, 79
Breton (language), 52, 79
Brinon de Caligny, Louis Henry, 148–49
Brittany, 52–54, 57–63, 67–68; sailors from, 79
Brossy, Pierre de, 74
Bru, Louis, 150
Buslé, Antoine, 145, 150
Buenos Aires, 98
Bussy, 44, 79, 103, 112, 114–16, 174n86

Cadillac, Antoine de La Mothe de, 24, 30
Cadot, Paulin, 112
Caillot, François, 41–42
Caillot, Marc-Antoine: on Capuchins, 120–21; career in India, 155, 157–59; death of, 153, 159; departure from Louisiana, 150–52; early life, 40–42; as employee of Company of the Indies, 39–40, 44, 64, 67, 102, 109, 153, 155, 157–59; family, 40–42, 153, 157–58; as militiaman, 145, 151; Paris-centric outlook, 47–48, 52–53; and petty trade, 77, 139, 157; "Relation du voyage," 3–5, 4, 6–7, 39–40, 48, 162n3; travel to Louisiana, 43–54, 60, 67–68, 86, 89–93, 94–96, 102–103, 105; and women, 6–7, 47, 50, 52, 81, 84, 91, 102–103, 110, 114–16, 145–46, 151
Caillot, Marie-Madeleine, 153, 157–58
Caillot, Pierre, 40–41
Calcutta, 26, 27
Cambry, Gilles, 78
Campeche, 136
Canada, 1–2, 15, 21–22, 33, 35, 43, 146, 147
Canary Islands, 63, 88, 96–97
Canton (China), 63
Cape Verde, 70, 88, 96–97
Capuchins, 82, 116, 119–22, 190n123
Caracas, 98
Caribbean Sea: maritime traffic in, 92–93, 95–96; piracy in, 95
Carolina, Charter of, 23
Carolina(s) (English colony/-ies), 12, 21, 24–25, 131, 137, 143, 166n41
Carrière, François, 109
Carrière, Joseph, 109
carrying trade, 18, 54, 73–74, 96
Cartagena, 98
Cartier, Jacques, 12
Cassimbazar, 26
Cassini maps, 8, 171n17
Castanier, François, 31
cemetery (Saint-Pierre), 117
Chalon, 101–102
Chamber of Justice, 26, 29–30
Chandernagore, 27, 69, 155, 157–59
Chaperon, Joseph, 85, 187n71
Charles, duc du Berry, 40
Charles II (England), 23
Charlevoix, Father Pierre-François Xavier de, 99, 189–90n120
Charpentier, François, 17, 165n17
Chartres, 9, 46–47, 52
Chastang, François, 112, 114–16
Chauvin brothers, 118
Chépart, de, 140
Chesapeake, 2, 3, 12, 19, 130, 137–39
Cheval Marin, 157
Chickasaw, 122, 134–35
Chierdel, Jean-Robert, 80
China: textile industry, 13, 23, 31, 35, 38–39, 63, 72, 135, 138, 146–47, 178n53
Choctaw, 143–44
church, Saint-Louis, 118, 120
Clark, Emily, 84
clerks. *See* Compagnie des Indes—personnel
Clive, Robert, 158–59
Code noir: 8; and bans on interracial unions,

82; and baptism of slaves, 125; and free people of color, 82
Coëtlogon, Abbé Charles-Elizabeth de, 12–33
Colbert, Jean-Baptiste, 16–20, 26, 31, 44–45, 54, 60–61
Compagnie d'Afrique (Africa Company), 31
Compagnie d'Occident (Company of the West), 30–31, 73, 83
Compagnie de Guinée (Guinea Company), 20, 23, 30, 54–56
Compagnie de Saint-Christophe, 13
Compagnie de Saint-Domingue (Saint-Domingue Company), 20, 23, 30, 61, 97–99
Compagnie de Sénégal (Senegal Company), 20, 30, 55, 61, 72, 131
Compagnie des Indes (Company of the Indies):
—finances, 64–67, 146–50, 155; sale of shares in, 30–32, 33–34
—headquarters: in India, 63–64; in Lorient, 62–63, 154; in Louisiana, 63–65, 115–16; in Paris, 36–38
—investments in infrastructure in France, 34–36, 154
—in Louisiana: coastal trade, 126, 135–36; investment in colony, 123–24, 126–29, 137–38, 149; plantations of, 122–27, 132–33, 137–38; retrocession of colony, 138–39, 146–50, 153–55; trade with Indians, 2, 75, 134–35, 143–44, 149
—organizational structure, 31, 36, 63–64
—passengers on ships owned by, 79–93, 94–95
—personnel: clerical, 38–39, 44, 64–67, 79–80, 112–16, 163n11; families of, 80, 153, 157–58; literacy of, 5–7, 38; maritime, 74–75, 78–79; scandals involving, 65–66, 112–14
—predecessors of, 13–20, 26–27, 30–31
—propaganda, 30–33, 32
—reorganization of, 35, 36, 62
—in Saint-Domingue, 99–101
—sale of trade goods: agricultural, 59; *grande vente*, 57–58; *petite vente*, 58–59; and *port-permis*, 59, 76
—selection of home port, 60–61
—and Seven Years' War, 158–59
—and shipment of women as prospective brides: to China, 83n53; to Louisiana, 81–82, 84–85
—ships: *Alexandre*, 73; *Amphitrite*, 35; *Annibal*, 73; *Atalante*, 155; *Aurore*, 151; *Badine*, 135; *Baleine*, 73, 84, 178n64; *Comte de Toulouse*, 79; *Dromadaire*, 78, 129; *Duc de Bourbon*, 73; *Duc de Chartres*, 69–70, 73, 77, 175n3; *Durance*, 69, 73–79, 74, 85–86, 88–93, 94–96, 101–103, 105, 106–107, 116–17, 136, 177n31; *Espérance*, 69, 70–71, 78; *Galathée*, 103–106; *Gironde*, 88, 90, 110–11; *Jupiter*, 135; *Neptune*, 157; *Néréide*, 72–73; *Prince de Conty*, 152, 192n47–48; *Saint-Louis*, 152; *Saint-Michel*, 141; *Solide*, 35, 135; *Vénus*, 73, 107, 109, 122–23, 151; *Vierge de Grace*, 35
—slave trade, 56–57, 74; to Louisiana, 72–73; in West Africa, 37, 70–73; in West Indies, 99–100
—trade monopolies, 30, 33–34, 56–57, 99, 101, 130–31, 136–37, 148, 150, 168n71, 191n28
—warehouses, 13, 36, 52, 57–59, 58, 62, 64, 65–66, 69–70, 76, 100, 109–10, 112, 115–16, 122, 136, 140, 150, 154, 183–84n61, 193n3
Compagnie des Indes Occidentales (West India Company), 18–20
Compagnie des Indes Orientales (Company of the East Indies), 17, 31, 60
Compagnie française de l'Orient (French Company of the Orient), 15–16
Compagnie Royale de la Chine (Royal China Company), 20, 31
Company of the Indies. *See* Compagnie des Indes (Company of the Indies)
concessions and concessionaires: Jesuit, 119–20, 122; in Louisiana, 77, 85–86, 118, 130–34, 141, 142, 188n94; in Saint-Domingue, 98–99; in Senegambia, 70–72, 107, 154–55
convicts. *See* immigration: forced
Coquelin, Marie-Anne, 157–58
Cossimbazar, 158
Council of Commerce, 17, 55–57
Council of the Indies, 36
cowrie shells, 59, 69–70, 135
Creole, 102–103, 182n28
crime: accusations of, 110; forgery, 66, 113; fraud, 67, 83; libertinism, 83; monopoly violations, 36, 76–77, 85; murder, 21, 113–14; profiteering, 109–10; slander, 112; smuggling, 36, 65, 77, 85, 97, 99, 191n18; theft, 112. See also *lettres de cachet*
Crozat, Antoine, 2, 97; and Louisiana charter, 20, 22–26; and mineral extraction,

Crozat, Antoine (*continued*) 23–24; and penalization by Chamber of Justice, 26; and tobacco monopoly, 23
Cuba, 130, 136
currency: banknotes, 29, 32–34, 66, 100; forgery, 66; shortages in Louisiana, 64, 65–66; specie, 28–29, 34, 37, 76, 90, 100–101

Dacca, 27
dancing, 52–53, 92
Darien Company (Company of Scotland), 28
Darnton, Robert, 5–6
Dauphin Island, 25–26, 106, 128–29, 136
Dawdy, Shannon Lee, 5, 119
debt: of colonists, 66, 72, 113, 123, 138, 150, 154–55, 183–84n61, 189n110; of French Crown, 28–29, 31; of Jesuits in Louisiana, 120
deerskin trade. *See* fur and peltry trade
Demorils, Suzanne, 81
Desfontaines, George, 133
Deshayes, Jacques, 80, 146–47
Deslandes, André Bourreau, 26–27
Detroit, 24
Deucher, Jean, 133
disease, 15–16, 22, 86–87, 89; scurvy, 95, 104–106, 109, 110, 122–23, 184n64, 189n107; venereal, 84, 103
Dodun, Charles-Gaspard, 36
domestic servants, 79, 84–86, 157; enslaved, 190–91n14; in Maison du Roi, 40–42
domestiques commensaux, 41–42
Du Codère, Commander (Yazoo), 144
Du Halley, Joachim Descasaux, 55–56
Dubuisson, Claude, 113–15
Duché, Jean-Baptiste, 22, 30–31
Dumont de Montigny, Jean-François Benjamin, 6, 50, 144, 172n33, 180n86, 189–90n120, 190–91n14
Durtal, 46, 51
Dutch East India Company (Verenigde Oostindische Compagnie), 2, 12–15, 18
Dutch War, 20, 165–66n28
Dutch West India Company (Geoctroyeerde Westindische Compagnie), 2, 18–19, 57
Dutisné, Claude-Charles, 118–19
Duval, Kathleen, 134
Duval de Leyrit, Georges, 159
Duvergé, Bernard, 106–107, 109

education, 120, 125
Elkins, Stanley: and shocks of enslavement, 87
Eltis, David, 8, 163–64n13
engagés. *See* indentured servants
engineers and surveyors, 5, 61, 62–63, 80, 85, 106, 115, 117–18, 154, 185n29, 187n56
English East India Company, 12–13, 15, 26
exiles, 43–44, 83–85. *See also* immigration: forced

Faucon Dumanoir, Jean-Baptiste, 133
Fayet, Pierre-Antoine, 86, 104, 141
feitorias, 11, 13
Feleme River, 70
Ferme générale (United General Farms), 33–34
Fleuriau, François, 145
food: and bakeries, 62, 75, 117; Caillot's commentary on, 47–48, 110; ceremonial consumption, 192n40; citrus, 75, 95, 101–102; flour, 26, 105, 119, 143; processing facilities, 61, 115, 119, 122, 126; *sagamité*, 119; at sea, 75, 79, 89, 94, 105; shortages, 25–26, 93; stipends for, 41, 67–68. *See also* agriculture and agricultural products—provisioning crops
Fort Condé, 114
Fort d'Orléans, 158–59
Fort de Chartres, 144
Fort Louis, 22–23, 109
Fort Rosalie (Natchez), 130–32, 140, 141–44
Fort St. James (English), 70
Fort Saint-Joseph, 70–71
Fort Saint-Louis, 70–71, 104
Fort Saint-Pierre, 144
Fournier (councillor), 159
Fox Indians, 151
free people of color, 82, 102–3
French and Indian War. *See* Seven Years' War
French economy: debt, 29, 31; and John Law, 29, 31, 33–34; national bank, 29–30, 32, 34, 36; paper money, 29, 32–34, 66, 100; specie shortage, 29, 34; under Louis XIV, 16–17, 29
French West India Company. *See* Compagnie des Indes Occidentales (West India Company)
French West Indies, 2, 12–14, 15, 18–20, 25, 30, 35, 54–57, 88, 99, 133–34. *See also* Guadeloupe; Martinique; Saint-Christophe; Saint-Domingue
frontier-exchange economy, 25–26, 64, 130–34, 139
fur and peltry trade, 2, 14, 20, 21, 30, 36, 75, 128, 131, 135–36, 139, 152

Galam, 70–71, 104
galériens (galley slaves), 70, 85
Galloway, Patricia, 132
Gambia River, 70
gambling, 27–29, 43, 49–51
Ganges River, 26, 157
Gaultier, Jean-Baptiste de La Renaudais, 107
Gauvry, Joachim de, 118
German Coast, 121
Germans, 33, 74, 131
Gilly, Simon, 31
Girard (company agent), 101
Giraud, Marcel, 83, 168–69n82
gold, 2, 11, 24, 33, 69
Gontier, Charles, 79, 112, 114–16
Gorée Island, 70, 71, 104–107, 122–23
Gouriou, Jacques, 75
grands chemins, 44–46, 51
Great Sun of the Natchez, 140
gros habitants, 110
Guadeloupe, 96
guildive. *See under* alcohol and drinking
Guinea, 72, 107, 146, 147
Guyonard, Pierre, 79

Hachard, Marie-Madeleine, 6, 83, 88, 90, 109–11
Haiti. *See* Saint-Domingue (Haiti)
Hall, Gwendolyn Midlo, 125
Hardancourt, Louis Boyvin d', 31
Harms, Robert, 4–5
Haudrère, Philippe, 38, 81, 162n1, 164n5, 168–69n82
Hauterive, Renaud d', 118–19, 145
Havana, 98, 114
Hennebont, 59, 60, 61–62, 63
histoires, 5–7, 162n8
Historic New Orleans Collection, 3
Hubert, Marc-Antoine, 132–33
Huet, Pierre-Daniel, 17
Hugli River, 26–27, 158–59
hybridity: of Louisiana, 2; of *histoires*, 6–7

Illinois country, 21, 23–24, 119, 129, 144, 150–51
Illinois Indians, 151
immigration, 32–34, 43, 79–86; forced, 25, 43–44, 83, 85; German, 33, 74, 131; policy, 14, 25, 85. *See also* indentured servants
indentured servants, 86, 100, 131–32
India, 1–2, 11–17, 26–27, 37, 38–39, 63–64, 72, 146, 154–55, 157–58
—settlements in: Dutch, 13, 27; English, 13, 26–27, 158; French, 26–27, 63–64, 155–59; Portuguese, 11–13, 26
indigo. *See under* agriculture and agricultural products
Ingrande, 52–53
inns: in Ingrande, 52–53; in La Fèche, 49–51; in Lorient, 59–60, 67, 174n85; in Nantes, 59–60; in New Orleans, 114, 151; and *relais de postes*, 45–46; in Saint-Marc, 47
insects, 6, 109
Isle de Bourbon (Reunion), 31, 35
Isle de France (Mauritius), 31, 35

Jackson, Jason Baird, 132
Jacmel, 100
Jarry, Anne, 114, 151
Jarry, Louis, 114, 151
Jesuits in Louisiana, 119–22, 138
Jolicoeur, 107

Kaskaskia, 24, 144
Khan, Ibrahim, 26–27
Khan, Shaista, 27
kinship ties, 38–39, 40–42, 157–58
Kolly, Jean-Daniel, 132–33

La Caye Saint-Louis, 94, 96–100; company plantation in, 104–105; population, 102–103; as provisioning port, 96–97, 101–102
La Chaise, Jacques de, 64–67, 83–84, 105, 109–10, 112–15, 116–17, 122–23, 129, 144–45
La Ferté-Bernard, 47
La Flèche, 9, 48–51
La Franqueri, Gilles Le Brun de, 65
La Goublaye, Antoine de Joye de, 113
La Jonchère, Girard Michel de, 133
La Loë, 68
La Motte, Guillaume de, 60–61
La Potière (councillor), 159
La Roche-Bernard, 60
La Salle, Nicolas de, 134–35
La Salle, René-Robert, Cavelier de, 21
La Vigne, Captain, 104
Labat, Jean-Baptiste, 98–99, 102, 181n17, 182n27–28
Lake Pontchartrain, 23, 119
land banks, 28–29
Langlois, Denis, 61
Larchevesque, Joseph, 85
Laudonnière, René de, 12
Lauray Ford, 45
Laval, Antoine-Francis, 90

Law, John, 26; and Banque Générale, 29; and Banque Royale, 30, 32; and Company of the Indies, 31–36, 43–44, 56, 85–86, 99; and Company of the West, 30–31; as controller general of France, 34; exile of, 34; in France, 27–29; life in England, 26–27; *Money and Trade Considered*, 28; system of, 7, 29–36; and tobacco, 30, 39, 130–31; training in economics, 28
Le Blanc, Louis Claude, 133
Le Blond de La Tour, Pierre, 117–18
Le Coq, François, 81
Le Coq, Margueritte, 81–82, 84–85
Le Coq, Marie-Louise "Catin," 84–85, 178n64–65
Le Havre, 57, 60, 78, 81, 173n48
Le Moyne, Jean-Baptiste, de Bienville: and French-Indian relations, 22, 135; and Indian slave trade, 24–25; and Jesuits, 120; on mineral wealth in Louisiana, 23; recall to France, 116, 185n22; on tobacco, 133
Le Moyne, Joseph, de Sérigny, 22
Le Moyne, Pierre, d'Iberville, 21–22, 83, 131
Le Page du Pratz, Antoine-Simon: *Histoire de la Louisiane*, 6; as slave overseer, 101, 126; on wheat, 119
Le Sueur, Pierre-Charles, 23
Léogâne, 105–106
lettres de cachet, 43–44
libres de savanne, 102–103
life at sea, 86–96; discipline, 91–92; divisions between passengers and crew, 89–90; entertainment, 89–92; rations, 84, 89, 94, 96–97; rituals, 89–91; sickness, 87–88, 93, 95; weather, 92. *See also* slave ships
Lind, James, 95. *See also* disease: scurvy
literacy, 5, 38, 120
Lorient, 35, 38, 44, 57, 58–59; establishment of, as company port, 60–62; improvements to, 31, 62–63, 154, 155; living conditions in, 62–63; as naval base, 26, 62, 64, 65, 66, 67–68, 69, 71, 73, 75, 77, 78, 80–81, 86, 88, 104–105, 107, 114, 116, 128, 135–36, 141, 142, 150; warehouse sales, 154
Louboey, Henry de, 119, 142, 143–44
Louis, duc de Bourgogne, 40
Louis XII de Rohan, Prince de Guéméné, 61, 63
Louis XIII, 15
Louis XIV: and *Code noir*, 82, 125; and Compagnie de Saint-Domingue, 97–99; and Compagnie des Indes orientales, 16–17; and Compagnie française de l'Orient, 16; death of, 29, 40; and domestic trade barriers, 16, 19; and French finances, 17, 20, 29, 168n65; and gambling, 50; and *grands chemins*, 44–45; and Louisiana, 1, 20–21, 25; and Maison du Roi, 40–41; and tobacco farm, 168n71; wars of, 14, 17, 20, 22
Louis XV: and Bienville, 185n22; and Compagnie des Indes, 136–37; and the regency, 29, 41
Louis de France (Monseigneur le Dauphin), 40
Louisiana: colonial diet in, 110, 119; colonization of, 21–26; education in, 120; as frontier-exchange economy, 25–26, 64, 130–34, 139; illicit trade in, 77; immigration to, 25, 32–34, 43–44, 74, 79–83, 85, 86, 131; investment in, 14–15, 22, 23–24, 25–26, 123–24, 126–29, 137–38, 149; military budget, 118; population, 31, 82, 131–32, 134; propaganda promoting, 32–33, 32; religious life in, 119–22; reputation of, 43–44, 48, 73; retrocession of, 138–39, 146–49, 150; rumors of mineral wealth in, 21, 23–24, 33; skilled labor in, 81, 127–28, 129; slavery in, 106–107, 122–30, 131, 137–38; starvation in, 22, 25–26, 66; and tobacco, 2–3, 24, 30, 55, 86, 120, 123, 130–34, 136–40, 143, 147–49, 189n110; trade with Indians in, 2, 22–23, 75, 134–35, 143–44, 149
—forts: Condé, 114; de Chartres, 144; de La Boulaye, 22; Louis, 109; Maurepas, 22; Rosalie, 130, 131, 132, 140, 143, 144; Saint-Pierre, 144
Lucas, Marie-Claire, 157
Lunel, 137, 141
Lusser, Joseph-Christophe de, 143–44

MacMahon, Laurent, 146, 191n18
Madagascar, 15–16, 17, 31, 35, 165n12, 165n17; Fort Dauphin, 16
Madeira Islands, 11, 88, 96–97
Mahé, 35, 155
Maison du Roi: benefits of membership in, 40–41; demise of, 41–42; multigenerational service in, 41
Maisonneuve, 66, 113
Maratha Confederacy, 158
Marine (French navy), 26, 59, 62, 67, 78;

clerks in, 163n11; in Louisiana, 151; and Phélypeaux, comte de Pontchartrain, 22, 83
maritime rituals, 88, 89–91, 180n82; Baptism of the Tropics, 90–91, 180n86
maritime technology: *Le Neptune François*, 18
Marquaysne, Jacques de, 69
marriage, 82–85, 103; and Caillot, 157; *Code noir* and, 82, 125; and company employees, 80; among company-owned slaves, 124–25; military men and, 80, 177n42. *See also* kinship ties
Martin, François, 26–27
Martinique, 13, 19–20, 55, 73, 96, 150, 155, 178n53, 180n1, 181n17
Mascarenes, 2, 31, 35
Masclary, 80, 177n40
Massachusetts Bay Company, 14
Mellier, Gérard, 59
Ménétra, Jacques-Louis, 5–6, 171n20
mercantilism, 18–19, 66; violations of, 19, 76–77, 98–99
merchants (private), 20, 22, 147; Bengali, 27; Nantais, 53–60; Portuguese, 27; and slave trade, 54–58, 59, 72, 101; and trade with Louisiana, 149–50. *See also* Crozat, Antoine
messageries, 45–46
Meudon, château de, 40–42, 170n104
Michel de Saint-Michel, Claude, 153
military: alliance with Choctaw, 142–44; budget in Louisiana, 118; engagements against the Natchez, 142–44, 150–51; personnel, 80–81, 85, 118–19, 139, 144–45. *See also* Plantin's Company
militia: in Louisiana, 144–45, 151; in Saint-Domingue, 100–101. *See also* Plantin's Company
Ministry of the Marine. *See* Marine (French navy)
Mississippi Bubble, 31–35, 48
Mississippi Company. *See* Compagnie d'Occident (Company of the West)
Mississippi River, 106; travel on, 109–11, 122–23, 128–29. *See also* Balize
Mobile, 22–23, 25–26, 65, 109, 114, 121, 128–29
Mobile Indians, 22–23, 25–26
Mocha, 2, 35, 59, 155
money. *See* currency
Monseigneur le Dauphin. *See* Louis de France (Monseigneur le Dauphin)
Montaudoin, René, 54, 56
Montplaisir de La Guchay, 132–33
Moreau, René, 31
mortality: in Lorient, 77, 177n29; in Louisiana, 39, 123; at sea, 72, 104–106
Mory, Pierre de, 153
Mouchard, François, 31
Mughal Empire, 26–27
music and musical instruments, 48, 54, 60; hunting horn, 47, 171n11; violin, 52–53

Nantes, 35, 53–60; and company warehouses, 57–59, 58; and slave trade, 54–57, 59. *See also* Montaudoin, René
Natchez (French settlement), 64–65, 86, 121, 188n94; and Indian slave trade, 131; population, 107, 123–24, 127, 131–32, 139, 183n53; settlement of, 130–32; tobacco cultivation in, 130–34, 136–39, 149
Natchez Indians, 131, 132, 139; First Natchez War, 130; Grand Village of, 131, 132, 142; land transfers, 132; settlement districts (Flour, Grigra, Jenzenaque, Tiou, White Apple), 131, 139–40, 188n86; trade with English, 131, 135; trade with French, 131, 134–35. *See also* Great Sun of the Natchez; Natchez War of 1729–1730
Natchez War of 1729–1730, 3, 139–45, 189–90n120, 190n123; and Choctaw, 142–44, 145; and destruction of tobacco infrastructure, 140, 142–43; and disruption of trade, 142, 143–34, 146–47; French retaliation, 141–45, 150–51; hostages, 140–42, 190n124, 190n3; and Natchez enslavement, 151; and pan Indian conspiracy, 144; survivors, 139–41
Natchitoches, 64–65, 121
New Orleans, 33, 64–65, 66, 102, 105–106, 112–15, *115*, 137–38, 139, 140, 143, 144, 146, 149, 150–52; capital of Louisiana, 39, 63–64; Capuchins in, 230–21; improvements to and layout of, 115–19, 120; population, 83–84, 86, 107, 114, 118, 123–28
New Spain, 3, 11–12, 55
Nicolas (councillor), 159
nobility, 48, 94, 171n17; and Maison du Roi, 41
Nogent-le-Rotrou, 47
North Carolina. *See* Carolina(s) (English colony/-ies)
Nos, Gilles de, comte de Champmeslin, 101
Nossa Segnora dos Prazeres, 159
Nouvelle-France. *See* Canada
Nunez River, 107

O'Kelly, Father Denis (Denys Oquely), 78–79
Orléans, duc de. *See* Philippe II, duc d'Orléans
Orry, Philibert, 148–50
Ouidah, 56, 71–72
outfitting, 21, 35, 69–70, 75–77, 154; provisioning, 62, 75, 89, 94, 96–97, 99, 101–102, 157, 180n1; ship repairs, 96. *See also* slave ships

Palaiseau, 9, 45
Paparel, Claude-François, 28
Pardimene, François, 78
Paris, 16, 27–28; communications with company administrators in, 38, 64–67, 86, 89, 104, 105, 114, 116, 121, 125, 129, 133, 136, 141, 143, 145–46, 157; company offices and operations in, 31, 36–39, *37*, 43, 44, 61, 80, 148, 153, 154; and Council of Commerce, 17, 55; as cultural reference point, 39, 47–48, 50, 52, 54, 73
Pâris brothers (Antoine, Claude, Jean, and Joseph), 33
Patna, 26
patronage: and Caillot, 7, 39–42, 157, 158; and Company of the Indies, 38–39; and Maison du Roi, 41–42
Pauger, Adrien de, 117–18
Pélican, 83
Pellerin, Gérard, 77
peltry trade. *See* fur and peltry trade
Pénicaut, André, 23
Penmanec, 68, 69
Pennautier, Pierre Louis de Reich de, 23
Pensacola, 25, 114, 128–29, 136
Périer, Catherine (Le Chibelier), 84–85
Périer, Etienne, 65, 84–85, 105, 112, 117, 121, 122–23, 129, 145, 150; and Caillot, 151–52; and campaign against the Natchez, 141–42, 151; on French-Indian relations, 134–35, 146–47; government offices of, 114, 116; plantation of, 107, 124, 127
Périer de Salvert, Antoine-Alexis, 151
petits blancs, 100
petty trade, 76–77, 139, 151, 157
Phélypeaux, Jean-Frédéric, comte de Maurepas, 56–57, 72, 141, 150, 158, 175–76n8
Phélypeaux, Jérôme, comte de Pontchartrain, 21, 30, 130; and attempts to charter Louisiana, 22–24; and slave trade, 56, 97
Phélypeaux, Louis, comte de Pontchartrain, 21
Philippe II, duc d'Orléans, 29–34, 41
Piganiol de La Force, Jean Aymar, 49, 53
Piou, Jean, 31
Pipli, 27
pirates and piracy, 73, 76, 95–96, 97
Plantin's Company, 80–81, 94, 118, 119, 177n43, 177n45
Poisson de Bourvalais, Paul, 28
Pondicherry, 27, 39, 63–64, 66, 69, 155–58, *156*
Pont-Scorff, 62
Pontchâteau, 50
Pontivy, 79
Port-Louis, 59, 61, 75, 77, 79, 141, 177n40
port-permis, 59, 76–77
Portobelo, 98
postal system in France, 45–46. See also *messageries*; *relais de poste*
Poulo Condore, 35
Prat, Louis, 145
Prévost, Antoine: *Manon Lescaut*, 178n56
Prevost, Jean-Baptiste, 183–84n61
propaganda, 32–33
provisioning. *See* outfitting
Puerto Rico, 96
punishment: at sea, 91–92; of women, 83–84

Quincampoix, rue, 34
Quinet de Préville, Captain, 104–105

race: census categories, 102–103; and *Code noir*, 82; Creoles, 102–103, 182n28; at sea, 129
Raguet, Abbé Gilles-Bernard, 121, 125
Ramont, 147–48, 191n22
Raphaël de Luxembourg, Father, 82, 120–21, 125
rations: in *captiveries*, 123; in Louisiana, 84, 101, 118; procurement of, at ports of call, 96–97, 101; at sea, 84, 88–89, 94–95, 100–101, 177n42
Raudot, Antoine, 31
Recollets, 121
Rediker, Marcus: and "language of punishment," 91–92; on pirate flags, 181n10
regency: of Louis XIV, 16; of Louis XV, 41, 50, 85, 148. *See also* Philippe II, duc d'Orléans
relais de poste, 45–46, 171n15, 171n17
religious orders, 119–22, 186n43; budget for, in Louisiana, 121; Capuchins, 120–22; Jesuits, 119–20, 122, 138, 144; missionary work by, 119–20, 121–22; Recollets, 121; Ursulines, 110–11, 120, 121. *See also* Beau-

bois, Father Nicole-Ignace; Hachard, Marie-Madeleine; Raphaël de Luxembourg, Father
Rémonville, Antoine Alexandre, 22
Reytet, Jean de, 80, 179n70
Riantec, parish of (Port-Louis), 77
Ribaut, Jean, 12
rice. *See under* agriculture and agricultural products
Richelieu, Cardinal (Armand-Jean du Plessis), 15–17
Roberval, Jean, 12
Royal African Company, 57, 166–67n41
Royal Council of State, 56
royal roads. See *grands chemins*

sagamité. *See* food
Saintard, Pierre de, 157
Saint-Christophe, 13, 178n53
Saint-Domingue (Haiti), 21, 44, *98*; Cap Français, 99–101, 151; Cap Tiburon, 97; debt of colonists in, 72; Léôgane, 105; Naybe River (Yaque del Sur), 97; Petit Goâve, 101; rebellion against Company of the Indies in, 100–101; slave trade to, 55–57, 99–100; sugar production, 19–20; tobacco cultivation, 19–20; trade with, 72, 98–99, 126, 136, 150, 155
—southern province, 97–99, *98*, 100, 102–103; demographics of, 102–103; La Caye Saint-Louis: 86, 94, 95, 96–99, 101–103, 104–105, 136; and outfitting and provisioning of company ships, 96–97, 101
Saint-Domingue Company. *See* Compagnie de Saint-Domingue (Saint-Domingue Company)
Saint Louis, parish of (Lorient), 77
Saint-Louis (Senegambia), 70–71, 104, 123
Saint-Malo, 15, 59, 78, 79, 147; and slave trade, 57, 173n48
Saint-Marc (family), 47–48
Saint-Marc (Saint-Mars-la-Brière), 47–48
Sainte-Catherine Company, 132
Sainte-Catherine concession, 132–33, 142
Saugrain, Claude-Marin, 46–49, 53, 171n15
Savennières, 52
Scipion, 129
Scorff River, 60–62
scurvy. *See under* disease
seasoning, 86–87
Seminary of Foreign Missions, 119–20
Senegal. *See* Senegambia
Senegal Company. *See* Compagnie de Sénégal (Senegal Company)
Senegal River, 70–71, 104
Senegambia, 70–72, 78, 99, 104–106, 107, 123, 154–55; disruption of slave trade in, 138
Seven Years' War, 158–59
sex ratios and efforts to balance: in French Caribbean, 82, 178n53; in Louisiana, 81–85, 123–24, 178n61; in New France, 82
ship building, 18, 35–36, 52, 53, 60–62, 74, 78, 126, 154
Sierra Leone River, 55, 72
silver, 69, 99; rumors of, in Louisiana, 2, 23–24, 32–33; in Spanish America, 3, 11, 14. *See also* currency
Siraj ud-Daulah, 158–59
Siroux (company agent), 101
skilled labor: enslaved, 107, 126–31; from Plantin's Company, 79–81; shift from free to enslaved, 126–29; shortage of, in Louisiana, 25, 129; tobacco workers, 131–33, 137
slave ships, 54–57, 71–72, 74, 76, 96, 99, 183n57; *Galathée*, 103–106; mortality on, 72, 104–105, 123; *Saint-Louis*, 152; *Vénus*, 107, 109, 122–23
slave trade, African, 163–64n13. *See also* smuggling
—commissions to ship captains, 76
—company monopolies on, 18, 20, 54–57, 72, 97–101
—and French-Atlantic ports, 54–56, 173n48
—leasing privileges/permits: *assiento*, 55, 97–99; *exclusif*, 72; to private traders, 54–57, 72, 148
—and Ministry of Marine, 56–57, 72
—and Nantes, 54–57, 59, 173n48, 173n51; and Montaudoin, 54, 56
—supply vs. demand, 99, 100, 122–23, 138
—trade goods, 37, 59, 70. *See also* Compagnie de Guinée; Compagnie de Saint-Domingue; Compagnie de Sénégal
—and West Africa, 11; Ouidah, 56, 71–72; Senegambia, 70–72, 78, 99, 104–106, 107, 123, 138, 154–55
slave trade, Indian, 24–25, 131
slaves, Indian, 20, 24–25, 110, 126, 131–32
Smallwood, Stephanie, 88
smoking, 19, 103, 130
smuggling, 43, 65, 76–77, 97–99, 181n17, 191n18; exile to Louisiana as punishment for, 85; of textiles into France, 36
Society of Jesus. *See* Jesuits in Louisiana
soldiers, 5, 20, 21–22, 25, 66, 73, 77, 79, 80–81, 83, 94, 103, 117, 118, 130, 132, 140,

soldiers (*continued*)
144, 149, 151, 177n42–43, 177n45. *See also* Dumont de Montigny, Jean-François Benjamin; Plantin's Company
Somme, 151
Soret, 77
Souel, Father Jean-François, 144
South Carolina. *See* Carolinas(s) (English colony/-ies)
specie. *See* currency
Suette, 51
sugar. *See under* agriculture and agricultural products
Superior Council: Bengal (Chandernagore), 158; Louisiana, 84, 89, 114–16, 118, 125, 126, 132, 145, 151–52, 183–84n61; Pondicherry, 157–59; Saint-Domingue, 100
Surat, 17, 69, 155
surgeons: at sea, 78, 176n22; Louisiana-bound, 80, 179n70
Système. *See under* Law, John

Tahomé, 22–23
taverns, 46, 47, 113, 114
taxation, 16; audit of Nantais merchants, 54; exemption, 40; by French Chamber of Justice, 26; and Le Coq family, 81; revenue, 29; in Saint-Domingue, 100; and United General Farms, 33–34, 148
Tchoupitoulas, 121
Te Deum, 151, 192n40
Terre Blanche, 132–33
textiles, 11, 12, 16, 27, 36–37, 47, 53, 58–59, 69–70, 77, 117, 135, 157, 176n20; and gum Arabic, 71; *petites étoffes*, 58, 69; protectionist policies in France, 36
theater, 48, 60; Destouches, 54; Molière, 49, 54
Tixerant, Louis, 109–10
tobacco. *See under* agriculture and agricultural products
tobacco farm (monopoly), 30, 131, 136–37, 168n71
tonnage, 73–74
Tonty, Henri de, 21
Toulouse, 90
trade: agricultural commodities, 18, 56, 59, 69, 98–100, 128, 133, 136, 138, 143, 155; in alcohol, 11, 14, 53, 69, 75, 117, 143; with American Indians, 2, 22–23, 75, 134–35, 143–44, 149; apothecary stores, 136; barriers to, in France, 16, 19; circum-Caribbean, 25, 98–99, 126, 136–37, 150; exotic woods, 56, 69, 136; fur and peltry, 2, 14, 20, 21, 30, 36, 56, 75, 128, 131, 135–36, 139, 152; gum Arabic, 71, 154–55; lumber, 25, 126, 135–36; naval stores, 126, 128; petty, 76–77, 139, 151, 157; protectionist policies, 36; with the Spanish, 25, 110, 126, 136–37; textiles, 11, 12–13, 16, 36–37, 57–59, 58, 70. *See also* slave trade, African; smuggling
trading companies. *See names of specific trading companies*
travel: in the Caribbean, 95–96; in France, 8, 44–49, 51–54, 60, 67, 171n17; and hospitality, 47–48, 50, 54, 59–60, 109–10, 114; in Louisiana, 106, 109–11, 114; measuring distances, 171n14; overland, 45–46, 171n15; at sea, 86–93, 94–95
travel narratives, 3–7; and censorship, 1, 6–7; and exoticism, 163n9; as eyewitness accounts, 6, 189–90n120; *histoires*, 5–6, 162n8; picaresque, 6, 50; as propaganda, 6
Treaty of Ryswick, 21, 27, 97
Troyes, de, 44–47, 48–49, 51–53, 60, 67, 79, 112, 114–15

Ulrich, Laurel Thatcher, 4
Ursulines, 6, 90, 110–11, 120, 121. *See also* Hachard, Marie-Madeleine
Usner, Daniel H., 82, 191n14

Valette de Laudun, 83
Vannes, 60, 192n48
Vera Cruz, 98, 136
Versailles, 7, 17, 40, 50, 149, 192n40
Victorin, Father, 121
Villegaignon, Nicholas Durand de, 12

Wabash, 122
War of Austrian Succession, 155
War of Spanish Succession, 22, 26, 62
Watson, Charles, 158–59
wheat. *See under* agriculture and agricultural products
Windward Islands, 94

Yazoo, 122, 144
Yazoo River, 144